Fundamentals of
Computer Organization and Architecture

FUNDAMENTALS OF COMPUTER ORGANIZATION AND ARCHITECTURE

JYOTSNA SENGUPTA

DEEP & DEEP PUBLICATIONS PVT. LTD.
F-159, Rajouri Garden, New Delhi - 110 027

FUNDAMENTALS OF
COMPUTER ORGANIZATION AND ARCHITECTURE

ISBN 978-81-8450-186-5

Typeset by RAHUL COMPOSERS
358, Pocket-B, Phase-II, Sector-16B, Dwarka, New Delhi - 110 075

Printed in India at MAYUR ENTERPRISES
WZ Plot No. 3, Gujjar Market, Tihar Village, New Delhi - 110 018

Published by DEEP & DEEP PUBLICATIONS PVT. LTD.,
F-159, Rajouri Garden, New Delhi - 110 027 • Phone : 25435369, 25440916
E-mail : ddpbooks@yahoo.co.in • ddpubs@gmail.com
Showroom :
2/13, Ansari Road, Daryaganj, New Delhi - 110 002 • Telefax : 23245122

Dedicated to

UDAYAN

AND

SIDDHARTHA

Contents

Preface

This book is written for all students and professionals who want to learn fundamentals of computer architecture or want to clarify doubts about what they have already learnt in the past through various books. The contents covered are appropriate for students of courses in B.Tech., MCA or M.Tech. with specialization in Computer Science, Information Technology, Electronics or Electrical Engineering. Even students who have no knowledge of computer architecture can comfortably learn the basics in the simple language used for explanation in the text.

THE DRIVING FORCE

There are many books of Computer Architecture available in India that have been written by foreign authors. It is a general observation of the author that the language used in these books is not easily understood by ordinary Indian students. Moreover, some texts start with a high level of complexity where student loses interest before understanding the concepts. The syllabus of Computer Architecture prescribed by most Indian Universities/Colleges is not available in one book. Rather than spending their time in trying to learn the subject, I have realized that they spend more time to locate the right book that would cover the syllabus prescribed for the course. As I have been teaching the subject of Computer Architecture for about 20 years, I strongly felt the need of writing a book for Indian students that would address all their problems and improve the learning process. The text, presented in a simple language, generally comprises of the lectures prepared for B.Tech., MCA and M.Tech. students by consulting various books and other sources of Computer Science specialization.

THE TEXT

The book of 'Fundamentals of Computer Organization and Architecture' presents basic principles and design concepts of different units of a computer. It explains the entire process of computation in different units of a computer that is involved in transforming a program written in high-level language within the computer till its output results. The need of the day is to improve the performance, and hence the speed, of the computer. The sequential flow of computation in the computer system can be increased considerably by using processes in parallel. The concepts of parallel processing have also been clarified in this manuscript.

The book is divided into eight chapters. The sequence of these chapters is based on treating study of computer architecture at different levels where each level requires some kind of decoding before it reaches the lowest level, the digital logic level, where the actual computation takes place.

Chapter 1 provides an introduction to the broad subject of Computer Architecture and describes the historical computers. The layered model of the study of the subject is explained. The concept of operating system is clarified for beginners.

Chapter 2 presents the concepts and design of logic circuits that are basic building blocks of the digital computer. The design of digital circuits, by using Boolean Algebra, is explained to construct combinational circuits. For building sequential circuits, methods like state-diagrams and state-tables are used which help in handling the various states of flip-flops to build an optimum design. Design of popularly used circuits like decoders, multiplexers and similar other circuits are presented.

Chapter 3 describes the fundamentals of the computer organization. The external and internal design and functioning of the CPU is thoroughly explained. The processing of an instruction requires the fetch and execute cycles following which the results are stored in the memory locations. This is explained in detail in this chapter, along with the need of various available registers in the CPU. The construction of the processor may be hardwired or microprogrammed, either one is used based on the needs of speed and cost. The basic difference is explained. The register transfer language is also introduced here.

Chapter 4 gives details of the Control Design of the CPU. Both the methods, i.e. Microprogrammed Control and Hardwired Control design have been clarified by providing suitable examples. Further, benefit of parallelism in microoperations that allows the speed of computation to be increased is explained in detail by providing concepts of horizontal and vertical microinstructions, microoperation timing and pipeline control.

Chapter 5 explains the architecture based on the Instruction Set of a Control Unit. Register transfer notation and assembly language notations are used to clarify the actions performed within the CPU. The effects of instructions with different number of addresses on the operations in the program are clarified, along with loops in those programs that have repeated instructions of the same kind. Tags that are used to store information related to either instruction or data for fast retrieval has also been explained. The issue of various addressing modes that also affect the speed of computation have been addressed. RISC and CISC are different design methodologies and neither of them is particularly superior, the choice depends on the performance of the application. This has been explained in detail.

Chapter 6 gives details of the memory unit of a computer. This chapter introduces hierarchy of memory available in a computer system. To solve the problem of attaining fast, large, and inexpensive memory, many different structures and organizations are presented. The memory structure characteristics as well as various memory technologies have been covered. Different organizations of the cache affect the speed in case of a hit or a miss. Four placement policies are covered. Multilevel memories and virtual memory technique have also been explained.

Chapter 7 describes the Input/Output or I/O sub-system that are the collection of interfaces that different functional units of a computer use to communicate with each other, or the outside world. Typical devices for communication between computers, such as modems and network cards, are for both input and output. It has been explained in detail. The various I/O bus standards that define connectors, signal amplitudes, and clock speeds for widely used standards like ISA, SCSI, USB and PCI are described. The functioning of input devices like keyboard, mouse, trackball and joysticks has also been covered. This chapter also considers different technologies like speech input to computers, image scanner, and many other I/O devices like CRT monitor, etc. are illustrated. Different methods of I/O such as Programmed I/O and DMA have also been examined.

The last chapter deals with the concepts of Parallel Processing, which are used to achieve very high performance and reliability. Chapter 8 provides the basic structures of Pipeline and Vector Processors and also introduces various characteristics of Multiprocessors. The characteristics and functions of processors are studied before considering them for the use as a multiprocessor. The explanation of the difference in tightly coupled, loosely coupled or massively parallel computer has been illustrated. Problem of cache coherence that arises when private cache is shared among processors has been investigated. Method to evaluate the performance of pipeline processors has been explained as well.

Appendices A, B and C cover the Number Systems, Character Codes and Karnaugh Map respectively.

Finally, I would like to thank all those who have directly or indirectly helped me in the preparation of this book.

JYOTSNA SENGUPTA

CHAPTER

1

Introduction to Computer Architecture

1. INTRODUCTION

Computer Architecture is the study of the basic principles, design concepts and functions of different units of digital computers. These primary units work with some extra units of the computer to accept inputs from external sources, like a keyboard, and provide information to the destinations, like a display or a storage device or a communication device.

1.1 ELEMENTS OF COMPUTERS

A computer consists of three independent units: memory, processor and input-output unit (I/O). The main components of a computer are connected as shown in Figure 1.1. The input unit accepts information from the external sources through input devices like a keyboard, or from communication devices. This information received is either used immediately or stored in the computers memory for later use. Memory unit contains various kinds of memory which might have different capacity and speeds of access. The processing of a program is also controlled by another program, which is stored in the memory. After the program is processed, the results are sent to the external destinations through the output unit. All these actions are controlled by the processor that consists of control unit and arithmetic-logic unit.

The information in the computer is in the form of either instruction or data. The function of the 'instruction' is to transfer information within a

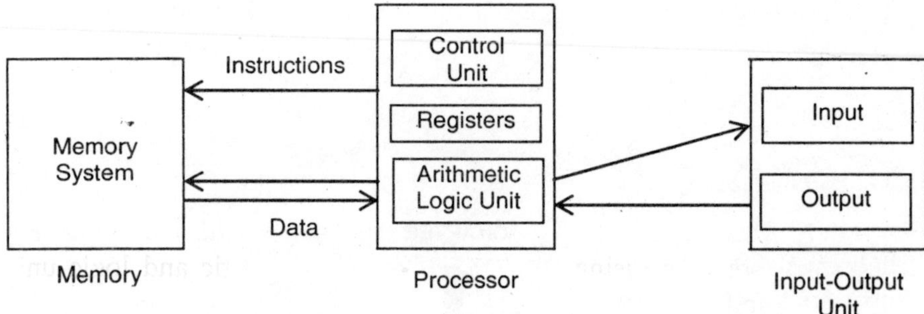

FIGURE 1.1 : The Three Main Components of a Computer

computer and the I/O devices. It also specifies the arithmetic and logic operation to be performed. The terms 'program' and 'data' are defined as under:

Program: A list of instructions that perform the required activity is called a program.

Data: Data are numbers and encoded characters that are used as operands by the instructions. Data also means any digital information. Thus, an entire program may be considered as data.

1.1.1 Memory Unit

The memory is in the form of large number of storage cells. Each cell is capable of storing one bit of information. These cells are never read or written as individual cells. They are generally processed in groups of fixed size units called words. The memory is organized so that the contents of one word can be stored or retrieved in one basic operation.

Address: All the cells in the memory have an address. Every word in the memory is also given a distinct address. This provides easy access to any word in the memory. The number of bits in each word is referred to as the *word length* of the computer. The capacity of the computer is the size of computer data that is processed within a computer in units of words. The function of the memory unit is to store programs and data.

Different types of storage devices are used in a computer depending upon the need of the speed of access and their cost. Various memory devices are provided in the computer as a memory hierarchy. There are two kinds of storage devices: Primary storage and Secondary storage.

Primary storage is a fast memory and program must be stored in this memory while they are executed.

Primary Memory: Programs must be in the primary memory during execution. This memory is referred to as Random Access Memory (RAM). In this memory, any location can be reached in a short and fixed amount of time after specifying its address. Typical range of access time of a RAM is a few nano seconds.

Secondary Memory: Although primary storage is essential, it is very expensive. Thus, additional cheaper memory, called the secondary memory, is used when large amount of data and programs have to be stored. Wide range of secondary memories are available (discussed in Chapter 6).

1.1.2 Processor

The processing of the program is performed in the hardware unit called processor comprising of three subunits: arithmetic and logic unit, control unit and registers.

Arithmetic Logic Unit

Most computer operations are executed in the arithmetic and logic unit (ALU) of the processor. For example, if two numbers stored in the memory are to be added, they are brought into the processor and the actual addition is carried out by the ALU. The result may then be stored in the memory.

Many other ALU operations like multiplications, division or comparison of numbers follow the same process. When operands are brought into the processor, they are stored in the processor's memory called registers. Access time of the register is faster than access time to the fastest primary memory.

Registers

A very small amount of memory with extremely fast speed, generally in the form of registers, is present in the processor to hold data brought from memory for computation. These registers also hold temporary results after processing of data in the ALU.

Control Unit

The memory, ALU and I/O units store and process the information. The operation of the above units is managed by a control unit (CU) that sends control signals to other units and starts their action. The CU is a well defined, physically separate unit that interacts with other parts of the computer. The control lines are physically distributed throughout the computer. The action performed by every unit is initiated by the CU. This is done by producing an appropriate control signal which initiates the operation to be performed. I/O transfer consists of input and output operations through I/O devices. The speed is very slow as compared to the speed of the CPU. The timing signals that govern the transfer of data from these I/O devices are generated by the control unit. These timing signals determine when a given action is to take place. These actions are data transfer between the processor and the memory or transfers between memory and memory.

1.1.3 Input/Output (I/O) Unit

The input and output of a computer is managed by input/output unit, more popularly known as I/O unit, which consist of an input unit where all the incoming data is accepted, and an output unit that allows the processed information to be available to the outside world.

Input Unit

The information to be processed by the computer is coded and accepted by the computer through input unit, which reads the data. The most used input device is a keyboard. Whenever key is pressed, the corresponding letter is translated into its corresponding binary code, and then, it is transmitted over to the memory or the processor.

Many input devices are available, which will be described in Chapter 7.

Output Unit

The output unit sends processed result to the external of the computer. The most common example of such a device is a printer. Though very fast printers that print up to ten thousand lines per minute are available these days, but this speed is very slow as compared to the speed of the processor units.

Some units provide both an input function as well as an output function. Graphic display is an example of such a device that does the simultaneous operation of input and output. Details of many more output devices will be discussed in Chapter 7.

Thus, the operation of the computer can be summarized as:

1. The computer accepts information in the form of program and data through an input unit.
2. The information is stored in the memory.
3. This information is processed in the arithmetic and logic unit.
4. The processed information is available to the external destinations through an output unit.
5. All activities inside the computer are controlled by the control unit.

1.2 HISTORICAL COMPUTER ARCHITECTURE

Many different kinds of computers have been designed in the past few centuries to reach to the level of the modern digital computers. Most of these earlier computers have been forgotten, but some of them have contributed significantly to reach the current knowledge. These innumerable computers are grouped into different generations according to the basic elements used as building blocks. These generations are as under:

First Generation: 1940-1956
Second Generation: 1955-1964
Third Generation: 1964-1971
Fourth Generation: 1975-present
Fifth Generation: Present and ahead

A brief sketch of different generation of computers will be provided in this section.

1.2.1. First Generation: Mechanical Era

The first mechanical computer was built by Blaise Pascal, in 1642, using mechanical elements like gears and cranks. This machine could only perform addition and subtraction. After 30 years, a German mathematician built a machine that could also perform multiplication and division.

About 150 years later, Charles Babbage designed a 'difference engine' which had memory, computation unit, input section and an output section. This machine could run a single algorithm by the method of finite differences using polynomials. Babbage designed the analytical engine. It was programmable in a simple assembly language to produce the software.

In late 1930s, mathematical calculators came into existence, which used electromagnetic relays. The language used was cryptic binary.

1.2.2 Second Generation: Electronic Era

The electronic era (1956-1963) of computers replaced mechanical elements with vacuum tubes. The first electronic computer was ENIAC (Electronic numerical integrator and computer) consisting of about 18000 vacuum tubes and 1500 relays. This machine had 20 registers, which could hold a 10 digit decimal number each. ENIAC weighed 30 tones and consumed 140 kilo watts of power. Later, a researcher, von Neumann, came up with its own computer (the IAS Machine). The architecture of this computer included memory, control unit, ALU, an input unit and an output unit. The details of the von Neumann Machine will be discussed in the next section.

The transistor was invented at Bell Labs in 1948. The transistor revolutionized the electronic industry by late 1950's, making it smaller, faster and cheaper. A few years later, DEC introduced the mini-computer which had a single bus that connected the CPU, memory, console terminal and I/O devices. The block diagram of general mini-computer is shown in Figure 1.2.

The languages used with these computers changed from binary to high level programming languages like COBOL and FORTRAN.

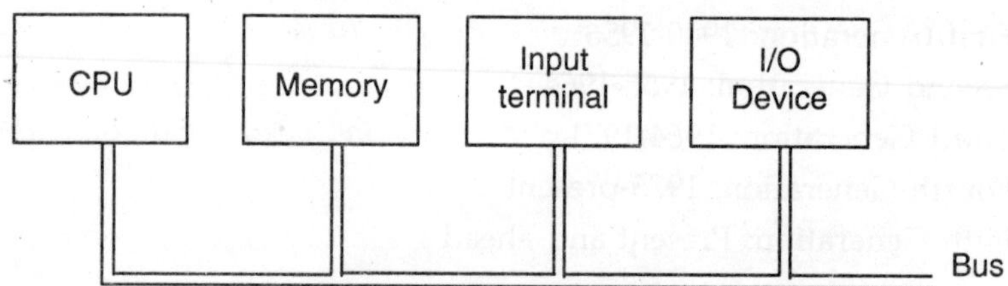

FIGURE 1.2 : Block Diagram of a Mini-Computer

1.2.3 Third Generation: Integrated Circuits : 1964-1971

The invention of the silicon integrated circuit allowed many transistors to be put on a single chip. The computers that came up during this era kept on improving in the range of prices and performance. The input-output methods changed from punched cards and printouts to keyboards, monitors, printers and operating system. IBM 360 introduced multiprogramming which had several programs in memory at once, so that when one is waiting for input/output to complete, another could compute. This computer also had a large address space of 2^{24} bytes. The word size was increased to 32 bits.

1.2.4 Fourth Generation: Microprocessors : 1971-present.

By the 1980s, VLSI (Very large scale integration) made it possible to put millions of transistors on a single chip. This made the size of the computers as well as their price smaller. Personal computers were used for word processing, spread sheets and highly interactive applications that the larger computer could not handle well. Each PC contained a printed circuit board having a number of chips, some cables, a power supply and an 8 inch floppy disc. The CP/M operating system was used. It was a disc operating system with a file system and user commands were typed in from the keyboard.

Apple was another popular personal computer. The Intel family of CPUs, starting from 4004, 8080, 8086 and so on, were used as CPUs for personal computers which kept on increasing their performance and decreasing the cost with time. Later on, the IBM PC came with MS-DOS operating system supplied by Microsoft Corporation. The Microsoft Corporation developed its own windows operating system that runs over MS-DOS.

By the mid-1980s, a new architecture called RISC appeared, which was fast and had much simpler architecture instead of the complicated architectures that were coming up. In 1990s, superscalar CPUs appeared. These machines could execute multiple instructions at the same time.

With the use of small powerful computers, networks were formed by linking different machines with each other, which eventually led to the development of internet.

1.2.5 Fifth Generation: Present and ahead

Fifth generation computers will be based on artificial intelligence and have the capability of voice recognition and natural languages. These systems will be based on nanotechnology.

1.3 COMPUTER ORGANIZATION AND ARCHITECTURE

The complete study of computer organization and architecture includes the study of both hardware of the computer system, and the software needed to make the computer system perform the computation. Thus, the structure of the computer and the functions performed by the various units of the computer are involved in the study of architecture and organization of the computer. There are a lot of computers available in the markets which change their versions after every few years. The change is not only in cost but also in size, performance and applications. These changes cover all aspects of computer technology, from the integrated circuit technology used to construct computer components to the changes in organization of combining those components. But the fundamentals of computer organization and architecture remain the same.

1.3.1 Difference between Architecture and Organization

The distinction between computer architecture and organization is difficult to define precisely. However, the general areas covered by each are as follows:

Computer Organization

The term 'Computer Organization' refers to the operational units of the computer and their interconnections. The main hardware units are the CPU, memory, I/O units, etc. The hardware details such as various computational units, control signals, interfaces between computer peripherals, and the memory technology used are included in the organization of the computer. Therefore, it can be said that the hardware units and their connection details cover the organization of the computer system.

Computer Architecture

By the term 'Computer architecture', it is generally meant those qualities of a system that are visible to a programmer, such as the number of bits used to represent various data types, the instruction set of the computer, techniques for addressing memory, methods used for input-output, etc. These qualities are known as architectural qualities and have an effect on the execution of a program.

In short, the quality associated with the functioning of software is linked to computer architecture whereas those associated to hardware aspects of the computer are related to computer organization. For example, if a computer is running multiple instructions, it is an architectural design issue. On the other hand, it is an organizational issue whether that instruction will be implemented by a special multiple unit or by a unit that makes repeated use of the add instruction.

Many computer manufactures offer a family of computer models, all with the same architecture but with differences in organization. These models have different price and performance characteristics. The architecture may not change for many years but the organization changes with the change of technology. This means that the same software can be used on different models of the computer, only the hardware changes to make the system improve in performance and speed.

1.3.2 Software/Hardware Interaction

A program is a set of instructions that specify the operations, the operands and the sequence by which processing has to occur. The procedure of entering a program in some high level language or in some low level language and receiving the output results involves the simultaneous working of software and hardware.

The computer program consists of a list of instructions which are stored in the memory. These instructions are brought from the memory into the processor and the specific operation is executed. The procedure involves the following steps:

1. Fetch the instruction
2. Decode the instruction
3. Fetch the operands
4. Execute the instruction
5. Store the results

For example, the following instruction adds the numbers available in register A and register B, and stores the results in register C.

ADD A, B, C

The execution of this instruction requires the following steps:

1. Instruction is fetched from memory to processor
2. Instruction is decoded
3. Operand of register B is fetched
4. ADD operation is carried out in the ALU
5. The results are stored in register C

The operand of the ADD instruction may be available in the memory location whose address is specified in register B. Actually, the operands may be located in any memory location and the results may also be stored in some memory location. How the data is accessed is part of the study of addressing modes.

Therefore, it can be seen that the desired output results from a computer are obtained because of the interaction of hardware and software.

1.4 LAYERED MODEL

The study of computer architecture involves the study of various actions performed at the hardware level, right from the point when a program is fed into the computer through its input unit and the results are available through its output unit. The architecture of the computer from the digital logic gates up to the solution of the problem in a form easily understood by everyone, involves many stages. The study of organization and functioning of a computer can be simplified by considering it to be consisting of many modules. Each of these modules can be regarded as a layer or a level. This section explains the structure and functioning of a computer system by regarding it to be constituted of many layers.

1.4.1 Concept of Layers

The functioning of various modules and their interconnection can be explained better by dividing them in layers. Each of these layers performs a particular job related to the organization and architecture of the computer system. Some machines may have just one level (digital logic level), like a calculator. Others may have more levels depending on the need. The interaction between other layers is either through data paths, which may be constituted of hardware circuits or of software programs. A layered model is shown in Figure 1.3, having 6 layers interconnected with each other through interfaces between them. Interconnection of layers exhibit the interface between the layer.

Level 1—Digital Logic

Level 1 of the machine, which is also the lowest level, is of the digital logic gates. This is the true hardware of the machine where actual computation at the gate level is taking place through digital circuits built from transistors. Each gate has a digital input that is either 0 or 1, which represents the analog low level or analog high level. All other digital circuits like memory and registers are formed by groups of these gates.

Level 2—Micro Architecture

The micro architecture level performs the execution of the most basic digital circuits by using software commands. This level also comprises of digital circuits to perform memory and ALU operations. The registers are

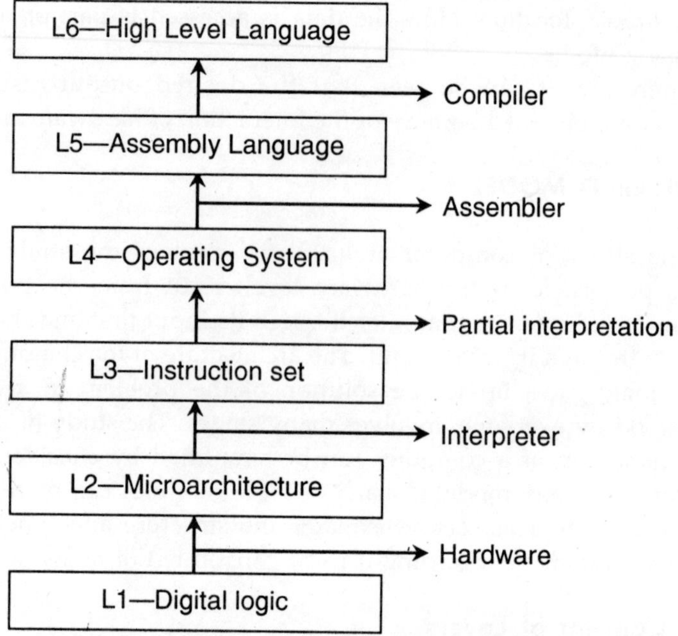

FIGURE 1.3 : Layered Model of the Computer

connected to the ALU and the connection path is called a data path over which the data flows.

The operation of the data path is controlled either by a software program called a microprogram, or by hardware. If the data path is controlled by software, the microprogram is called an interpreter. The interpreter fetches, examines and executes the instruction one by one using the data path. After the execution, the result is stored at a specified location. With the hardwired control of the data paths, similar steps take place except storing of the result.

Level 3—Instruction Set Architecture

The instructions that the machine uses is decided by the architect of the machine. These instructions are carried out through an interpreter and use machine language. Thus, by using the instruction set in its machine language, the required computation is performed.

Level 4—Operating System Machine Level

Operating system level has instructions to control the operation of the computer. Though most of the instructions of the operating system level are also present in the instruction set architecture level, the level 4 also has a set of new instructions. It requires a different memory organization. It can also run more than one program simultaneously. The programs are run by an interpreter which operates at level 2.

Level 5—Assembly Language Level

The assembly language level is a symbolic form used by the specific processor to solve the problem. The programs in assembly language are translated to lower levels and then interpreted by the concerned machine. The program that performs the translation is called an assembler.

Levels 5 & 6 are used by the applications programmer. The language used by levels 1, 2, and 3 are machine languages, where the programs consists of a series of binary numbers that only the machine can understand. Starting from level 5, the language contains words and abbreviations that are easy to understand.

Level 6—High Level Language

This level is used by the applications programmer to solve the problems. There are many different high level languages that exist. For example, BASIC, C, C++, C-Sharp, Java, Prolog. Programs written in these languages are translated to levels 4, 5 by compilers. Compilers are primarily used at Level 6.

1.4.2 Cost benefits of Layers

From the above explanation of the layering of different modules in the structure of a computer, it can be seen that the complex working of computers is made simpler by studying it as a series of levels, each one built on the levels below it. Every level is an abstraction with different objects and operations. Each of these levels can be studied and designed independently.

1.5 VON NEUMANN ARCHITECTURE

The world's first general purpose computer was ENIAC (Electronic Numerical Integrator and Computer) that was completed in 1940. The major problem in this computer was of I/O operations which made the tasks of entering and altering the programs for the ENIAC extremely complicated. The concept of stored program was initiated by John von Neumann to facilitate the programming process by storing the program along with data in the memory. The architecture of ENIAC is explained in this section.

1.5.1 General Features of von Neumann Architecture

In 1946, von Neumann and his colleagues designed a new stored-program computer in Princeton, USA. This computer has a CPU for executing instructions, a main memory for storing active programs, and input-output equipment. This design is quite modern and acts as a prototype for most general purpose computers.

1.5.2 Functional Units of von Neumann Architecture

The organization of the von Neumann computer is shown in Figure 1.4. The size and high cost of electronic elements in those times was responsible for small size of the CPU and the instruction set. The main memory was 1K, expandable up to 4K. Along with this, 16K cheaper and slower secondary storage was provided.

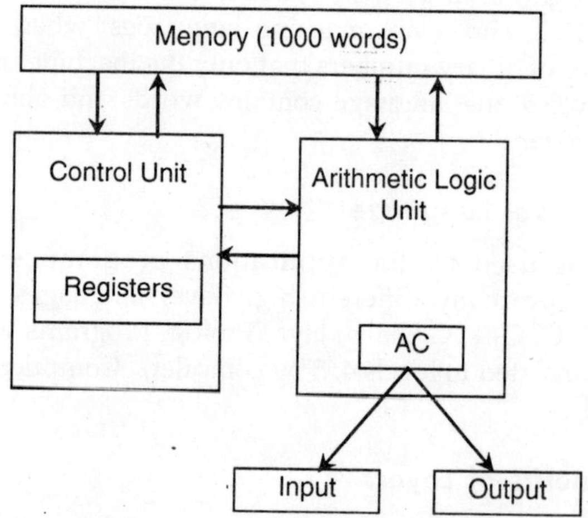

FIGURE 1.4 : Organization of the von Neumann Computer

Memory

The memory consists of 1000 storage locations, called words, each having 40 binary digits (bits). Both data and instructions are stored here. The numbers are in binary form and every instruction has a 39-bit binary code. All the numbers are represented by a sign bit.

Register

The CPU contains storage locations called registers. These registers are:

Memory Buffer Register (MBR)

It contains words to be stored in memory, or used to receive a word.

Memory Address Register (MAR)

This 12 bit register specifies the address in memory and the word to be written or read into the MBR.

Instruction Register (IR)

It contains 8 bit opcode of the instruction being executed.

Instruction Buffer Register (IBR)

It holds the temporary instruction from a word in memory.

Program Counter (PC)

It contains the address of the next instruction to be fetched from memory.

Accumulator (AC)

It holds temporary operands and results of ALU operation.

CPU

The CPU has two main parts which are responsible for fetching information from main memory and interpreting it. The first part is known as program control unit (PCU) while the second is known as data processing unit (DPU) or data path.

Instruction Set

There are about 30 types of instructions. These instructions include data transfer instructions, data processing instructions and program control instructions. Examples of these instructions are to transfer contents of one register to another, transfer contents of memory to accumulator or to transfer absolute value to AC.

1.5.3 Criticism of von Neumann Architecture

Although von Neumann computer was a great invention of it's times but considering the computers of today, the limitations of this computer may be listed as under:

1. While writing a program and later debugging it, some instructions may get changed by themselves, which causes lot of problems.
2. Before every execution of program, the version of the program must be loaded in the memory.
3. The amount of memory in registers is so small that a lot of time is spent in data transfer between the CPU and the main memory.
4. Because of this small storage of CPU and the data transfer instructions, the length of program is increased a lot.
5. This computer has no instruction to link different programs. For example, there are no procedure calls all return instructions.
6. The instruction set of this computer is made only for numerical

computation. Therefore programs for non-numerical computations such as text processing are difficult to type and they execute slowly.

7. Not many input output instructions were provided in the instruction set of this computer.

1.5.4 Requirements for Improved Architecture

Though von Neumann architecture had many limitations on its size and speed, but the innovative construction of the CPU with internal registers, its memory and input-output capabilities are used in the modern computers. The basic architecture has improved on many aspects:

1.6 FUNCTION OF OPERATING SYSTEM

An operating system is a program that controls the execution of application programs and acts as an interface between the user of a computer and the computer hardware. It has two objectives, convenience and efficiency. Thus, an operating system makes a computer more convenient to use and it allows the computer system resources to be used in an efficient manner.

Operating system is the most important system program of the hardware for the programmer and provides a convenient interface for the programmer for using the system. A layered model of hardware and software used to provide processing power to a user is as shown in Figure 1.5. The user treats a computer system in terms of an application. This application is expressed in a programming language and is developed by an applications programmer. A set of system programs are evolved to control the computer hardware. Some of these programs are referred to as utilities. These utilities are implemented frequently and use functions to create programs, management of files and control of I/O devices.

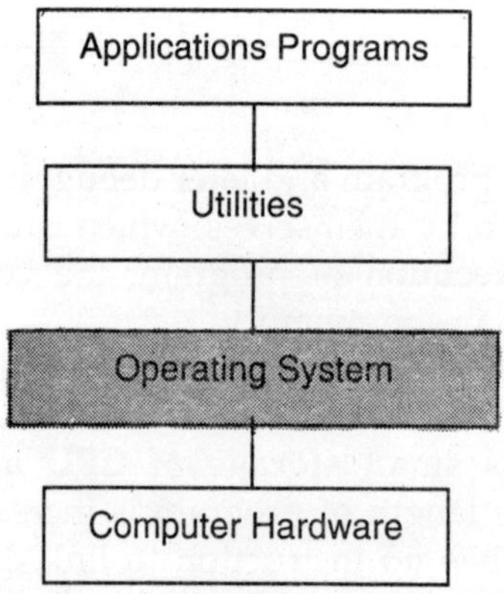

FIGURE 1.5 : Operating System Layer in middle of other Layers

The operating system provides the following services:

1.6.1 Program Creation

Programs such as editors and debuggers are provided by the operating system for creating programs. These services are in the form of utility programs that are not actually part of operating system but are accessible through the operating system.

1.6.2 Program Execution

The execution of a program requires an instruction to be fetched, decoded and executed. The tasks of the instruction and data to be loaded into main memory and the execution of instruction are handled by operating system. The I/O devices and files must be initialized, which is also handled by the operating system.

1.6.3 Access to I/O Devices

The operating system makes the access to I/O devices simpler by having read and write instructions. Each I/O device has its own set of instructions and control signals for the operation. The operating system takes care of managing these I/O devices so that the programmer can use them by issuing a simple read and write operation.

1.6.4 Shared System

The access to whole of the shared system is controlled by the operating system. The specific system resources as well as the protection of resources is also controlled by the operating system.

1.6.5 Error Control

Errors may occur in the memory or in the devices connected to the system because of failure in the device. In such cases, the operating system program must clear the error condition.

1.6.6 Statistics

The information about the use of resources like amount of memory, time of use of resources, etc. is also collected by an operating system. These statistics convey the performance parameters and response time on a multi-user system and can be used for billing.

Types of Operating System

Operating systems are of two kinds: Batch processing or Interactive type.

Batch System

In this kind of operating system, user programs are submitted in batches by a computer operating system to the required resource after the program is completed. The results are printed out for the user. These kinds of systems are rare these days.

Interactive System

In this kind of operating system, the user program interacts directly with the computer through a keyboard. Thus, request for the execution of a job or a transaction is performed in an interactive manner. The user may communicate with the computer during the execution of the job is completed.

Time-Sharing System

In a time-sharing system, multiple users access the system simultaneously through turns. This technique is known as time sharing because the time of the processor is shared among multiple users. For the use of dedicated microcomputers, the requirements for interactive computing facility are essential

1.7 PERFORMANCE METRICS

Though the basic building blocks of computers these days are the same as those used fifty years ago, but the performance of these systems has increased manifold. The cost of computer system continues to decrease year by year, but the performance and capacity of these systems remains on the increasing path. Work stations are used for highly developed engineering and scientific applications. The servers are used to handle a client-server network and are very powerful and have replaced the main frame computer of the past.

The most important metric of the performance of a computer is the speed of execution, which is affected by the design of its hardware and its machine language instructions. The performance is also affected by the design of the compiler that translates high level language programs into machine languages. Thus, for best performance, the machine instruction set, the hardware, and the design of the compiler matter the most. Along with these, the execution of the programs of the operating system affects the performance of the system. There are times when the processor is idle and there are times when the processing is active. The performance of processor only in the periods during which the processor is active are considered. The following metrics are used to measure the performance of the processors.

1.7.1 Processor Clock

Processor circuits are controlled by a timing signal called a clock. The clock defines regular time intervals called clock cycles. For the execution of a machine instruction, the processor divides the action to be performed into a sequence of steps such that each step can be completed in one clock cycle. The lengths L of one clock cycle affects the processor performance. The clock rate is R = 1/L and is measured in clock cycle per second. Clock rates of a few hundred million to over a billon cycles per second is a normal situation these days. Clock rate is measured in hertz (Hz), Megahertz (MHz) or Gigahertz (GHz).

1.7.2 Performance Equation

Let T be the processor time required to execute a program of some high level language. The complier generates a machine language object program of the source program. The whole program has N machine language instructions. However N is not the number of machine instructions in the object program but is the number of actual instructions being executed. This number is different because of the presence of a program loop or because of some other conditional execution. Each basic step is completed in one clock cycle, where the clock rate is R cycle per second. If the number of basic steps needed to execute one machine instruction is S, then the program execution time is given as:

$$T = \frac{N \times S}{R}$$

This is known as the basic performance equation. The performance parameter T is the program execution time, which is much more important to the user than the individual values of the parameters N, S or R. To achieve high performance, the value of T should be reduced which means that value of N, S are reduced and the value of R is increased. This shows that to reduce the value of S, instructions should have smaller basic steps to perform. Value of R is increased by using a clock of higher frequency. It can also be seen that N, S and R are not independent parameters as changing the value of one of them affects the values of the other two. Therefore, an optimal design of the system is needed.

1.8 OUTLINE OF THE BOOK

This book explains the fundamental concepts of the organization and architecture of a standard computer which involves the design of various logic circuits used for computation, storage or similar units. The internal details of all the units and subunits are explained with the details of the working of a computer.

The book is divided into eight chapters. Chapter 1 provides a set up to begin the learning of the subject by giving the architecture of historical computers. The functioning of a computer at all the levels is explained with the layered model of the machine, which is then explained in later sections. The beginner's concepts of operating system are taken up here.

Chapter 2 provides design concepts of the digital logic circuits used as building blocks of any computer. This chapter provides the specific circuits used within a computer, including the circuits of memory unit.

Chapter 3 describes the external design of the three main components of a computer. The explanation of organization of the Central Processing Unit and its functioning has been done at the register transfer level. Along with these, the other basic concepts needed for the functioning of a computer have also been explained.

Chapter 4 describes the Control Design in depth. Both the methods, i.e. Microprogrammed Control and Hardwired Control design have been clarified by providing suitable examples.

Chapter 5 explains the architecture based on the Instruction Set of a Control Unit. The types of instructions and their management have been elaborated. The architectures based on other attributes of the machine have also been dealt with.

Chapter 6 gives details of the computer's memory unit. The memory structure, it's characteristics as well as various memory technologies have been covered, giving an emphasis to cache memory and virtual memory.

Chapter 7 makes clear the Input-Output subsystem. The Bus Architecture and its characteristics are explained. Different methodologies utilized for I/O have been described.

Chapters 8 deals with concepts of Parallel Processing, which are used to achieve very high performance and reliability. The basic structure of Uniprocessor to realize parallelism is dealt with. Various organizations that may use multiple processing elements used for parallelism are addressed. Various characteristics of Multiprocessors are covered.

1.9 SUMMARY

This chapter considers the basic elements and operation of the structure of a computer. The development from the times when mechanical elements constituted the structure of computers, up to the present age are described. The overall study of computer architecture is simplified by learning it methodically through layers. General features of von Neumann architecture are explained. A beginner's concept of operating system is also put forth.

REFERENCES

Tanenbaum, Andrew S., Structured Computer Organization, 4th ed., Prentice-Hall of India, New Delhi, 2001.

Patterson, D.A. and J.L. Hennessey, Computer Architecture: A Quantitative Approach, San Mateo, CA: Morgan Kaufmann Publishers, 1990.

Hamacher, C., Vranesic, Z., and Zaky, S., Computer Organization, 5th edition, McGraw-Hill, NY, 2002.

M. Morris Mano, Computer System Architecture, Third Edition, Pearson Education (Singapore), 1993.

Gibson, G.A., Computer Systems: Concepts ND Design, Englewood Cliffs, NJ: Prentice Hall, 1991.

PROBLEMS

1. Explain the design of a basic computer.
2. How is processing of a program controlled in a computer.
3. Explain the difference between an instruction and data in a program.
4. Name the smallest unit of memory where information is stored.
5. What is 'word length' of a computer?
6. What is the difference between 'primary memory' and 'secondary memory'?
7. Give details of main features related to different units in a processor.
8. How is the action of different units of a processor initiated?
9. Discuss features of various generations of computers.
10. What is the most important difference between distinct generations of computers?
11. Describe the architecture of the Von Neumann Machine and explain how the basic features of this architecture are incorporated in present day computers.
12. List the differences between the study of computer organization and computer architecture.
13. When a company launches a new model of computer, what changes in the hardware and software do you expect?
14. What steps are involved for a software instruction to be executed in the computer hardware?
15. How does the concept of layered model of computer architecture reduce the complications of study of the subject?
16. Clarify the advantage of cost involved by studying the subject of computer architecture as a hierarchy of layers.

CHAPTER

2

Digital Logic Circuits

2. INTRODUCTION

Digital circuit is the true hardware of the computer where the real computing and processing of computer programs takes place. In this chapter, the basic digital components, the design of gates and basic combinational and sequential circuits will be explained. The structure of a computer is a combination of these circuits utilized in building the bigger blocks. The memory of the computer is built with some special components. The organization of memory will also be explained.

2.1 GATES

The basic component of digital circuits is the transistor which has two logic levels, either 0 or 1. The transistor works as a two-way switch which can turn on or off depending on the input voltage fed to it. If the input voltage is low, output voltage is high and if input voltage is high, output voltage is low. Thus, if the electronic circuit is closed (short), the output is zero. On the other hand, if they are left open, the output is 1.

The three basic gates with their truth tables are shown as under:

(i) *OR Gate*

The OR gate has at least two inputs and one output. Figure 2.1(a) depicts a two input OR gate. The truth-table of this gate shows all the possible combinations of the input, and the corresponding output. If the inputs A and B are both 0, the output X would be zero. But in all other combinations of A and B, where at least one input is 1, the output X will be 1. Thus, if either A or B is 1, the output X is 1.

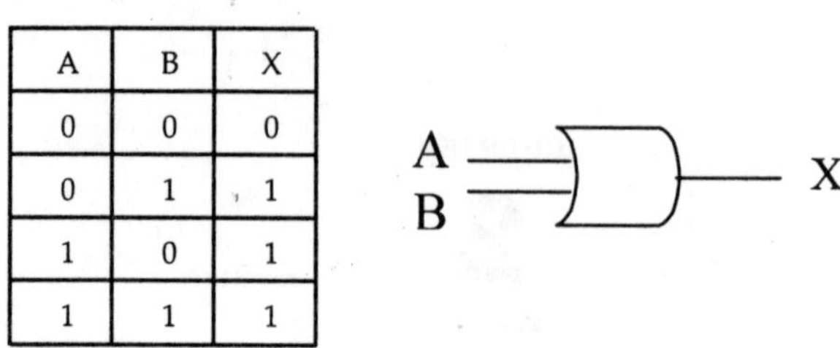

A	B	X
0	0	0
0	1	1
1	0	1
1	1	1

FIGURE 2.1(a) : A two input OR gate

(ii) *AND Gate*

The AND gate has at least two inputs and one output. Figure 2.1(b) shows a two input AND gate. The truth-table of this gate shows all the possible combinations of the inputs, and the corresponding output. If either of the inputs A and B are 0, the output X would be zero. Only in the case that both the inputs A and B are 1, the output X will be 1. Therefore, if either A or B is 0, the output X is 0. When both inputs A and B are 1, the output is 1.

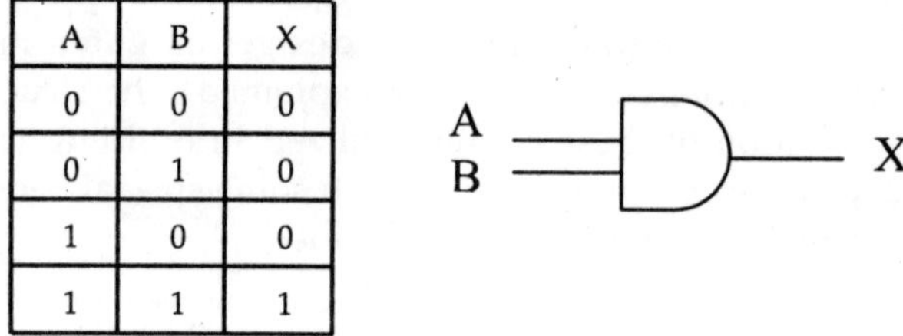

A	B	X
0	0	0
0	1	0
1	0	0
1	1	1

FIGURE 2.1(b) : A two input AND gate

(iii) *NOT Gate*

The NOT gate, which is more popularly known as INVERTER, has only one input and one output. Figure 2.1(c) shows the NOT gate. The truth-table of this gate shows the possible inputs, and the corresponding outputs. If the input A is 0, the output X is 1. If the input A is 1, the output X will be 0. Thus, the output X is the inverse of the input A, represented as X′ or $\overline{X}$.

A	X
0	1
1	0

A X

FIGURE 2.1(c) : A NOT gate

Apart from these basic gates, some other primary gates are also popular in their use. By placing an inverter in front of the OR and AND gates, NOR and NAND gates are built. It has been seen that these gates, with the inverter in the front, are easy to fabricate and use. These gates and their truth-tables are shown in Figure 2.2.

(iv) *NOR gate*

A	B	X
0	0	1
0	1	0
1	0	0
1	1	0

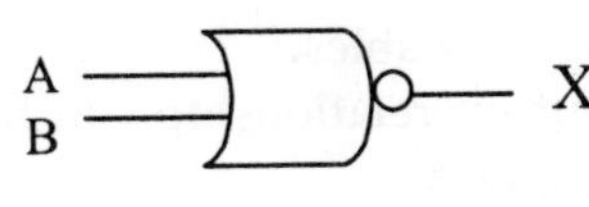

FIGURE 2.2(a) : A two input NOR gate

(v) *NAND Gate*

A	B	X
0	0	1
0	1	1
1	0	1
1	1	0

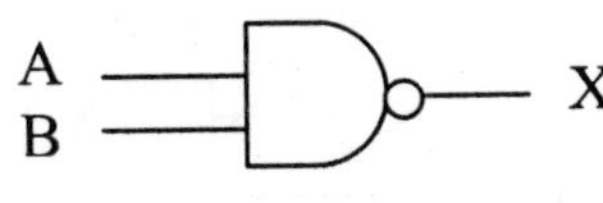

FIGURE 2.2 (b) : A two input NAND gate

The NAND and NOR gates are easier to fabricate and, therefore, are used more in the final design circuit.

AND, OR and NOT are the three basic logic gates and when used in combination, are sufficient to perform all kinds of computations. They can generate any Boolean function, which is a mapping of a binary input of M bits to a binary output of N bits. The three basic logic gates can be combined, with the output (s) of one becoming the input (s) of another, to build up any Boolean circuit.

2.2 BOOLEAN ALGEBRA

Boolean algebra is used to solve the logic equations dealing with binary variables and logic operations, after the name of the mathematician George Boole (1815-1864). Equations are formed for the different inputs of the circuits to give the desired output. These logic equations are then used for the construction of digital circuits from the basic gates. The inputs are in the form of variables which can take up only two values, either 0 or 1. This algebra is also known as switching algebra. The Boolean function has one or more input variables and produces an output that depends only on the inputs. An output function can be completely described by the different combinations of the input values which can be expressed by its corresponding truth table. A logic diagram composed of basic AND, OR, NOT gates is formed from the algebraic expression.

Thus, by using Boolean algebra, the following can be achieved:

1. A truth-table can be formed which expresses the relationship among binary variables.
2. The input-output relationship can be expressed in algebraic form and logic diagram.
3. By simplifying the relationships among the variables, simpler circuits for the same function can be found.

Let A, B, C and D be input variables of a circuit which realizes a function $F = A\bar{B} + C\bar{D}$, where $\bar{B}$ and $\bar{D}$ are complements of B and D. The logic diagram is shown in Figure 2.3.

$$F = A\bar{B} + C\bar{D}$$

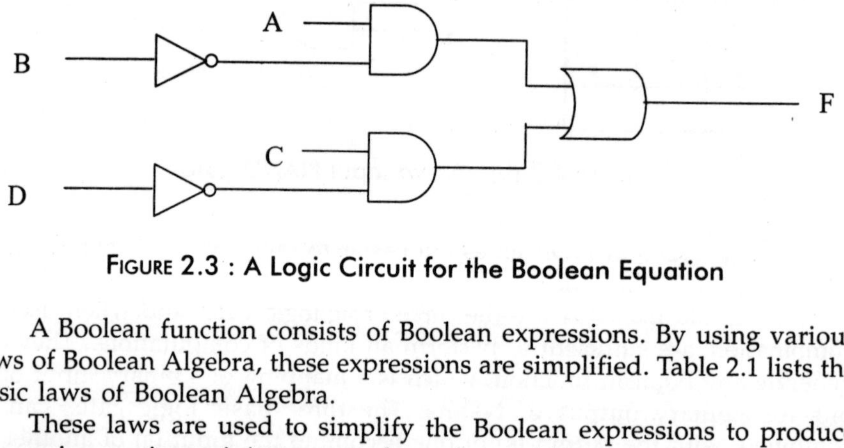

FIGURE 2.3 : A Logic Circuit for the Boolean Equation

A Boolean function consists of Boolean expressions. By using various laws of Boolean Algebra, these expressions are simplified. Table 2.1 lists the basic laws of Boolean Algebra.

These laws are used to simplify the Boolean expressions to produce expressions using minimum number of variables, popularly known as minterms. For example, the following Boolean expression can be simplified by using the above laws:

$$Z = \bar{A}BC + \bar{A}$$

Let $X = \bar{A}$ and $Y = BC$

By using Identity law, the expression simplifies to:

$$Z = X + XY = X(1 + Y) = X = \bar{A}$$

Another example is:

$$Z = [A + \bar{B}C + D + EF][A + \bar{B}C + \overline{(D + EF)}]$$

Substituting A + $\bar{B}$C = X, D + EF = Y and using Identity law and Inverse law, the above expression simplifies to:

$$Z = [X + Y]\,[X + \bar{Y}] = X = A + \bar{B}C$$

Principle of Duality—DeMorgan's Law

From Table 2.1, it can be seen that each law has two forms that are duals of each other. This means that if '+' sign is replaced by '.' i.e. OR gate is replaced by AND gate, relations become equivalent. Thus, either form can produce the desired results. This is stated by DeMorgan's theorem.

'+' sign → '.'
OR gate → AND gate,

FIGURE 2.4 : Principle of Duality

TABLE 2.1
Laws of Boolean Algebra using Variables A, B and C

OR Gate	*AND Gate*
Null law	
A + 0 = A	A . 0 = 0
Identity law	
A + 1 = 1	A . 1 = A
Idempotent law	
A + A = A	A . A = A
Inverse law	
A + $\bar{A}$ = 1	A . $\bar{A}$ = 0
Commutative law	
A + B = B + A	A . B = B . A
Associative law	
A + (B + C) = (A + B) + C	(AB)C = A(BC)
Distributive law	
A (B + C) = AB + AC	A + BC = (A+B)(A+ C)

This theorem states that a NOR gate that performs the function of $\overline{A+B}$ is equivalent to the function $\overline{A}\,.\,\overline{B}$. Similarly, a NAND gate can be expressed as: $\overline{(AB)} = \overline{A}+\overline{B}$

Consider the function F.

$$F = A\overline{B} + C + 0.\overline{D}(1 + E)$$

Then, dual of this function is expressed as:

$$F^D = (A + \overline{B}).C\,(1 + \overline{D} + 0.E)$$

Function F is equivalent to function F^D with the OR gate replaced by AND gate.

2.3 COMBINATIONAL CIRCUITS

Combinational circuits are circuits with multiple inputs and multiple outputs where the output depends exclusively on the inputs. These circuits are formed by interconnection of logic gates. The design of the logic circuit is formed by making Boolean expressions of the problem and solving them by constructing truth-tables of input variables and the output variables. Combinational circuits do not contain any memory.

2.4 DESIGN OF COMBINATIONAL CIRCUIT

The design of a combinational circuit involves stating the problem, identifying the input variables and output variables. The variables are identified and given symbols. The truth-table of the relationships between inputs and outputs is developed. The functions are simplified by using Boolean algebra or other techniques to construct the logic diagram.

The examples of half-adder and full-adder will be taken up to clarify the design of a combinational circuit. These circuits are the most basic arithmetic circuits which serve as the basic building blocks of a computer.

2.4.1 Half-Adder

A half-adder adds two binary digits or bits which are the two inputs of the half-adder. The logic circuit produces a 'sum' digit and a 'carry' digit as the outputs.

(a) Problem: To design a half adder

Inputs – Two binary digits X and Y
Output – Sum digit (S) and Carry digit (C)

The truth-table of a half-adder is given in Figure 2.5(a).

The truth-table exhibits the addition of two variables X and Y. The output variables are the sum S and carry C. Two output variables are needed for sum and carry as addition of two 1's will be 10, which gives sum

X	Y	C	S
0	0	0	0
0	1	0	1
1	0	0	1
1	1	1	0

FIGURE 2.5 (a) : Truth Table of Half-Adder

S as 0, and carry C as 1. The truth-table for half-adder is shown in Figure 2.5(a). The C output is 0 unless both inputs are 1. The Boolean function for the outputs can be directly obtained from the truth-table. These are given as under:

$$S = \bar{X}Y + X\bar{Y}$$
$$= X \oplus Y$$
$$C = X.Y$$

(b) Karnaugh Map for Simplification

The simplification may be performed by using Karnaugh maps

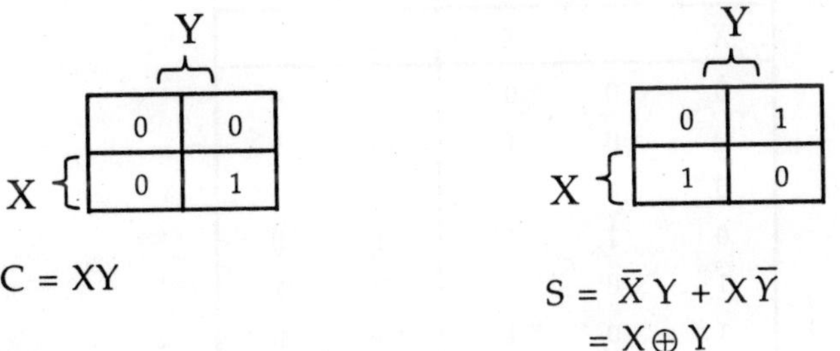

(c) Circuit diagram

The logic diagram of half-adder is formed by using appropriate gates as are shown in the output equations. In this case, an AND gate and an exclusive OR gate are required as is depicted in Figure 2.5(b).

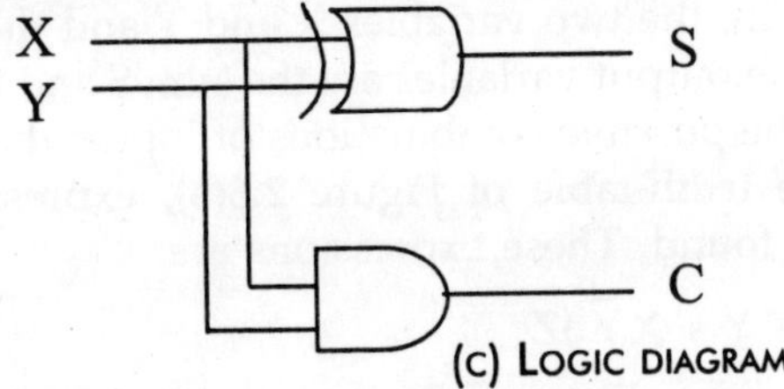

(c) LOGIC DIAGRAM

FIGURE 2.5(b) : A Half-Adder Circuit

2.4.2 Full-Adder

Half-adder has just two inputs of the digits to be added whereas the full-adder has three inputs. These inputs are the two digits for addition, augend and addend, and a carry produced from the previous significant bit. Thus, the full-adder has provision for carrying forward the carry from previous columns (least significant bits), and adding and carrying it forward to the higher order bits of the multi-bit number. For higher-order columns, a full-adder has to be used. As discussed above, a half adder can only add two inputs and does not have provision to add carry coming from the lower order bits when multi-bit addition is performed. In a full-adder, a third terminal is added and this circuit is used to add augend, addend (the two bits to be added) and carry generated from the previous bit addition. Thus, full-adder is a combinational circuit that performs sum of three input bits. A full-adder adds two binary digits along with a 'carry', if it exists from the previous bit addition. The circuit produces two outputs, one is for sum and the other is for carry. The truth table is as shown in Figure 2.6(a).

Problem: To design a Full-Adder

Inputs – Two binary digits X and Y and a carry from previous column, Z
Output – Sum digit (S) and Carry digit (C)

The truth-table of a full-adder is given in Figure 2.6(a)

Inputs			*Outputs*	
X	Y	Z	C	S
0	0	0	0	0
0	0	1	0	1
0	1	0	0	1
0	1	1	1	0
1	0	0	0	1
1	0	1	1	0
1	1	0	1	0
1	1	1	1	1

FIGURE 2.6 (a) : Truth Table for Full-Adder

The inputs are the two variables X and Y and the third input Z is the possible carry. The output variables are the sum S and the carry C. The truth table shows all the possible combinations of inputs that can exist in the full adder. From the truth-table of Figure 2.6(a), expressions for the output variables can be found. These expressions are:

$$C = XY + (\bar{X}Y + X\bar{Y})Z$$

$$S = \bar{X}\bar{Y}Z + \bar{X}Y\bar{Z} + X\bar{Y}\bar{Z} + XYZ$$

A Karnaugh map is utilized to find out the simplified expressions for the construction of the logic circuit of the full-adder.

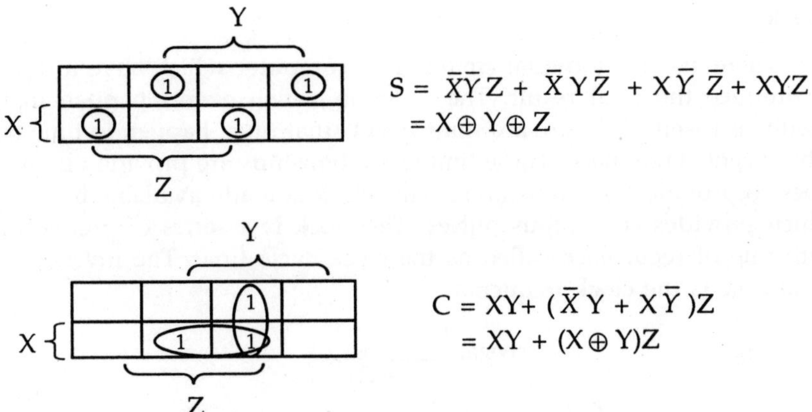

The circuit diagram for full adder is shown in Figure 2.6(b).

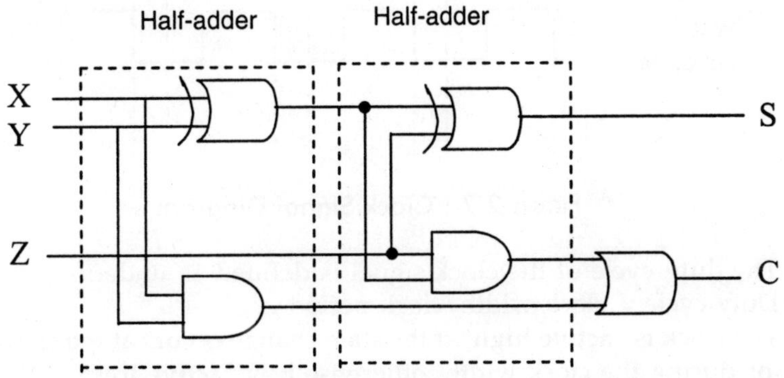

FIGURE 2.6(b) : Logic Circuit for a Full-Adder

2.5 SEQUENTIAL CIRCUITS

The circuits that need to remember the past history of inputs to produce the present outputs require memory. Sequential circuits are the circuits with feedback from output of later gates that is fed back to input of earlier gates. They contain memory, which means that output depends on the sequence of inputs and outputs. The output depends on present and past inputs. In combinational circuits, the output depends only on the present input

Sequential circuits are of two types: Asynchronous and Synchronous. The asynchronous sequential circuits change their state and output values whenever a change in input occurs. They are not clocked. The synchronous sequential circuits are clocked and change their state and output values only at fixed time points, i.e. at the rising or falling edge of a clock signal.

Clock

There are many digital circuits in a computer which have to function to produce the final result. The order in which events happen in these circuits is essential. There are some events that must happen in time before other events take place. These timing relationships are provided by using a clock to provide synchronization. This clock is made available by a crystal which provides continuous pulses. The clock is a series of precise pulses with rate of recurrence called as the clock cycle time. The inverse of this cycle time is the clock frequency.

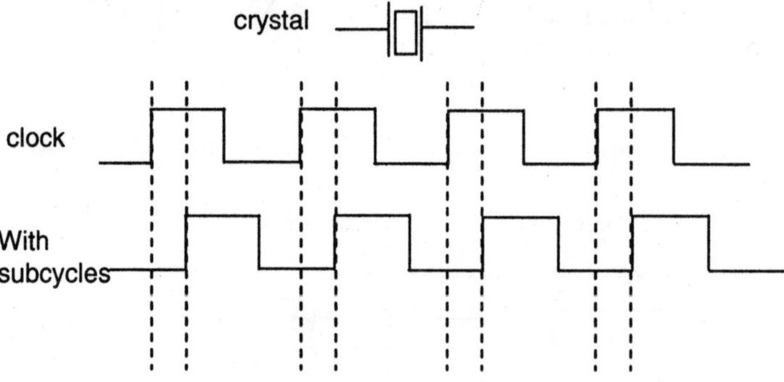

FIGURE 2.7 : Clock Signal Diagram

The duty cycle of the clock signal is defined as under:

Duty cycle = clock width/clock period

The clock is "**active high**" if the state change occurs at the clock's rising edge or during the clock width, otherwise it is "**active low**".

2.5.1 Flip-Flops

Flip-flops are bistable memory devices that remember their past state. They are the basic building blocks of sequential circuits. The clock tests its inputs, and changes its output only at times determined by a clocking signal.

Edge Triggered Flip-Flops

An edge triggered flip flop changes state either at the positive edge (rising edge) or the negative edge (falling edge) of the clock input. The basic types of edge-triggered flip-flop are S-R, J-K and D. The inputs are called synchronous inputs because data on these inputs are transferred to the outputs of the flip-flops only on the triggering edge of the clock pulse. On the other hand, the flip-flops that are not dependent on the clock for the change of their state are called asynchronous flip-flops. The direct set (SET) and clear (CLR) inputs are called asynchronous inputs, as they are the inputs that affect the state of the flip-flop independent of the clock.

In the explanation of the change of state of flip-flop output, present state means the output Q before pulse is applied. Q(t+1) refers to 'next state', which is the output Q pulse has been applied.

SR Flip-Flop

SR (Set-Reset) flip-flop is a flip-flop that is either set or reset. There is no third state. The characteristic table of SR flip-flop shows the states through which it can pass when the clock signal is set. If there is no clock signal, the output cannot change. If both S and R inputs are 0, the output Q(t+1) remains in the original state t. There is no change. For S=0 and R=1, the output Q(t+1) is cleared to 0. It means whether Q(t) is 0 or 1, the next state Q(t+1) is always equal to 0 for the S, R states of 0 and 1 respectively. For the states S=1 and R=0 and the clock signal C is set, the next state Q(t+1) will always be set to 1, no matter what the state Q(t) is.

The fourth state of this flip-flop is an indeterminate state. When both S and R are equal to 1, the output Q(t+1) can be either 0 or 1, depending on the internal clock of the circuit. This state should not be produced by setting both S and R equal to 1 as the output state cannot be determined.

S	*R*	*Q(t+1)*	*State*
0	0	Q(t)	No change
0	1	0	Clear to 0
1	0	1	Set to 1
1	1	?	Indeterminate

FIGURE 2.8(a) : Characteristic Table

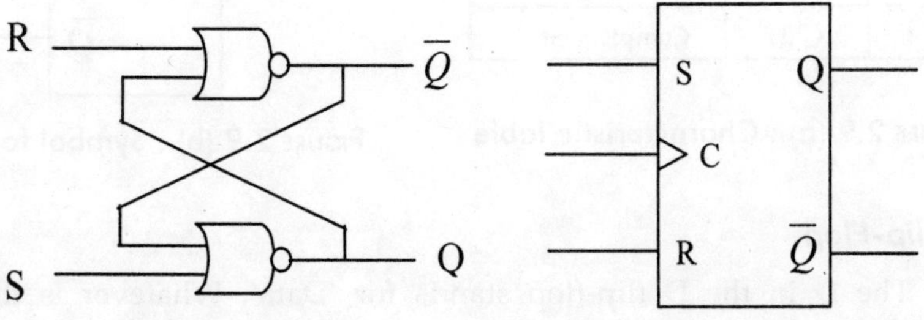

FIGURE 2.8(b) : Circuit and Symbol

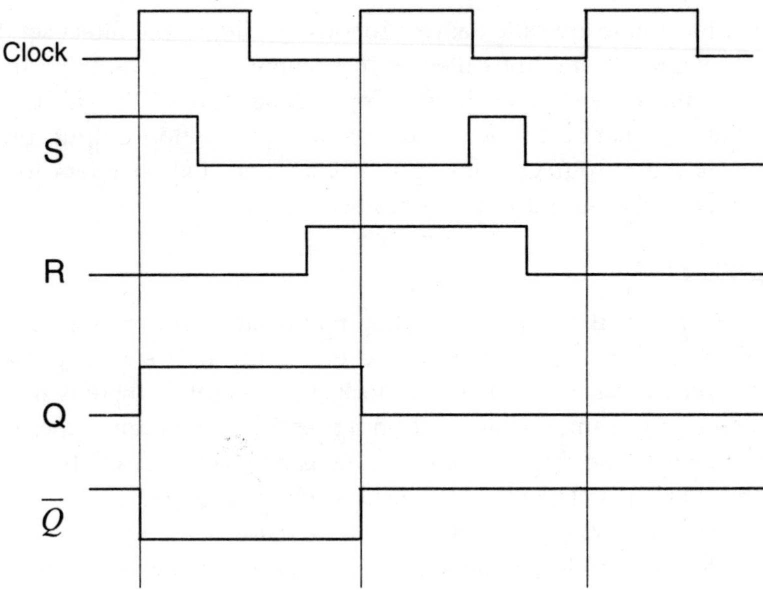

FIGURE 2.8 (c) : Timing Diagram

Trigger Flip-Flop

The T in the T Flip-Flop stands for 'Trigger' which changes state whenever a clock pulse arrives. The T flip-flop and its truth-table are shown in Figure 2.9.

The characteristic table of the T flip-flop shows that there are just two states. When T is set to 0 and the clock pulse is high, the next state is the same as the present state. If T is 1, next state is the complement of the present state.

T	Q(t+1)	Output
0	Q(t)	No change
1	Q′(t)	Complement

FIGURE 2.9 (a) : Characteristic Table

T Q
C
$\overline{Q}$

FIGURE 2.9 (b) : Symbol for T FF

D Flip-Flop

The D in the D flip-flop stands for 'Data'. Whatever is the data available at the input at time t, the same data will be available at the output at time (t+1) during the occurrence of next clock pulse. The D flip-flop and its truth-table are shown in Figure 2.10. The SR flip-flop can be converted to a D flip-flop by inserting an inverter between S and R.

The characteristic table of the D flip-flop shows that it has just two states. When D is set to 0 and the clock pulse is high, the next state is set to 0 at time (t+1). If D is 1, output is set to 1 at time (t+1) which is the next state.

D	Q(t+1)	Output
0	0	Clear to 0
1	1	Set to 1

FIGURE 2.10 (a) : Characteristic Table

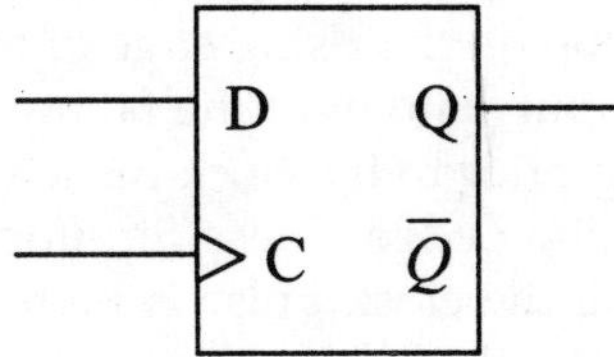

FIGURE 2.10 (b) : Symbol

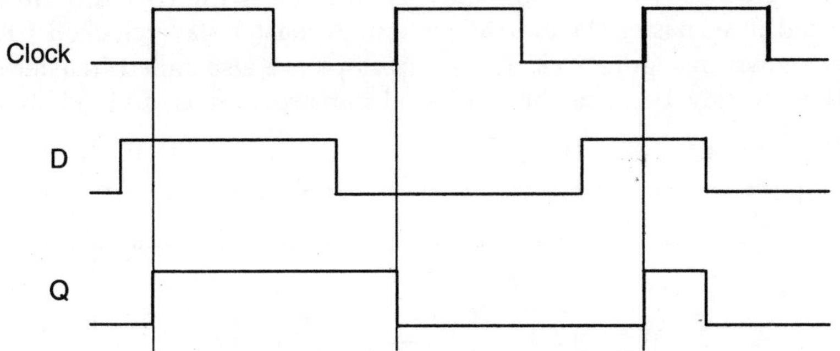

FIGURE 2.10 (c) : Timing Diagram

JK Flip-Flop

The JK flip-flop is similar to SR flip-flop with the difference that all the four states are defined and there is no indeterminate state. Figure 2.11 presents the characteristic table of JK flip-flop which shows the states through which the JK flip-flop passes when the clock signal is set. When both J and K inputs are 0 at time t, the next state Q(t+1) remains in the original state t. For J=0 and K=1, the next state Q(t+1) is cleared to 0. For the states J=1 and K=0, the next state Q(t+1) will always be set to 1.

J	K	Q(t+1)	
0	0	Q(t)	No change
0	1	0	Clear to 0
1	0	1	Set to 1
1	1	$\overline{Q}$	Complement

FIGURE 2.11 (a) : Characteristic Table

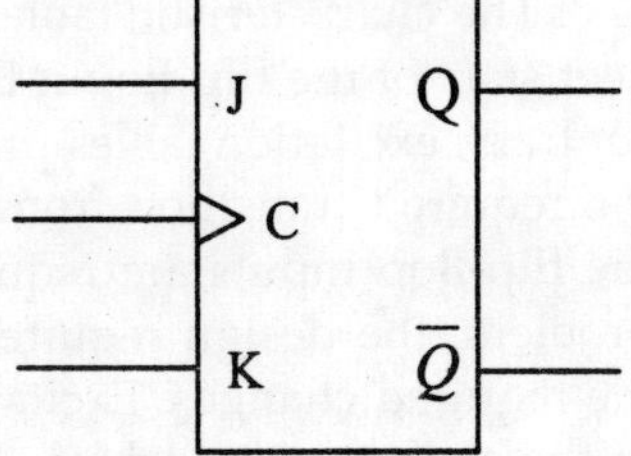

FIGURE 2.11 (b) : Symbol

The fourth state of this flip-flop is the toggle state. When both J and K are equal to 1, the next state Q(t+1) is the complement of the present state Q(t). This is also known as the toggle state.

Pulse-Triggered Master Slave Flip-Flops

The pulse triggered flip-flop is such that the data are entered into the flip-flop on the rising edge of the clock pulse, but the output does not show the input state until the falling edge of the clock pulse. The inputs must be set up prior to the clock pulse's rising edge and must not be changed before the falling edge. These flip-flops are sensitive to any change of input levels during the clock pulse is high. Otherwise, uncertain results will happen.

The three basic types of pulse triggered flip-flops are S-R ,J-K and D. The truth table for the pulse triggered flip-flops are the same as that for the edge triggered flip-flops, except for the way they are clocked.

The clocked J-K flip-flop may be formed with two R-S flip-flops connected in a master-slave arrangement. A master-slave clocked J-K flip-flop is shown in Figure 2.12. These flip-flops are also called 'master-slave' flip-flops simply because their internal construction is divided into two sections.

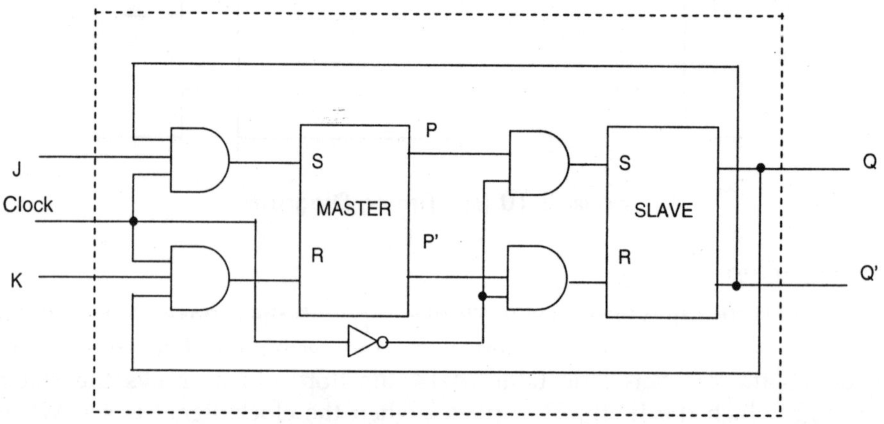

FIGURE 2.12 : Master-Slave Flip-Flop

2.5.2 Excitation Tables

The characteristic tables of the flip-flops are formed which specify the next state of the flip-flop if the present state and the input is known. On the contrary, excitation tables produce the opposite conditions. The outputs and the required transition from present state to the next state are known, and the flip-flop inputs are required. To design a sequential circuit for a given problem, the design requires the flip-flop input conditions that will cause the required changes. Excitation tables produce just the opposite conditions of the characteristic tables. This means that based on the present state and the next state, the excitation table specifies the input conditions of the flip-flops. These excitation tables are constructed from the characteristic tables only, going backwards, to see what the conditions of states of flip-flop exist for a particular transition to take place.

SR Flip-Flop

Table 2.2 shows the excitation table for SR flip-flop. The first two columns of the excitation table are for Q(t) and Q(t+1). The last two columns show the conditions of S and R to produce the required next states.

In the first case, Q(t) and Q(t+1) are both 0. Looking carefully at the characteristic table of Figure 2.8(a), it can be seen that when Q(t) is 0 and Q(t+1) is also 0, then S is always 0 while R can be either 0 or 1. Thus, the excitation table shows that for Q(t) and Q(t+1) to be both 0, S is always 0 whereas condition of R does not matter. Thus, R is a 'don't care' condition.

The second row is for the condition Q(t) = 0 and Q(t+1) = 1. Again, looking at the transition table of Figure 2.8(a), for the present state to be 0 and next state to be 1, S is always 1 while R is always 0. Similarly for Q(t) = 1 and Q(t+1) = 0, S is always 0 and R is always 1. In the last row, Q(t) and Q(t+1) are both 1. To produce this condition, S is 'don't care' condition. This means that it can be either 0 or 1. But R has to be 0.

TABLE 2.2
Excitation Table for SR Flip-Flop

Q(t)	*Q(t+1)*	*S*	*R*
0	0	0	x
0	1	1	0
1	0	0	1
1	1	x	0

T Flip-Flop

The excitation table for T flip-flop is shown in Table 2.3. The first two columns of the table show the possible present states and the corresponding next states.

TABLE 2.3
Excitation Table for T Flip-Flop

Q(t)	*Q(t+1)*	*T*
0	1	0
0	1	1
1	0	1
1	1	0

D Flip-Flop

The excitation table for D flip-flop is shown in Table 2.4. The first two columns of the excitation table are for Q(t) and Q(t+1). The last two columns show the conditions of D to produce the required next states.

In the first case, Q(t) and Q(t+1) are both 0. Looking carefully at the characteristic table of Figure 2.10(a), it can be seen that when Q(t) is 0 and Q(t+1) is also 0, then D is always 0. The second row is for the condition Q(t) = 0 and Q(t+1) = 1. From the transition table of Figure 2.10, for the present state to be 0 and next state to be 1, D is always 1. Similarly for Q(t) = 1 and Q(t+1) = 0, D is 0. In the last row, Q(t) and Q(t+1) are both 1. To produce this condition, D is 1.

TABLE 2.4
Excitation Table for D Flip-Flop

Q(t)	*Q(t+1)*	*D*
0	0	0
0	1	1
1	0	0
1	1	1

JK Flip-Flop

The Table 2.5 shows the excitation table for JK flip-flop. In the first case, Q(t) and Q(t+1) are both 0. From the characteristic table of Figure 2.11(a), it can be seen that when Q(t) is 0 and Q(t+1) is also 0, then J is always 0 while K can be either 0 or 1. Thus, the excitation table shows that for Q(t) and Q(t+1) to be both 0, J is 0 while K is a 'don't care' condition. For Q(t) = 0 and Q(t+1) = 1, again looking at the transition table of Figure 2.11(a), J is 1 and K is don't care condition. For the states Q(t) = 1 and Q(t+1) = 0, J can be either 0 or 1, but K is always 1. In the last row, Q(t) and Q(t+1) are both 1. To produce this condition, J is 'don't care' condition and K=0.

TABLE 2.5
Excitation Table for JK Flip-Flop

Q(t)	*Q(t+1)*	*J*	*K*
0	0	0	x
0	1	1	x
1	0	x	1
1	1	x	0

From the above excitation tables, the characteristic equations of these flip-flops can be formed, which are given below:

$Q^{+} = S + \bar{R}Q$ (for SR flip-flop)
$Q^{+} = J\bar{Q} + \bar{K}Q$ (for JK flip-flop)
$Q^{+} = D$ (for D flip-flop)
$T^{+} = \bar{T}Q + T\bar{Q}$ (for T flip-flop)

2.5.3 State Table

A sequential circuit is specified by its inputs, the outputs and the states of the flip-flops. All these states are interdependent on each other. A state-table is a table that exhibits the desired behavior of the sequential circuit. It shows relationship between the inputs, present states, next states and outputs of the sequential circuit.

Counters are sequential circuits and are constructed from two or more flip-flops. These flip-flops change state in a set sequence when input pulses are received. The flip-flop input equations are formed based on the set sequence to make a counter. This procedure will be explained in the following sections for two counters.

Binary Counter

The design of a synchronous binary counter will be discussed. The synchronous operation will change the states of the flip-flops when an input pulse is received.

The binary counter follows the sequence:

000, 001, 010, 011, 100, 101, 110, 111

This is also how the flip-flops will change state. The 3-bit counter needs three flip-flops. Three T flip-flops are used in this example and are depicted in Figure 2.13.

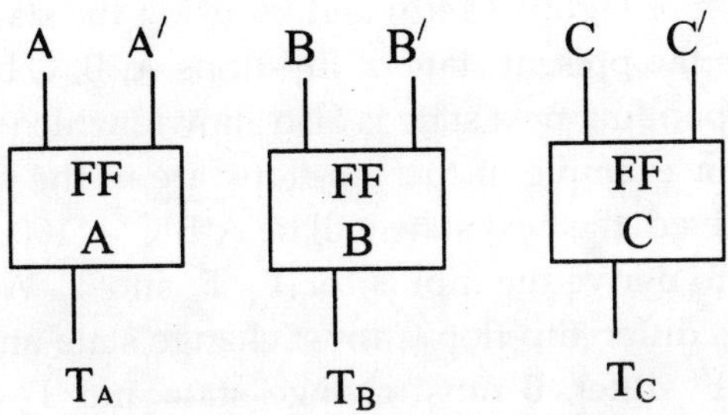

FIGURE 2.13 : Flip-Flop for Binary Counter

From the sequence of events, it can be seen that the flip-flop changes state when an input pulse is received. It should be known what the inputs to T_A, T_B, and T_C will produce these outputs. It can be judged that C changes sequence after every clock pulse. Thus, C is connected directly to T_C. Next, B changes state only if C=1. Therefore, an AND gate is connected to T_B so that if C=1 and a pulse is received, B will change state. Similarly, A changes state when a pulse is received and B and C are both 1. An AND gate is connected to T_A so that A will change state when B=1, C=1 and a pulse is received.

To see how this counter works, initially ABC = 000. When the first pulse arrives, it reaches T_C. The state changes to 001. When second pulse arrives, it reaches to T_B and T_C and the state changes to 010. This process continues until the state 111 is reached. The next pulse reaches T_A, T_B and T_C and all flip-flops return to the state 000. The synchronous binary counter is shown in Figure 2.14(a).

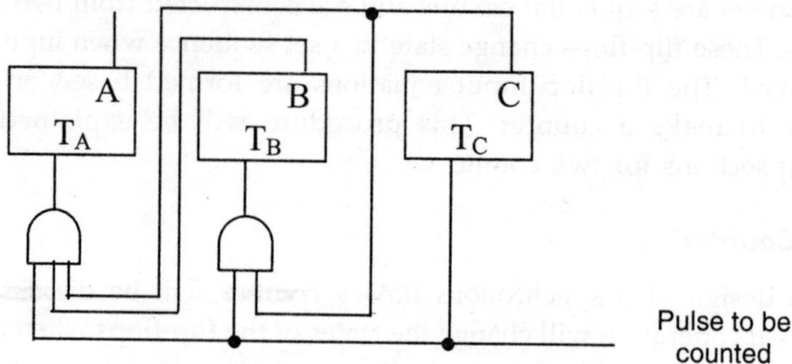

Figure 2.14(a) : Synchronous Binary Counter

2.5.4 State Diagram

A state diagram shows the sequence of events in the form of a directed graph. The output states of binary counter of Figure 2.14(a) can be represented in the state diagram of Figure 2.14(b).

The synchronous binary counter of Figure 2.14(a) will be redesigned by using a state-diagram of Figure 2.14(b) and by using the state-table of Table 2.6. The table shows the present state of flip-flops A, B, C before a pulse is received. The corresponding next state is also shown, which is the state after getting the pulse. For example, if the flip-flops are in the state ABC = 011 and the pulse is received, the next state will be $A^+B^+C^+$ = 100. A third column in the table is used to derive the inputs for T_A, T_B and T_C. Whenever entries in C and C^+ columns differ, flip-flop C must change state and T_C must be 1. Similarly, if B and B^+ differ, B must change state and T_B must be 1. For example, if ABC = 011, $A^+B^+C^+$ = 100 then all the three flip-flops must change state, so $T_AT_BT_C$ = 111.

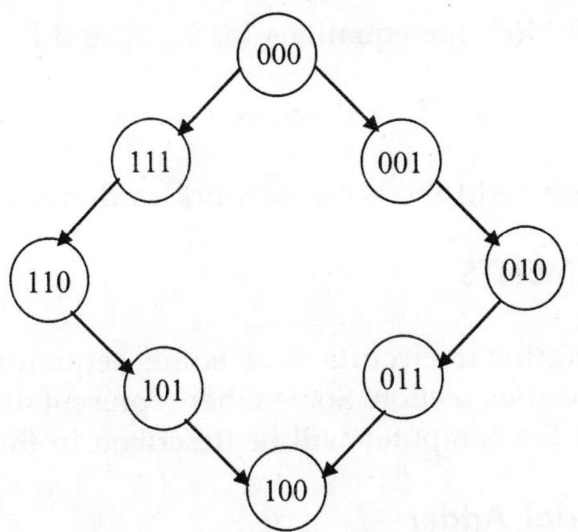

FIGURE 2.14(b) : State Diagram for Binary Counter

TABLE 2.6
State Table for Binary Counter

Present State	*Next State*	*Flip-flop Inputs*
A B C	*A⁺ B⁺ C⁺*	$T_A\ T_B\ T_C$
0 0 0	0 0 1	0 0 1
0 0 1	0 1 0	0 1 1
0 1 0	0 1 1	0 0 1
0 1 1	1 0 0	1 1 1
1 0 0	1 0 1	0 0 1
1 0 1	1 1 0	0 1 1
1 1 0	1 1 1	0 0 1
1 1 1	0 0 0	1 1 1

T_A, T_B and T_C are derived from Table 2.6 as functions of A, B and C. Karnaugh maps are plotted for T_A and T_B. By inspection, $T_C = 1$.

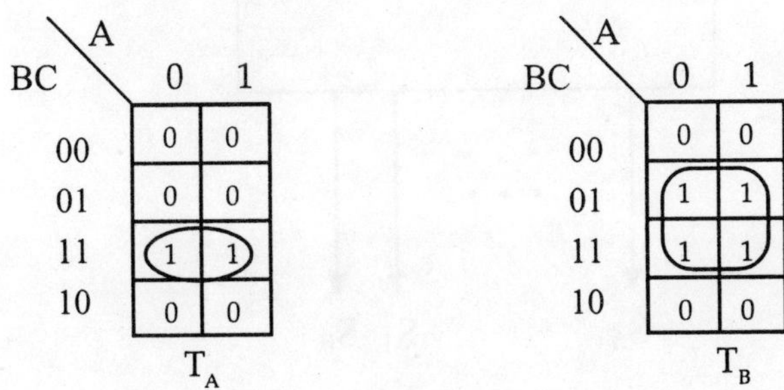

FIGURE 2.14(c) : Karnaugh Maps for Binary Counter

From Figure 2.14(c), the equations for T_A, T_B and T_C are:

T_A = BCP, T_B = CP and T_C = P, where P is the clock pulse.

These equations yield the same network as derived in Figure 2.14(a).

2.6 DIGITAL ELEMENTS

Some combinational circuits and some sequential circuits were explained in the previous section. Some other representative circuits used in the organization of the computer will be described in this section.

2.6.1 Parallel/Serial Adder

Binary addition may be performed in a parallel mode or in serial mode. The design of a parallel adder and a serial adder is explained in this section.

Parallel Adder

Parallel adder is a digital circuit that performs arithmetic sum of two binary numbers in parallel. The addition of two numbers $x = (x_0 x_1 \ldots x_n)$ and $y = (y_0 y_1 \cdots y_n)$ in parallel is done to corresponding bits of each number. This parallel addition is needed as in computer circuits, the number (x) is generally stored in a register and added to a second number (y) stored in

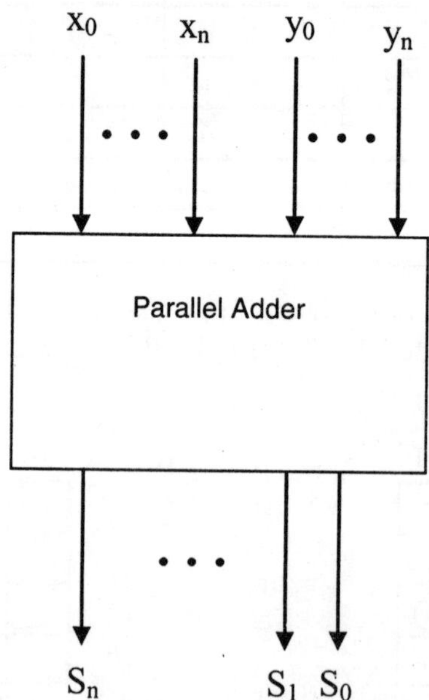

FIGURE 2.15(a) : Functional Diagram of a Parallel Adder Circuit

another register, leaving the sum S = ($S_0 S_1 \ldots S_n$) in the third register. The functional diagram for parallel adder is shown in Figure 2.15(a). The accumulator register is used for addition. A parallel adder is constructed by using full-adders of Figure 2.6 and by using flip-flops and other digital elements as shown in Figure 2.15(b), which makes the use of JK flip-flops. First, the number x is entered into the accumulator. The number y is applied to the full-adder inputs, and after the carry has propagated through the adders, the sum appears at the adder outputs. An Add Pulse is used to transfer the adder outputs into the accumulator flip-flops. The addition of two numbers takes place as follows: If $s_i = 1$, $J_i = 1$ and $K_i = 0$, then the next state of the flip-flop x_i will be 1. If $s_i = 0$, $J_i = 0$ and $K_i = 1$, then the next state of the flip-flop x_i will be 0.

Thus, $x_i^+ = s_i$, and when the Add Pulse occurs, the number X in the accumulator is replaced by the sum of x and y.

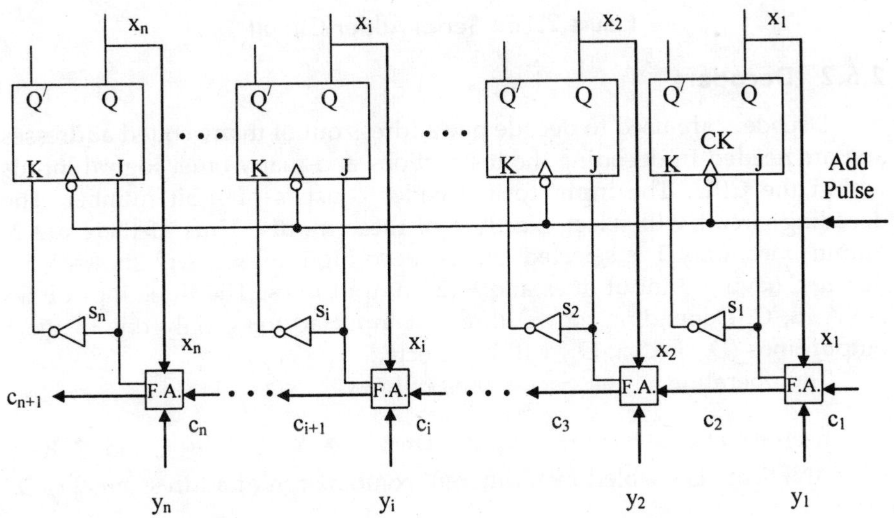

FIGURE 2.15(b) : A Parallel Adder Logic Circuit

Serial Adder

In a serial adder, the binary numbers x and y are fed in serially. Serial adders are used to add two numbers x = ($x_0 x_1 \ldots x_n$) and y = ($y_0 y_1 \ldots y_n$) to produce the sum S = ($S_0 S_1 \ldots S_n$). The bits of x and y enter the adder one at a time. First x_1 and y_1 are fed in. A sum digit S_1 is generated and carry c_2 is stored. At the next clock pulse, x_2 and y_2 are fed and added to give the sum digit S_2 and the new carry c_3 is stored. This process continues till all the bits have been added.

The logic circuit of serial adder has a full adder circuit of Figure 2.6 to generate the sum and carry bits. The carry passes through a delay unit. It is assumed that the inputs are synchronized with the delay so that the new x and y inputs are present at the same time the previous carry is available at the delay output. Figure 2.16 shows a serial adder using a D Flip-Flop to introduce the delay.

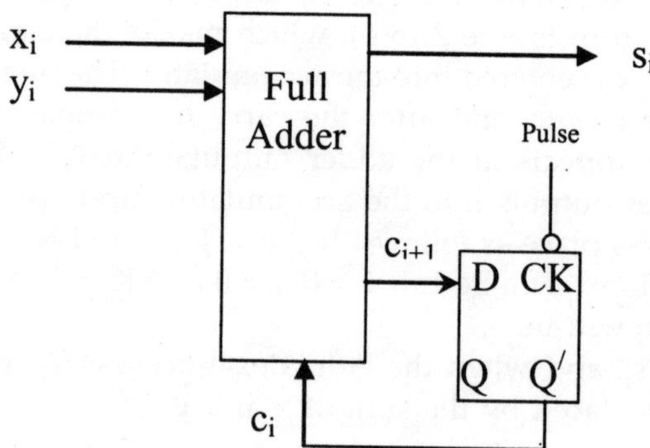

FIGURE 2.16 : Serial Adder Circuit

2.6.2 Decoders

Decoders are used to decode one address out of many coded addresses and are needed in decoding the instructions and many other logical inputs within the CPU. The input to a decoder consists of n-bit number. The decoding circuit will select exactly 1 of these inputs. Thus, if there are 2^n output lines, only 1 is selected and is set to high. Figure 2.17 shows a 3-8 decoder, having 3 input lines and 8 (2^3) output lines. The three input lines are A, B, C. Depending on the three bit input address, only one of the 8 output lines (D_0, D_1, ..., D_8) will be selected.

The operation of the circuit is as follows:

Each AND gate has three inputs. These are A, $\overline{A}$, B, $\overline{B}$, C and $\overline{C}$. Each AND gate is enabled by a different combination of address bits D_0, D_1,

TABLE 2.7
Truth-Table for Inputs and Outputs of a 3-8 Decoder

Enable	*Inputs*			*Outputs*							
E	*A*	*B*	*C*	D_7	D_6	D_5	D_4	D_3	D_2	D_1	D_0
0	X	X	X	0	0	0	0	0	0	0	0
1	0	0	0	0	0	0	0	0	0	0	1
1	0	0	1	0	0	0	0	0	0	1	0
1	0	1	0	0	0	0	0	0	1	0	0
1	0	1	1	0	0	0	0	1	0	0	0
1	1	0	0	0	0	0	1	0	0	0	0
1	1	0	1	0	0	1	0	0	0	0	0
1	1	1	0	0	1	0	0	0	0	0	0
1	1	1	1	1	0	0	0	0	0	0	0

. . ., D_8, and the inputs A, B, C or their complements. The final output F is through the OR gate whose inputs are the outputs of the AND gates. As only one AND gate is enabled at any time, therefore only one input is selected from the 3-bit combination of inputs.

Encoders

Encoders are digital circuits which act as the inverse of decoders. The encoder has 2^n input lines. The output is a set of n lines which generate a binary code that is related to the input lines. Table 2.8 shows the truth table of an eight to three (8 to 3) encoder. The truth table has 8 input lines, D_0 - D_7, and 3 output lines A, B, and C. Only one input line is selected at any time. The output lines show a binary code of 000 to 111.

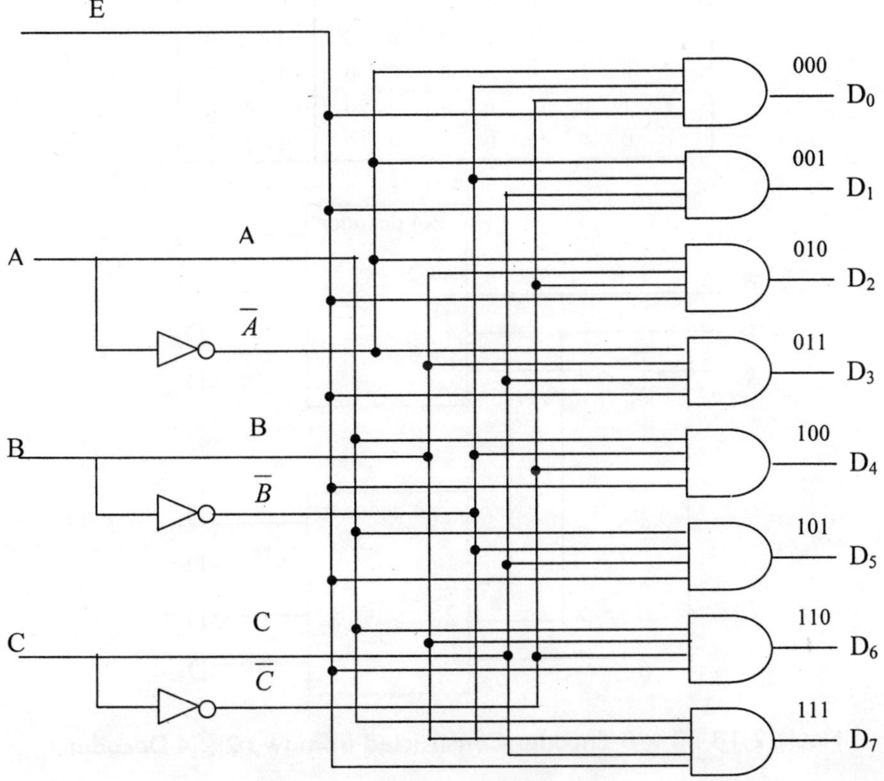

FIGURE 2.17 : A 3-8 Binary Decoder

Figure 2.18(b) shows an 8-3 binary encoder constructed by using two 2x4 encoders.

An encoder can be constructed with OR gates whose inputs are the different lines as given in the truth table of Table 2.8 below. The equations are:

$A = D_1 + D_3 + D_5 + D_7$
$B = D_2 + D_3 + D_6 + D_7$
$C = D_4 + D_5 + D_6 + D_7$

TABLE 2.8
Truth-Table of 8-3 Encoder

Inputs								*Outputs*		
D_7	D_6	D_5	D_4	D_3	D_2	D_1	D_0	C	B	A
0	0	0	0	0	0	0	1	0	0	0
0	0	0	0	0	0	1	0	0	0	1
0	0	0	0	0	1	0	0	0	1	0
0	0	0	0	1	0	0	0	0	1	1
0	0	0	1	0	0	0	0	1	0	0
0	0	1	0	0	0	0	0	1	0	1
0	1	0	0	0	0	0	0	1	1	0
1	0	0	0	0	0	0	0	1	1	1

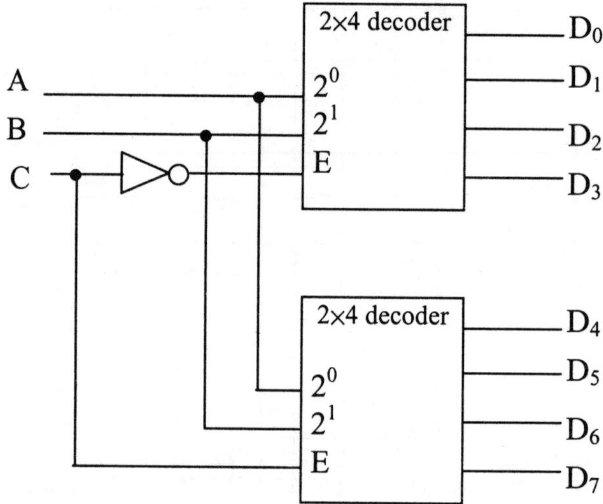

FIGURE 2.18 : 3 × 8-Encoder Constructed from two 2 × 4 Decoders

2.6.3 Multiplexers

Multiplexers are used to select one input line out of many input lines based on the control information available. The circuit has 2^n input lines and only one of these inputs is selected based on the control information that makes the single output line high. Thus, a 2^n to 1 multiplexer has 2^n input lines and n selection inputs, whose bit combination determines which input data will be placed on the output line.

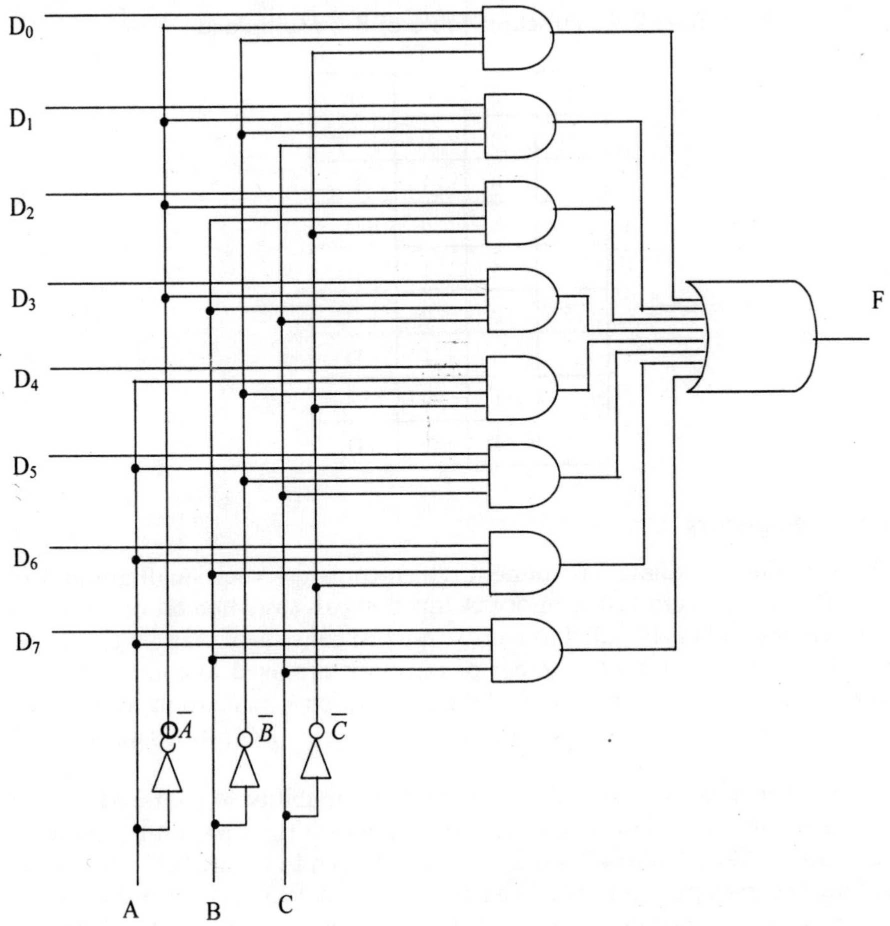

FIGURE 2.19 : A Multiplexer with 8 Inputs

Figure 2.19 shows a multiplexer with 8 (2^3) data inputs (D_0 - D_7) and 3 selection inputs (A, B, C). These three selection inputs control the three control lines to route the desired input data to the output line. The encoding of the three control inputs is the encoding of a three bit number that specifies which input is to be produced at the output OR gate. There are eight AND gates giving inputs to the final OR gate. But as the control lines will make only one input to the eight AND gates as 1, therefore only one AND gate will be enabled. Only this output of the AND gate will appear as the final output.

The Function Table 2.9 shows combinations of various inputs to produce the desired output. When A, B, and C are 000, the output line selected will be D_0. For ABC = 001, D_1 will be selected, so on and so forth.

TABLE 2.9 : Function Table of 8-3 Multiplexer

A	B	C	F
0	0	0	D_0
0	0	1	D_1
0	1	0	D_2
0	1	1	D_3
1	0	0	D_4
1	0	1	D_5
1	1	0	D_6
1	1	1	D_7

2.6.4 Registers

Register is a digital component which can store very small amount of data and acts as very fast memory. A flip-flop can store one bit of data. But in machines, data is handled in words. A word consists of many bits, maybe 8 or 16 or even 64 bits. A number of flip-flops are used in combination to form a register. The operation of all these flip-flops is synchronized by using a common clock. The data can be read or written in all flip-flops at the same time.

Shift register is a register which has the capability of shifting the data by one bit at a time. The data can be shifted left or right per bit position for each clock pulse. A four-bit shift register is shown in Figure 2.20. It consists of four D flip-flops connected to each other so that each clock-pulse causes the transfer of the contents of the first flip-flop FF_1 to the next flip-flop FF_2, of flip-flop FF_2 to FF_3, and flip-flop FF_3 to flip-flop FF_4. Proper operation of a shift register requires that its contents be shifted exactly one bit position for each clock pulse.

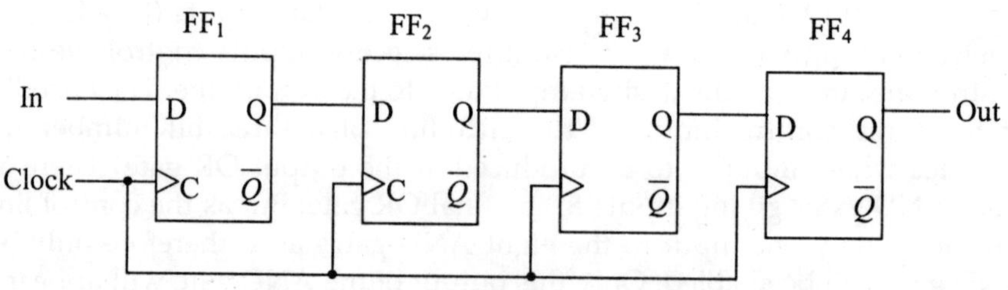

FIGURE 2.20 : A Shift Register

2.6.5 Counters

Binary counter is generally used to count a continuous sequence of numbers. But there are counters where the sequence of the states is not in straight binary order. Any sequence can be conveniently shown by a state graph that shows the graphical representation of the counter. Such a graph is shown in Figure 2.21(a).

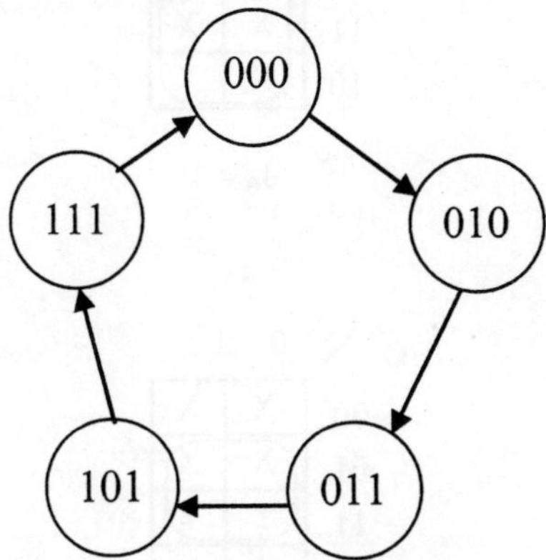

FIGURE 2.21(a) : State Graph for a General Counter

This counter has a sequence of numbers as: 000, 010, 011, 101, 111, which is not the normal binary counting from 000 to 111. Many states such as 001, 100, 110 are missing in this counting. To make a counter of the required sequence of states, a state table is used. The corresponding state table for this counter is given in Table 2.10.

TABLE 2.10
State Table for Counter of Figure 2.21(a)

Present State	*Next State*	*J states*	*K states*
A B C	A^+ B^+ C^+	J_A J_B J_C	K_A K_B K_C
0 0 0	0 1 0	0 1 0	x x x
0 0 1	— — —	x x x	x x x
0 1 0	0 1 1	0 x 1	x 0 x
0 1 1	1 0 1	1 x x	x 1 0
1 0 0	— — —	x x x	x x x
1 0 1	1 1 1	x 1 x	0 x 0
1 1 0	— — —	x x x	x x x
1 1 1	0 0 0	x x x	1 1 1

From this table, it is seen that the next state is unspecified for present states 000, 100 and 110. Next J_A, J_B and J_C, along with K_A, K_B and K_C, are derived from the table as functions of A, B and C. Karnaugh maps are plotted.

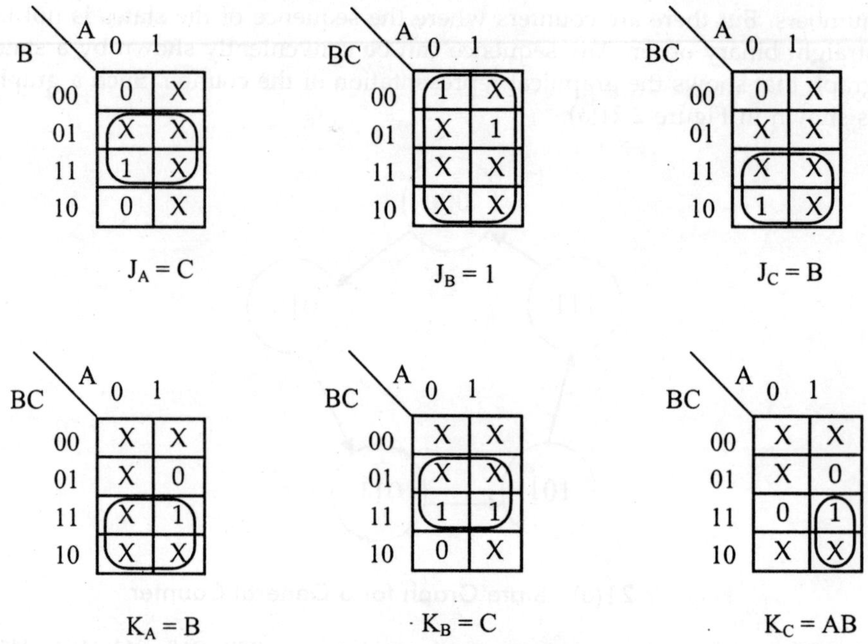

FIGURE 2.21(b) : Karnaugh Maps for a General Counter

The circuit for this counter is given in Figure 2.21(c)

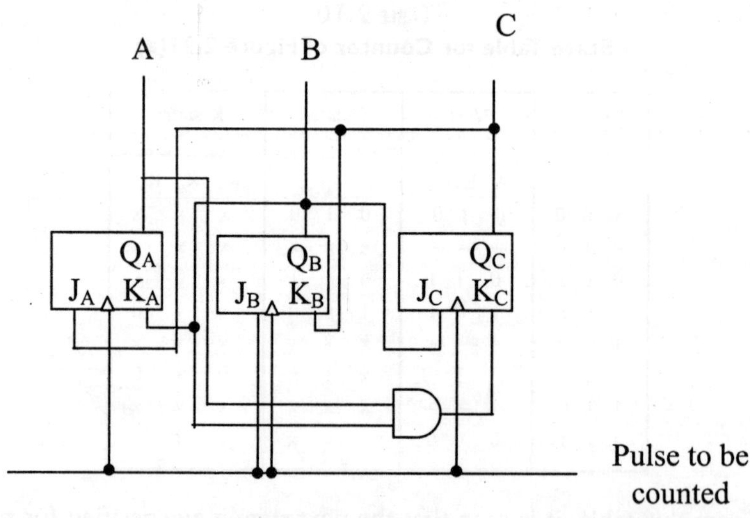

FIGURE 2.21(c) : Logic Diagram for the General Counter

2.7 MEMORY UNIT

The memory unit of a computer comprises of primary memory and secondary memory. Each of these units can have a variety of memory types ranging from flip-flops, transistors, optical memory, magnetic memories, etc. The primary memory consists of random-access memory (RAM). Read-only memory stores the instruction set used by the processor. Mostly, these two units are made of basic electronic elements. Though these two memories are available in large number of designs, a basic structure of these two will be discussed in this section.

2.7.1 RAM (Random Access Memory)

A random-access-memory (RAM) is a very high speed volatile memory and is available in wide range of speeds. The cycle-time ranges from 100 ns to less than 10 ns. The cost of these semiconductor memories is decreasing day by day because of LSI technology, and has become very less as compared to the cost of memories in the recent past.

In these memories, each cell is capable of storing one bit of information and these cells are organized in the form of an array from where the data bits can be either read or written. A memory word consists of data bits in a row of cells.

The organization has an address decoder which is connected to address lines. The cells in each column are connected to Read/Write circuit bit lines. The data input/output lines come out from the read/write circuit.

Read Operation

During a Read Operation, the data that is stored in the cells is read in the word line which has been selected by the decoder. This information is then transmitted to the output data lines.

Write Operation

During the Write operation, the data that has to be written is received at the input and is stored it in the cells of the selected word.

The organization of a 16 × 8 RAM consists of 16 words of 8 bits each. The structure of such a RAM is shown in Figure 2.22. The outputs of Read/Write circuit are connected to the data bus of a computer. Address lines $A_0 - A_3$ are decoded to locate one of the 16 × 8 cells where data is to be read from or written into. Two control lines $R/\overline{W}(Read/\overline{Write})$ and CS (chip select) are connected to the Read/Write circuit. The data bits d_0 ... d_7 represent the data in or data out.

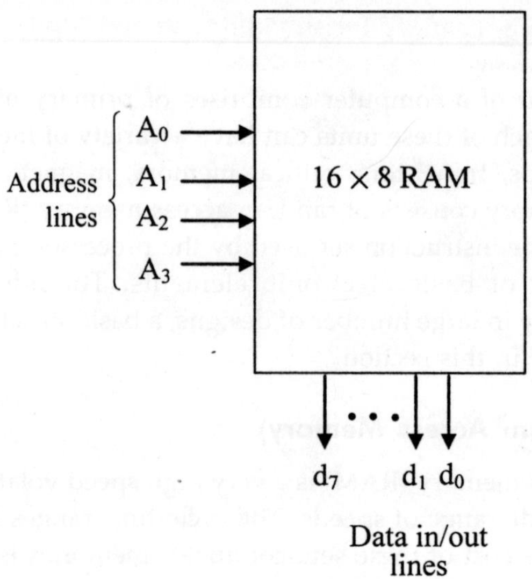

FIGURE 2.22 : RAM Circuit

2.7.2 Read-Only-Memory (ROM)

The Read-Only-Memory (ROM) is a non-volatile memory which consists of an array of transistors or similar electronic elements, from where the data is allowed to be read only. The binary data of the ROM is stored in these transistors at the time of its fabrication. This data can be read out when desired, but the data which is stored cannot be changed under normal operating conditions. A ROM that has four input lines and four output lines is presented in Figure 2.23. A typical truth-table which associates the ROM inputs and outputs is shown in Table 2.11. The data in a ROM are inserted during its manufacture. The data stored in the ROMs are fixed. The data

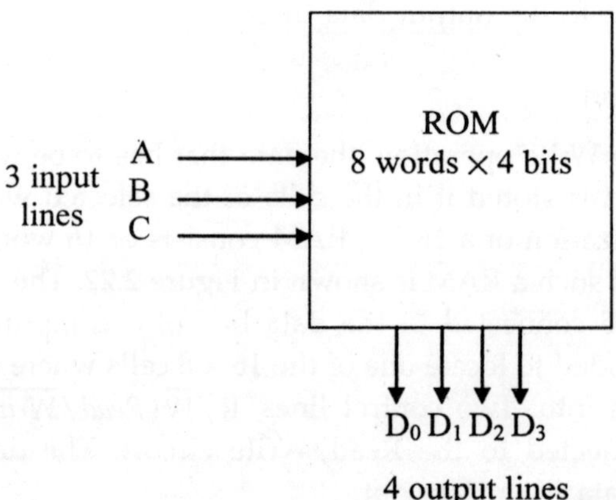

FIGURE 2.23 : ROM Circuit

stored in the ROM can be changed by providing different kinds of ROM like PROM, EPROM, EEPROM, flash memory, etc.

The truth-table for the ROM of Figure 2.23 is presented in Table 2.11 that shows the different data words (D_0 – D_3) stored at various addresses (ABC).

TABLE 2.11

Truth-Table for ROM Inputs and Outputs

A	B	C	D_0	D_1	D_2	D_3
0	0	0	1	0	1	0
0	0	1	1	0	1	0
0	1	0	0	1	1	1
0	1	1	0	1	0	1
1	0	0	1	1	0	0
1	0	1	0	0	0	1
1	1	0	1	1	1	1
1	1	1	0	1	0	1

Relative speed of reading the ROM is less than speed of reading the RAM. The writing speed of those types of ROM which can be written, the speed is very slow.

2.8 SUMMARY

Electronic gates constructed from transistors do the computing of the computer. The logical arithmetic is controlled by Boolean Algebra which manages the number of switches to be used in a chip. Combinational circuits are used to do the different kinds of computations in the processor, like addition. Sequential circuits comprise of flip-flops which are the basic memory elements. To construct sequential circuits, methods like state-diagrams and state-tables are used which help in handling the various states of flip-flops to build an optimum design. Numerous digital components like decoders, multiplexers, registers, counters etc., are used in the computer system. The design of these elements are the combinational circuits and sequential circuits built from the gates. Parallel adders are used to add all the bits of two numbers simultaneously. Serial adders add the two numbers bit wise. A decoder decodes the input bits by selecting one output from 2^n output lines depending on the control information. An encoder acts just the opposite of a decoder. A multiplexer has many inputs and selects one out of them. A flip-flop can store just one bit. But a word of a computer contains more than one bit, may be 8 or 16 or 64 bits. A register is made up of many flip-flops and stores a word. Registers are also used to handle many logical operations. Counters help in counting clock pulses. These counters can be designed to count any sequence. The design of RAM and ROM should have a convenient method of read/write so that the speed of access can be increased.

References

Gibson, G.A., Computer Systems: Concepts ND Design, Englewood Cliffs, NJ: Prentice Hall, 1991.

M. Morris Mano, Computer System Architecture, Third Edition, Pearson Education (Singapore), 1993.

Patterson, D.A. and J.L. Hennessey, Computer Architecture: A Quantitative Approach, San Mateo, C.A.: Morgan Kaufmann Publishers, 1990.

Hill, F.J. and G.R. Peterson, Digital Systems: Hardware Organization and Design, 3rd ed., New York: John Wiley, 1987.

Tanenbaum, Andrew S., Structured Computer Organization, 4th ed., Prentice-Hall of India, New Delhi, 2001.

PROBLEMS

1. In which unit of the computer does the processing of a program takes place?
2. Construct NOT, AND and OR gates using NAND gates only.
3. Draw the circuit that implements : ((w'x)'+(yz'))'
4. Show the truth tables for the following functions, and minimize using K-map:
   (a) wx+xz+y'
   (b) w'x'yz+w'xyz+w'x'yz'+w'xyz'
5. For the following equation, draw K-map and generate minimal equations:
   w'x'y'z'+w'xy'+wy'z'+wxy'z+wyz'
6. Explain the functioning of a R-S Flip-Flop by constructing the next state truth-table.
7. Convert a clocked D flip-flop to a clocked J-K flip-flop by adding external gates.
8. Draw a clocked S-R flip-flop and its truth table.
9. Show the internal organization and schematic representation of a 4-1 multiplexer.
10. Design a decade counter with the help of a state table and by using JK flip-flops.
11. Design a BCD to 7-segment decoder.
12. Design an 8-to-1 encoder using two 4-to-1 encoders and additional logic gates.
13. Draw the circuit for 8-bit register.
14. Show the truth-table and draw the circuit for 4-bit left-shift register.
15. Draw the diagram and explain the functioning of RAM.
16. Show the truth-table and draw the circuit for 4-bit up-down counter.

CHAPTER

3

Computer Fundamentals

3. INTRODUCTION

This chapter explains the fundamentals of various units of a digital computer that do the computation and store the information. Computer hardware essentially consists of electronic circuits which cover the basic components within the processor. This chapter introduces many hardware and software concepts, the terminology used and explains the basic concepts of the computer organization.

3.1 FUNCTIONAL UNITS

Computer organization is the structure of high level parts of the computer like—CPU, memory and input-output devices, whereas computer design is the structure of low level parts like gates, flip-flops, logic arrays, etc. The organization of a computer consists of study of three main functional units which are:

- Processor
- Memory
- Input/Output devices

These units are interconnected to each other through buses. The internal organization of a simple bus-oriented computer is shown in Figure 3.1, which depicts that the three main units of the computer, the Central Processing Unit (CPU), the memory and the input-output devices are interconnected through a system bus.

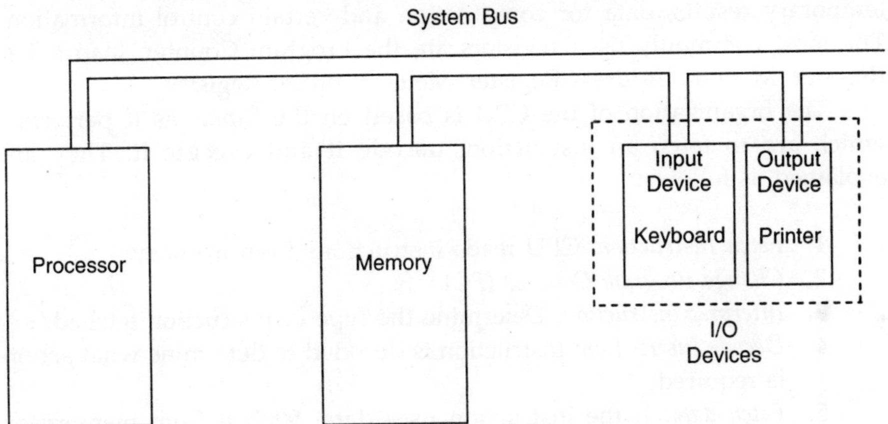

FIGURE 3.1 : Functional Units of a simple computer with two I/O devices

3.1.1 Processor

A central Processing Unit (CPU) is the 'brain' of the computer and controls its functioning. It has the responsibility of fetching the instruction, interpreting and executing it. The sequence of events that take place are that the processor fetches instructions from the memory by providing the address and control signals needed by the memory to access the data. The CPU then decodes the instructions, and provides control signals for the execution to be completed. Some operations are performed internally by the CPU to supply the address, data, and control signals required by memory and I/O devices to execute the instruction. The CPU makes everything to happen within the computer.

Thus, the function of the CPU is to execute the programs stored in the main memory by fetching their instructions, examining them, and then executing them one after another. The CPU is a synchronous sequential circuit whose clock period is the basic unit of time of the computer. It consists of the following components:

Control Unit

The control unit fetches the instructions from the main memory and determines their type. It generates control signals and microoperations.

ALU

The arithmetic and logic unit (ALU) performs operations like addition, subtraction, Boolean AND, OR, etc. that are needed to carry out instructions.

Registers

Registers are a very high speed memory within the CPU that stores temporary results, data for computation and certain control information. The most commonly used registers are the Program Counter, Instruction Register, Memory Address Register, Memory Buffer Register.

The organization of the CPU is based on the functions it performs, which are to fetch an instruction, decode it and execute it. They are explained as follows:

1. *Fetch Instruction*: CPU reads instructions from memory.
2. *Change Program Counter (PC).*
3. *Interpret instruction*: Determine the type of instruction fetched.
4. *Decode Instruction*: Instruction is decoded to determine what action is required.
5. *Fetch data*: If the instruction uses data, fetch it from memory or I/O devices.
6. *Execute instruction*: The execution of the instruction may require arithmetic or logical operations on data.
7. *Write data*: The results are stored in the memory location.

To do these operations, CPU needs to store some data temporarily in the CPU registers. Figure 3.2 shows the block diagram of a processor. The input to the processor is thc instructions from the memory that are to be executed, and data from the memory that is needed for executing these instructions. The output of the processor is the resulting data from execution and is stored in the memory. The three units are interconnected through internal buses, which are different from the system buses.

3.1.2 Memory

The external memories store the programs and data required by the processors. Many memory technologies exist which vary in capacity, performance and cost. Faster memories like cache will cost more, and slow devices, like secondary storage will cost very less.

The memory of a computer can be divided into several subsystems.

1. Main Memory

It is a relatively fast storage and is reasonably expensive, consisting of storage cells. This memory is connected directly to the CPU and is controlled by the CPU itself.

2. Secondary Memory

It is a quite slow, less expensive device and has a very large storage capacity. They are generally not connected directly to the CPU and form part of the I/O system.

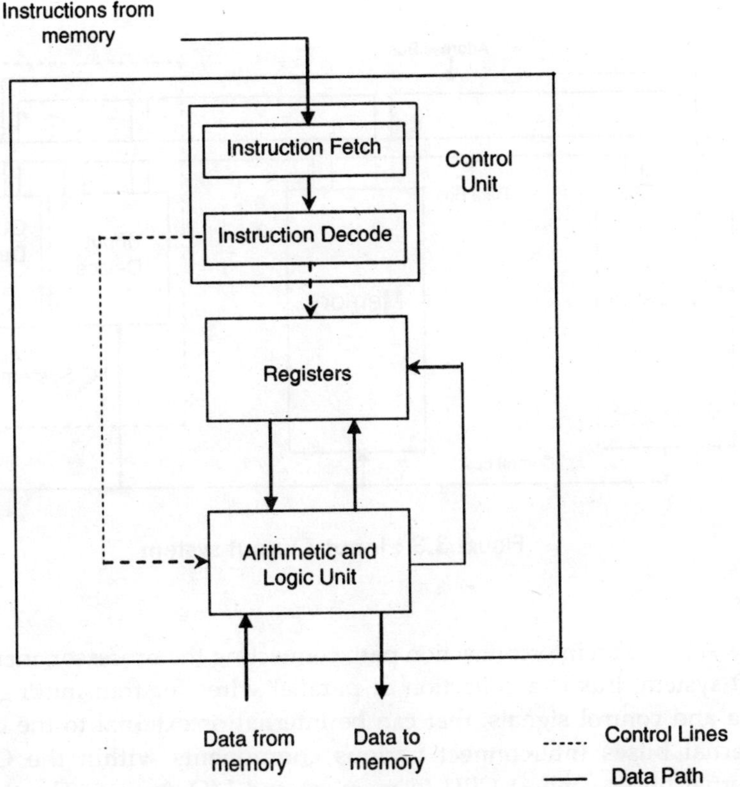

FIGURE 3.2 : Processor Block Diagram

3. Cache Memory

Cache memory is positioned between the CPU and the main memory. The purpose of having a cache is to reduce the delay in accessing the main memory by the CPU. The capacity of cache is very low and it is a very expensive memory.

3.1.3 Input/Output

The third main functional unit of the computer system is its Input/ Output (I/O) system. The computer system takes input data and provides output results through its I/O buses. Separate memory and I/O buses are used to communicate with the I/O system. Interfaces are used with the I/O bus that allows the processor to get connected with a wide range of I/O devices. The architecture consists of a set of I/O modules. Each module interfaces to the system bus and controls one or more peripheral devices. The block diagram of the connection of processor and memory with the

I/O system is shown in Figure 3.3. The address lines, data lines and the control lines are connected to each peripheral device.

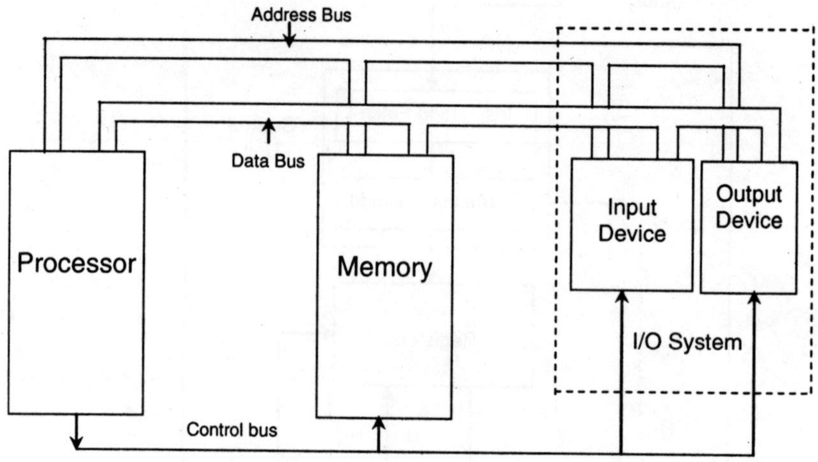

FIGURE 3.3 : Input-Output system

Bus

A bus is an interconnection path connecting the processor, memory and I/O system. Bus is a collection of parallel wires for transmitting address, data and control signals, that can be internal or external to the CPU. The internal buses interconnect various components within the CPU. The external buses connect CPU to memory and I/O devices. The three main buses are data bus, address bus and control bus, which are illustrated in Figure 3.4.

3.2 REGISTER ORGANIZED COMPUTER

In a register organized computer, the CPU has a set of registers used for various purposes. The logic of the control unit executes a particular instruction set and data paths are provided for flow of data and instructions. The general purpose registers (GPR) are used to read instructions, perform operations and store the results, and they are different for every CPU. Each register has a name, or number (used synonymously). The registers are allowed to be accessed in any order by specifying the register number of the register to be accessed. This is similar to specifying the address of the memory location in the memory system in any order. Reading the contents of a general-purpose register does not change their contents. Within the CPU, there are two different set of registers: User-visible Registers and Control and Status Registers.

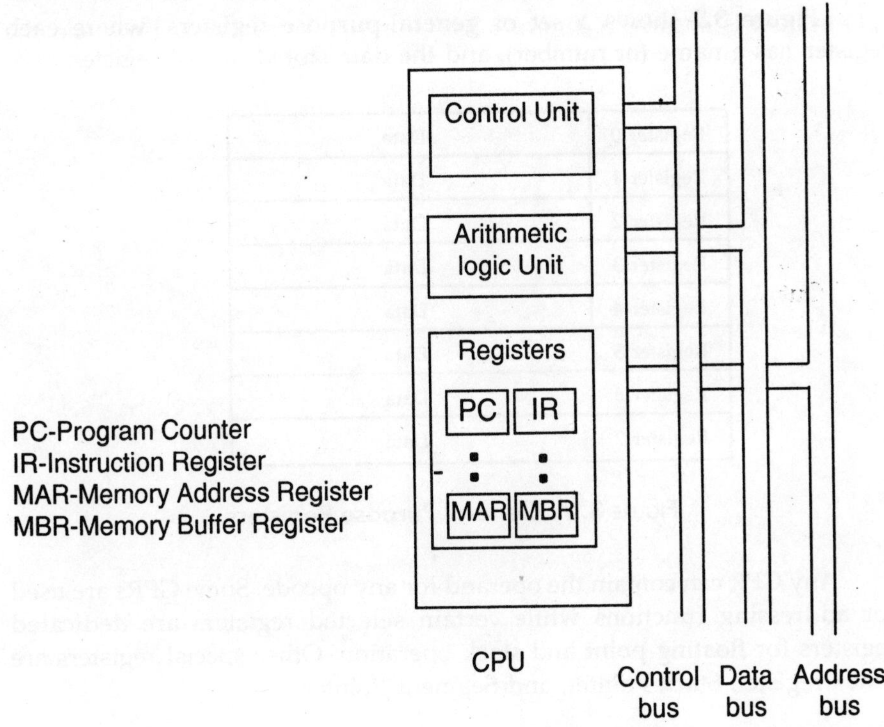

FIGURE 3.4 : CPU and the System Buses

User-Visible Registers

User-visible registers are referenced by means of machine language that the CPU executes. These registers store the data from the main memory that will be used during execution. Thus, they minimize the main memory references.

They are categorized as under:

- General Purpose registers
- Data register
- Address register
- Flag registers

General Purpose Registers

The general-purpose registers (GPR) allow an instruction to access the registers in any order. These are used by the control unit to control the operation of the CPU, and by operating system programs to control the execution of the program.

Figure 3.5 shows a set of general-purpose registers, where each register has a name (or number), and the data stored in that register.

Register 0	Data
Register 1	Data
Register 2	Data
Register 3	Data
Register 4	Data
Register 5	Data
Register 6	Data
Register 7	Data

FIGURE 3.5 : General Purpose Registers

Any GPR can contain the operand for any opcode. Some GPRs are used for addressing functions while certain selected registers are dedicated registers for floating point and stack operation. Other special registers are Index register, Stack Pointer, and Segment Pointer.

Data Registers

Data registers may be used only to hold data and cannot be used for calculations.

Address Registers

Address registers hold the address of the instruction. They may act as general-purpose register when they are used for a particular addressing mode.

Flag Registers

Flag registers are partially visible to the users and they hold the **condition codes,** which are the bits set by the CPU hardware as a result of operations. For example, an arithmetic operation may produce a positive, negative, zero, or an overflow result. The result of the operation is stored in the flag register, and the condition of the result, which can be of the form of a code, is also set

Control and Status Registers

The control and status registers are not visible to the user. They are used to control the operation of the CPU. These registers may have names that are specific to the CPU. The following four registers are essential for execution of an instruction:

Program Counter (PC): Contains the address of the next instruction to be fetched.
Instruction Register (IR): Contains the most recently fetched instruction.
Address Register (AR): Contains address of a location in memory.
Data Register (DR): Contains a word of data that has been most recently read from memory, or written to memory.

These registers are used for the movement of data between the CPU and main memory. Some commonly used registers with their more used attributes for 8-bit computer are described in Figure 3.6.

Register Symbol	*Register (Size Bits)*	*Register Name*	*Function*
PC	12	Program Counter	Holds address of next instruction
IR	16	Instruction Register	Holds Instruction Code
AC	16	Accumulator	Processor Register
MAR	16	Memory Address Register	Holds address for memory
DR	12	Data Register	Holds Memory Operand
INPR	8	I/P Register	Holds I/P Characters
OUTR	8	O/P Register	Holds O/P Characters

FIGURE 3.6 : Various Register for a General Computer

The program counter (PC) holds the address of the next instruction to be used from the memory after current instruction is executed. The instruction read from memory is placed in the instruction register (IR). The accumulator register (AC) is a general purpose processing register. The memory address register (MAR) has 16 bits of a memory address. The data instead of register (DR) holds the operand read from the memory. The input register (INPR) receives an 8-bit character from an input device. The output register (OUTR) holds an 8-bit character for a output device.

There is a special register known as Program Status Word (PSW), to hold the information of the status of the results in the CPU. It is also known as flag register. Common flags include the following:

Sign : Holds sign bit of the result of the last arithmetic operation.
Zero : It is set when the result is 0.
Carry : Set if addition result has a carry, or a subtraction needs a borrow.
Equal : If logical compare result is equality.
Overflow: Used to indicate arithmetic overflow.
Interrupt enable/disable: Used to enable or disable interrupts.

3.3 BUSES

Different components of the computer need a path to communicate. A bus is a shared transmission medium where multiple devices are connected. A signal transmitted by one device is received by all other devices attached to the bus. But only one device is allowed to transmit at any one time, otherwise the signal gets corrupted. A number of buses are provided in a computer to supply paths within different components. The bus that connects the major components like processor, memory and input-output, is called the system bus.

3.3.1 Bus Organization

A bus is a physical path that carries all electronic signals through a set of common lines, one for each bit of a register. Physically, the system bus is a number of parallel electrical conductor wires. There are three main functional buses in a computer system: data, address and control bus, as depicted in Figure 3.4.

Data Bus

The data bus provides a path for moving the data. This bus typically consists of 8, 16 or 32 separate lines, each line being capable of transferring one bit. The number of lines is referred to as the width of the data bus, which is a key factor to determine the performance of the system, as number of lines determines how many bits can be transferred at a time.

Address Bus

The address lines are used to specify the source and destination address of the data to be read or written. For example, to read a word from the memory, the address of the desired word is put on the data lines.

Control Bus

Control bus transmits both the command and timing information between system modules and is used to control the functioning of various components of the computer system. The operations that the CPU has to perform are identified by the command signals, whereas the timing signals indicate the time during which the data and address are present and are valid.

The functioning of the bus is that if a module wants to send data to another module then permission is obtained for the use of the bus and data is transferred. If a module wants to request data from another module then permission is obtained for the use of the bus transfer, the request is sent to the other module via control lines, and waits for second module to send data.

3.3.2 Hierarchical Bus

Generally, many components are attached to a bus for transferring information between them. The time taken by the bus to transfer data between modules depends on how many devices are connected to the bus, as the bus shares the time of information transfer. When multiple devices are connected to the bus, two problems arise: the length of the bus becomes very large, which increases the propagation delay and affects the performance of the system. The second problem is that when the total data transfer demand reaches the capacity of the bus, the bus restricts access to data transfer.

Because of these problems in a single bus, many computer systems use multiple bus architecture which is laid out in a hierarchy. A hierarchical bus structure is shown in Figure 3.7. There are three kinds of buses: local bus, system bus and an expansion bus.

Local bus connects the processor to the cache memory, or to specialized devices like an I/O controller. The cache memory controller connects the cache to the local bus and to the system bus. Main memory is connected to the system bus. The I/O devices are connected to the memory through the system bus so that I/O module transfers do not interfere with the functioning of the processor. An expansion bus interface allows the data transfer between the system bus and other I/O devices. This allows a wide variety of I/O devices to be used, but without interference between processor and memory traffic.

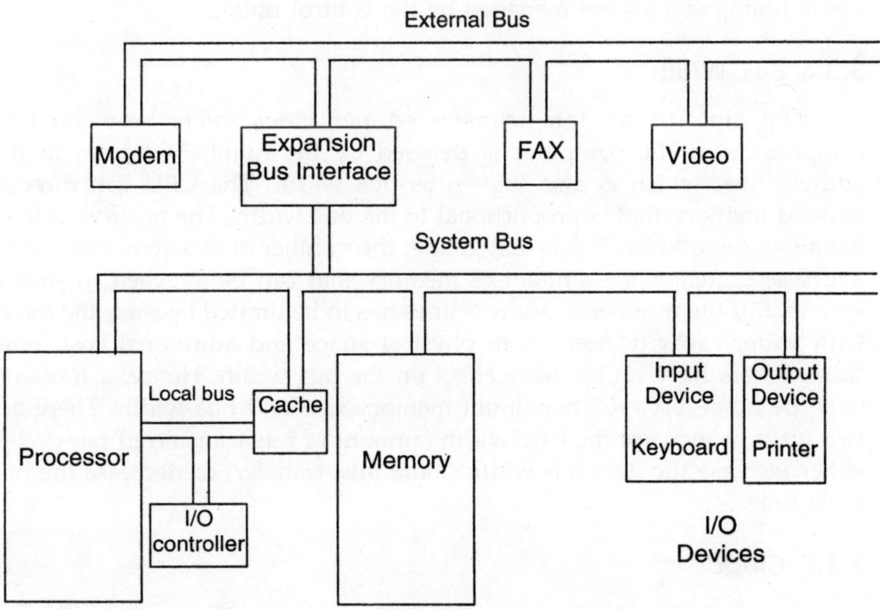

FIGURE 3.7 : Hierarchical Bus Architecture

3.3.3 Bus Types

There are generally two types of buses: dedicated buses and multiplexed buses. Dedicated buses are allocated a permanent function of computer components. For example, dedicated bus is the control bus that will carry only the control signals. On the other hand, multiplexed buses use the same lines for more than one purpose. Example of a multiplexed bus is the address bus that carries address and data information over the same set of lines. In the beginning of the data transfer cycle, address is placed on the data bus; the control signal indicates the presence of address on the data lines. The address is then removed from the data bus and this bus is used for transferring data for read or write. Thus, line multiplexing is achieved.

3.3.4 Bus Control

Only one unit can transmit information on the bus at any time. If many units need to use the bus at the same time, some method is needed to decide as to who will use the time of the bus at a particular time. Various methods are used which can be centralized or distributed. In centralized system, a bus controller is responsible for allocating time to the bus. In distributed control, each module contains access control logic and the modules act together to share the bus.

3.3.5 Timing

A clock provides timing signals that coordinate the events on a bus. These timing signals are managed by the control unit.

3.3.6 Bus Width

The amount of data transferred per clock cycle between two components of the computer is decided by the number of lines in the address bus, which is also known as bus width. The CPU can directly address memory that is proportional to the bus width. The positive side of having wider address bus is that greater the number of locations that can be addressed, greater the amount of memory that can be attached to such a system. But the number of address lines has to be limited because the buses with wider capacity need more physical space and additional cost. Both these factors have an opposite effect on the bus width. Hence, a trade-off must be made between maximum memory size and bus width. There are two ways to increase the bandwidth (amount of bits transferred per cycle), either increase the data bus width (more bits/transfer) or decrease the bus cycle time.

3.3.7 Clock

The clock provides timing signals to control operations of the CPU. The clock defines regular time intervals, called cycles. To perform any basic operation, the CPU divides the action into sequence of basic steps. Each basic step is completed in one clock cycle. The actions performed by the CPU can be synchronous or asynchronous.

The classification of buses can be done based on the clock, which is of two categories: Synchronous bus and Asynchronous bus. A Synchronous bus has all devices deriving timing information from a common clock line. This clock line is driven by a crystal oscillator and has equally spaced pulses that define uniform time intervals. Each of these intervals constitute a bus cycle during which one data transfer can take place

On the other hand, asynchronous bus is used for asynchronous operations, like I/O. In this case, data transfer on the bus is performed using

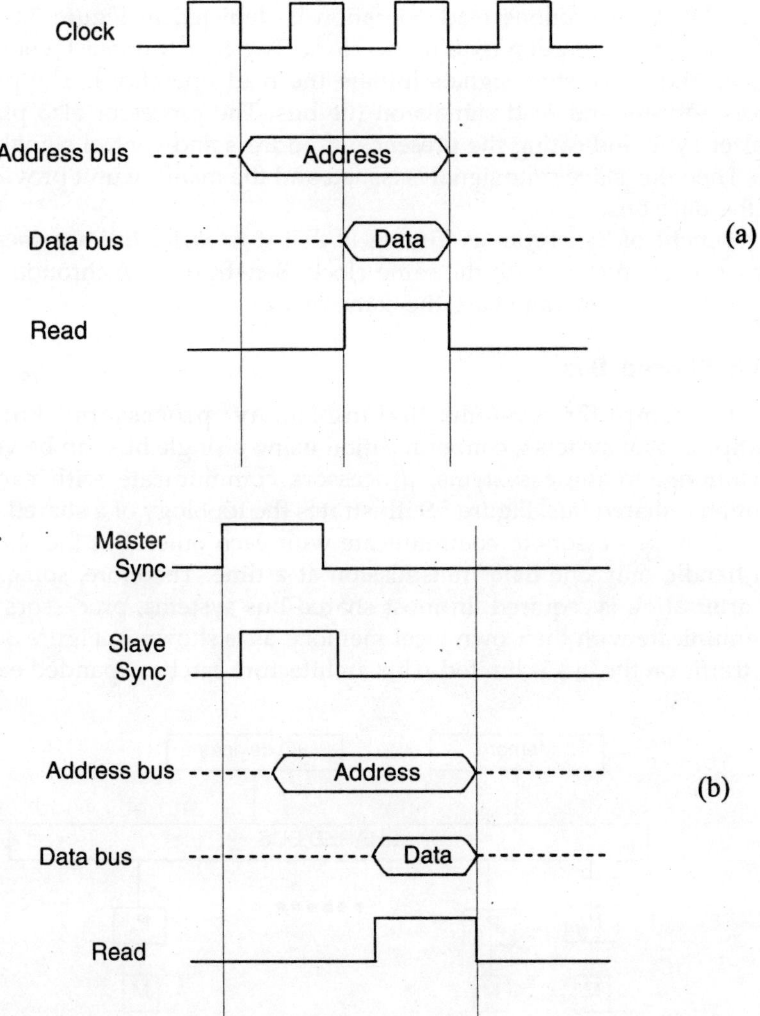

FIGURE 3.8 : Timing Diagram (a) Synchronous Bus (b) Asynchronous Bus

the concept of handshaking between the master and the slave. In these buses, the common clock is replaced by two timing control lines, Master-Sync and Slave-Sync. The first is furnished by the master, indicating it is in ready state for transaction. The second is a slave response.

Figure 3.8 (a) shows the timing diagrams for synchronous read operation. The 'clock' is the system clock. This clock is used to synchronize the operations of the system. The CPU places the address on the address bus at the beginning of the clock cycle. During this time, the address is decoded and data is accessed from the memory. The memory places the data on the data bus. The Read operation is activated during this time and the processor reads the data from the data bus, and stores it in one of the registers.

With Asynchronous timing, the occurrence of one event follows the other. An Asynchronous read operation is depicted in Figure 3.8(b). This Asynchronous operation requires no clock. Two Synchronous (sync) signals, Master and Slave sync signals initiate the read operations. The processor places address and read signals on the bus. The processor also places the 'master sync' indicating the presence of address and control signals on the bus. Then the 'slave sync signal is issued and the memory unit provides data on the data bus.

Benefit of Synchronous Timing is that it is easier to implement as all devices change state with the same clock. Benefit of Asynchronous Timing is that fast devices can share the same bus.

3.3.8 Shared Bus

In computer systems having many processors, known as multiprocessor systems, communication using a single bus can be very time consuming. In these systems, processors communicate with each other through a shared bus. Figure 3.9 illustrates the topology of a shared bus that is used by processors to communicate with each other. But the shared bus can handle only one data transmission at a time. Therefore, some method for arbitration is required. In most shared bus systems, processors directly communicate with their own local memory, as is shown in Figure 3.9. Thus, the traffic on the bus is limited. This architecture can be expanded easily, but

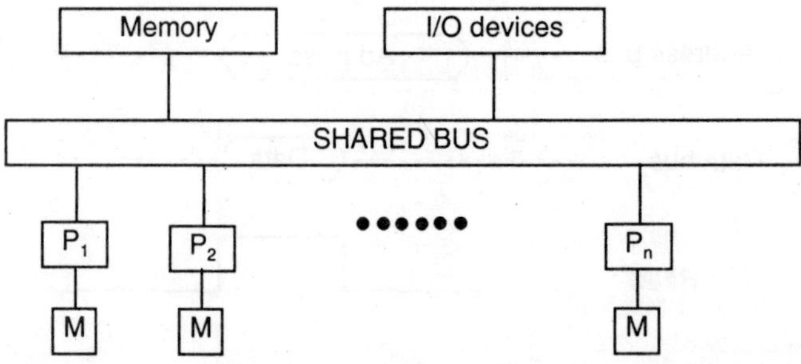

FIGURE 3.9 : Shared Bus with Processors, Memory and I/O Units

as the number of processors increases, the demand on the bus increases, which leads to an increase in the delay.

3.4 INSTRUCTION IMPLEMENTATION

A computer program comprises of a sequence of instructions. Each instruction is executed by the CPU through a sequence of steps. This process consists of execution of a set of instructions stored in the memory. The instructions constituting the program are made to go through various execution cycles, one for every instruction. Each step is executed as a set of microoperations. These instruction cycles consists of the following phases:

1. Fetch an instruction
2. Decode the fetched instruction
3. Get data from the effective address of operands (if any)
4. Execute the instruction

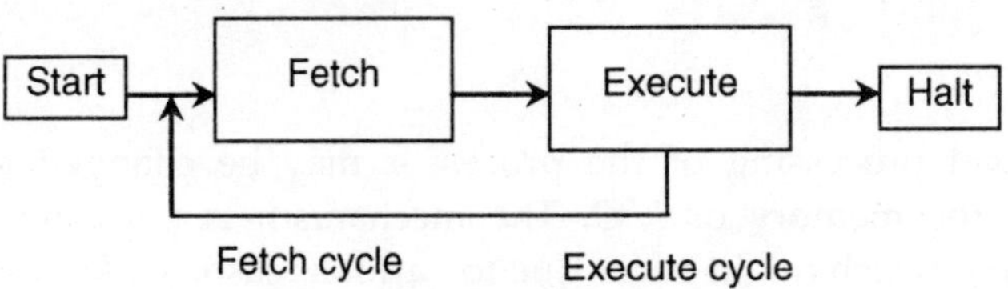

FIGURE 3.10 : Basic Instruction Cycle

In the beginning of each instruction cycle, the processor fetches the instruction from the memory. Program Counter (PC) is a register of the processor that contains the address of next instruction to be fetched. In the beginning, the address of the first instruction is entered into PC. After the instruction is fetched, the PC is incremented. The fetched instruction is loaded in the instruction register (IR). This instruction is interpreted by the decoder and the required action is performed. Accumulator (AC) is a special register which holds one of the operands for the operation to be performed, and is directly connected to the ALU. After this, the instruction is fetched from the address, decoded and executed by the processor. Similarly, other instructions are also executed one by one.

The execution of an instruction that adds two numbers is illustrated below:

> Two 16-bit numbers stored in memory locations with addresses 100 and 101 have to be added. The instruction is 16 bits: 4 bits for the opcode, 12 bits for the operand. The memory words at addresses 830 and 831 are to be added. Instructions of a program add the contents of the memory word at address 830 to the contents of the memory word stored at address 831. The results are stored at address 831. The

implementation requires three fetch and three execute cycles, as described below:

1. PC contains address 100, which is the address of the first instruction. The instruction is loaded in the IR.
2. The first 4 bits of the IR are for the opcode, which indicates that AC is to be loaded. The remaining 12 bits hold the address 830.
3. The PC is incremented.
4. The contents of AC (location 830) and the contents of 831 are added. The result is stored in AC.
5. PC is incremented and the next instruction is fetched.
6. The contents of AC are stored in location 831.

As can be seen from the above mentioned 6 steps for the addition of two numbers, three instruction cycles are used. Each of this instruction cycle consists of a 'fetch' and 'execute' cycle.

Interrupts

The normal processing of the processor may be changed by other modules, like the memory or I/O. The mechanism is performed by an 'interrupt' signal which might occur due to various reasons, like result of an execution, timer within the processor, by an I/O controller or due to some hardware failure. Depending on the type of interrupt, the normal execution of the instruction cycle is disturbed. Interrupts are provided to improve the processing efficiency. Most external devices are much slower than the processor. An example is the data being transferred by the processor to the printer. After each write operation, the processor must pause and remain in idle state till the printer has printed the data. The length of the pause may be many hundreds or thousands of instruction cycles. Various classes of interrupts are shown below:

- Program—Due to condition that occurs because of result of instruction execution like division by zero, arithmetic overflow, etc.
- I/O—Generated by I/O controller signal error conditions, or completion of an operation
- Timer—Generated by timer within the processor, to allow the operating system to perform certain functions at the right time
- Hardware failure—Generated by power failure

For the user program, interrupt is just an interruption to the normal sequence of execution. When the interrupt processing is completed, normal execution resumes.

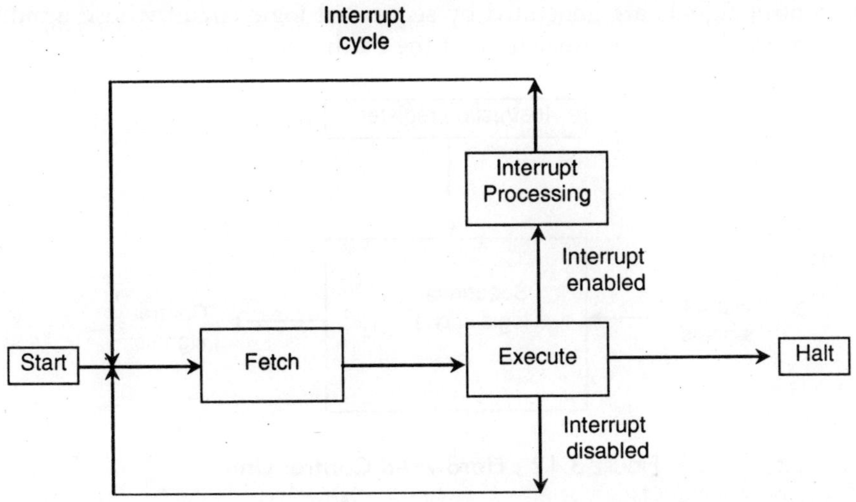

FIGURE 3.11 : Instruction Cycle with Interrupts

3.5 TIMING AND CONTROL

The various steps of instruction cycle take place in a particular time slot. The timing is handled by a master clock generator, which manages the timing for all operations in a basic computer. All electronic elements have an ENABLE pin activated by the control unit to obey the timer. These control signals have their origin in the control unit and act as control input to multiplexers of shared bus, registers, etc. To understand the various control signals necessary for timing in a computer, it is very important to first understand the structure of a control unit of that particular computer.

3.6 CONTROL DESIGN

Control design is the design of the control unit of a CPU that would execute the instructions. This is achieved by the processor with some kind of hardware or software construction to generate control signals in the proper sequence. To approach this problem, a computer designer has to design models of generating such control signals, which might be one of the following types:

(a) Hardwired Control
(b) Micro programmed Control

3.6.1 Hardwired Control

In hardwired control, control signals are generated by hardware assembly. Structure of a hardwired control unit is as shown in Figure 3.12.

The control signals are generated by sequential logic circuit whose inputs are from the Instruction Register and the Status signals.

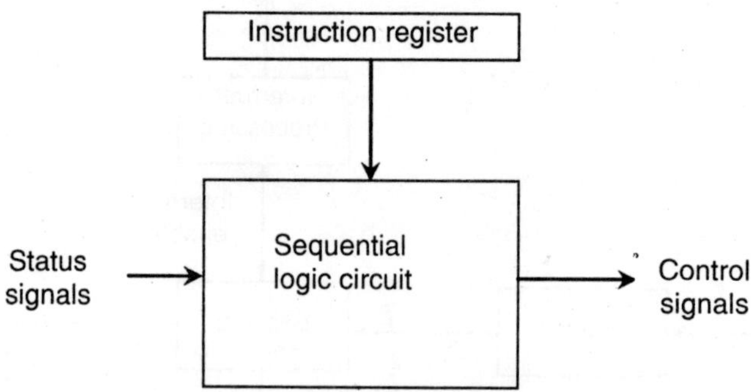

FIGURE 3.12 : Hardwired Control Unit

The sequential logic circuit is direct combinational logic for all next states and outputs. It gets a set of inputs from IR, flags, clock and system buses. The output signals are a function of the current state and inputs.

3.6.2 Microprogrammed Control

An alternative to hardwired control is microprogrammed control, where control signals are sent out by a program similar to machine language programs. The hardware does not execute the instructions directly. Rather, the hardware executes very simple microoperations. Here, each instruction comprises of a sequence of microoperations that are used to implement the instruction.

Figure 3.13 shows the structure of a microprogrammed control unit. It is built around a storage unit called a control memory. All the control signals

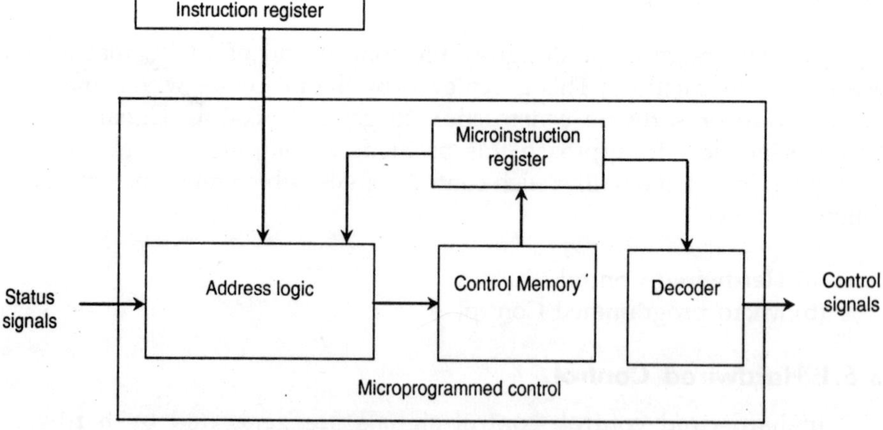

FIGURE 3.13 : Microprogrammed Control Unit

are stored in this control memory in a programmable format. The control memory stores a set of microprograms designed to implement a given instruction set. Each instruction initiates the corresponding microprogram and its control information to be fetched, similar to the fetch-execute cycle of a program from the main memory of the computer. Finally, the decoder decodes the required control signals.

3.6.3 Hardwired Control *vs.* Microprogrammed Control

These days, the control unit of computers are either hardwired or microprogrammed, depending on the needs of the application. Microprogrammed CPUs basically gain on flexibility. Once the control unit of a hardwired computer is designed and built, it is virtually impossible to alter its architecture and instruction set. In the case of a microprogrammed computer, however, the microprogram stored in the control memory can be easily changed by changing the computer's instruction set. Another advantage to using microprogrammed control is the fact that designing the computer is simplified. The process of specifying the architecture and instruction set is that of software (micro-programming) as opposed to hardware design.

Therefore, the alternative is chosen between these two options keeping in view that hardwired control is difficult to design for complex architectures. Once it is designed, no further change is possible. On the other hand, microprogramming is slow because the control memory is accessed in every cycle, and this memory access makes it slow. Hardwired control is fast because the cycle time depends on the combinational logic delay of the control unit, which is much less than the memory access time. Nevertheless, for certain applications, hardwired computers are used where speed is more important. Thus, hardwired control may be required for faster speed because it is quick to have the hardware issue the required control signals than to have a "program" do it.

3.7 INSTRUCTION CODES

A computer instruction is a binary code that represents a sequence of microinstruction for the computer.

3.7.1 Stored Program

All the instructions of the program that has to be executed are stored in the computer memory. Each instruction is then read from the memory and placed in a control register. The binary code of this instruction is interpreted, and finally it is executed by the control unit. The operation code (also known as opcode) of an instruction is a group of bits that define operations such as add, subtract, multiply, shift, complement, etc. The opcode must consist of at least 'n' bits for a given 2^n (or less) different operations to be performed. The operation which the opcode specifies must be performed on some data stored in the memory. An instruction code, hence, must specify not only the operation but also the registers or the memory words where the operands are to be found. The register or memory words where the operands are to be stored need also be specified.

Figure 3.14(a) is an illustration of the stored program in the memory of size 4096 × 16 bits. This means 4096 words of 16 bit each. A part of this memory is used to store the instructions. Operands are stored in a different

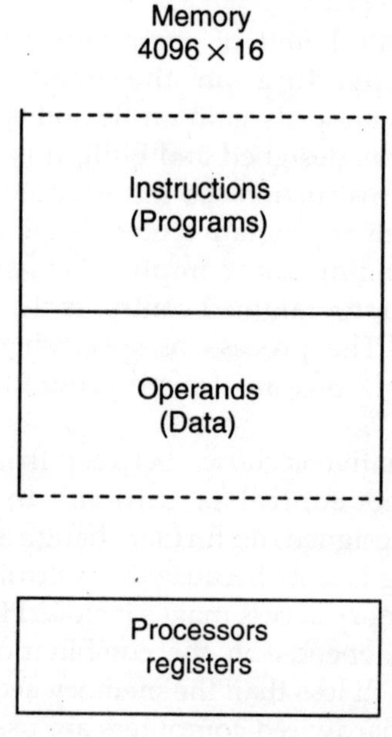

FIGURE 3.14(a) : Stored Program

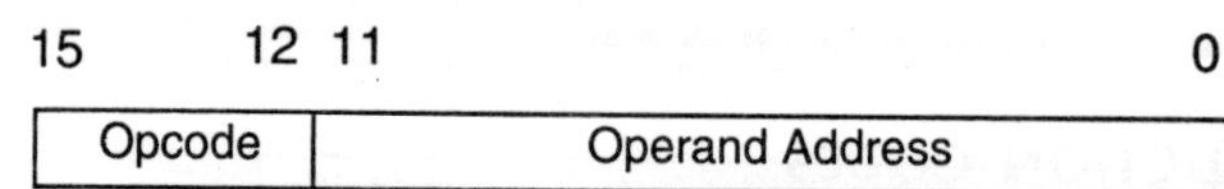

FIGURE 3.14(b) : Instruction Format

region of the memory. Processor registers are temporary storage and also hold instructions and operands. Figure 3.14(a) depicts instructions and data stored in the storage memory and registers. The format of the instruction in Figure 3.14(b) shows that it is a 16 bit instruction, with bits 12-15 used for the opcode and bits 0-11 used for the address of the operand.

3.7.2 Instruction Representation

Each instruction is represented as a sequence of binary digits within a computer. The instruction is divided into different fields, corresponding to the elements of the instruction. The format of a simple instruction is given in Figure 3.15, where the instruction has 16 bits that are divided as: 4 bits for opcode, 6 bits for source address, and 6 bits for destination address.

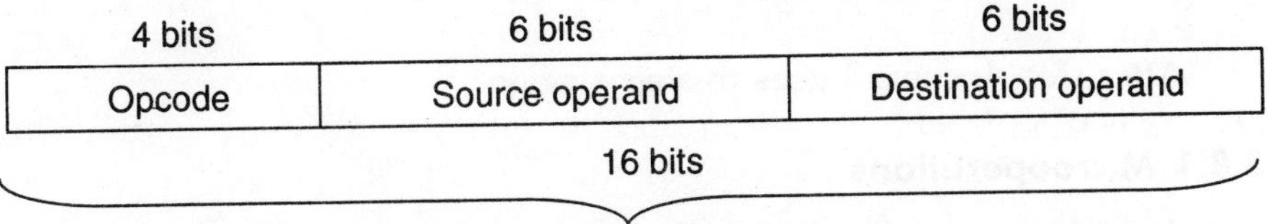

FIGURE **3.15 : Instruction Format**

The instruction contains the information required by the CPU for its execution. To accomplish this, the instruction must contain the following essential parts:

1. Operation Code: To specify the operation to be performed, like ADD, Read, etc. The operation is specified by binary code, called operation code or opcode.
2. Source operand: The operation may involve one or more source operands that are inputs to the operation.
3. Result operand: The operation may produce a result operand.
4. Next instruction reference: After the execution of the current instruction, the CPU fetches next instruction from this location.

As it is not easy to deal with binary representation of machine instructions for anyone, therefore, symbolic representation of machine instructions is used. Opcodes are represented by abbreviations, called mnemonics, that indicate the operation. Some of the common ones are:

ADD for Add
SUB for Subtract
LDA for load Data from memory
STO for store data into memory

3.8 INSTRUCTION CYCLE

A central processing unit normally contains three main components: a control unit, an arithmetic and logic unit and a register section. It is the control unit which is responsible for the control and synchronization of the actions of the CPU. The program consists of a sequence of instructions, which is executed by going through a cycle for each instruction. Every instruction cycle is further comprised of a sequence of subcycles. An instruction cycle consists of the following subcycles or phases.

1. Fetch instruction from memory.
2. Decode the instruction.
3. Read effective address from memory.
4. Execute the instruction.

After step 4, control goes to step 1 again.

3.8.1 Microoperations

A microoperation is the smallest operation that can be performed by the CPU. Every microoperation is executed in one clock cycle and they may be overlapped. Each machine code instruction is made up of a number of such microoperations.

3.8.2 Register Transfer Language (RTL)

Register Transfer Language is a kind of intermediate representation that is very close to assembly language. It is a symbolic representation of the transfer of data between the registers of the CPU and the memory of the system to express microoperation sequences. Each microoperation involves the transfer of data to or from a register. For convenience, the sequence is represented in terms of register transfer language. The statement R2 ← R1 denotes a transfer of contents of register R1 to contents of register R2. The contents of R2 are replaced by contents of R1. But the contents of R1 remain unchanged.

For this register transfer to take place, electronic circuits are available from the output of the source register to the input of the destination register, and the data is transferred in parallel when the control signal 'C' is true, active or high. The control function is a Boolean variable that is equal to either 1 or 0. The notation, including the control function, is:

C: R2 ← R1

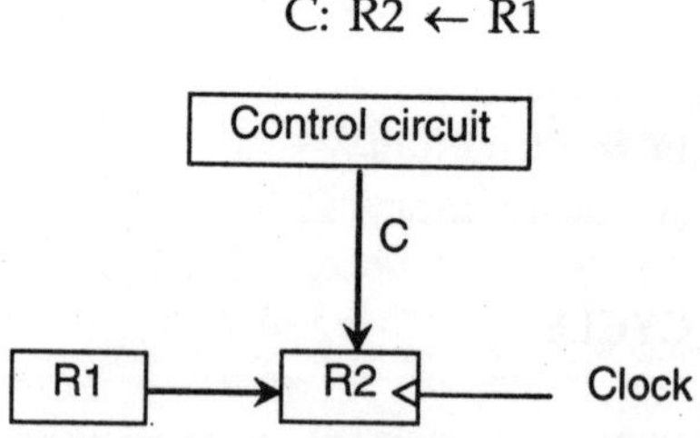

FIGURE 3.16 : Parallel Register Transfer when C=1

Figure 3.16 represents a register transfer of the contents of R1 to contents of R2. The transfer takes place when the control signal C is passed from the control circuit and the clock is high.

3.8.3 Fetch-Execute Cycle

The fetch-execute cycle is a sequence of controlled data transfers within the components of the CPU. The organization of the internal components of the CPU is shown in Figure 3.17 to explain the data transfers during the implementation of an instruction. The instruction comprises of small microoperations during which data is transferred between different registers of the CPU, and arithmetic and logic operations are performed during these transfers. Some registers transfer data within the internal CPU bus while others transfer data both on the internal CPU bus as well as on the external bus, which is the system bus. The main registers that transfer data on the internal CPU bus are: Program Counter (PC), Instruction register (IR) and Accumulator (AC). The address register (AR) gets information from the internal bus and passes it on the external bus. This way, address is transmitted on the address bus. Data Register (DR) may get data from the address bus or it may pass data from the internal bus to the external system bus. The control unit (CU) issues timing and control signals for the microoperation to be implemented. The Arithmetic and logic unit (ALU) receives two inputs; one from the DR, and the other from AC, which is the data register used in arithmetic and logical operations. The PC holds the address of the next instruction to be executed while IR holds the current instruction. AR is connected to the address bus. It specifies the address in memory for a read or write operation. DR is connected to the data bus and contains the data to be read from or written to memory. INC is the Incrementer. It adds one to its input to produce its output. A sequence counter (SC) is used to provide the sequence of timing signals to the decoder. Timing signals go through a sequence T_0, T_1, T_2, ... The microoperations for fetch-decode cycle are:

T_0 : [AR] ← [PC]
T_1 : [IR] ← M[AR], [PC] ← [PC+1]
T_2 : [DR] ← Memory, [IR] ← [DR]

Consider the sequence of events during the fetch and execute of an instruction to add the contents of the accumulator to some data from memory, and store the result back in the accumulator.

(1) Send the address of the next instruction to be executed to memory, through the AR.
(2) Increment the PC.
(3) Load the next instruction from memory into the DR.
(4) Move the instruction from the DR to the IR.
(5) Move the instruction from the IR to the control unit for decoding.
(6) Send the address of the required data to memory, through the AR.
(7) Read the data from memory into the DR.
(8) Move the data from the DR to the ALU.

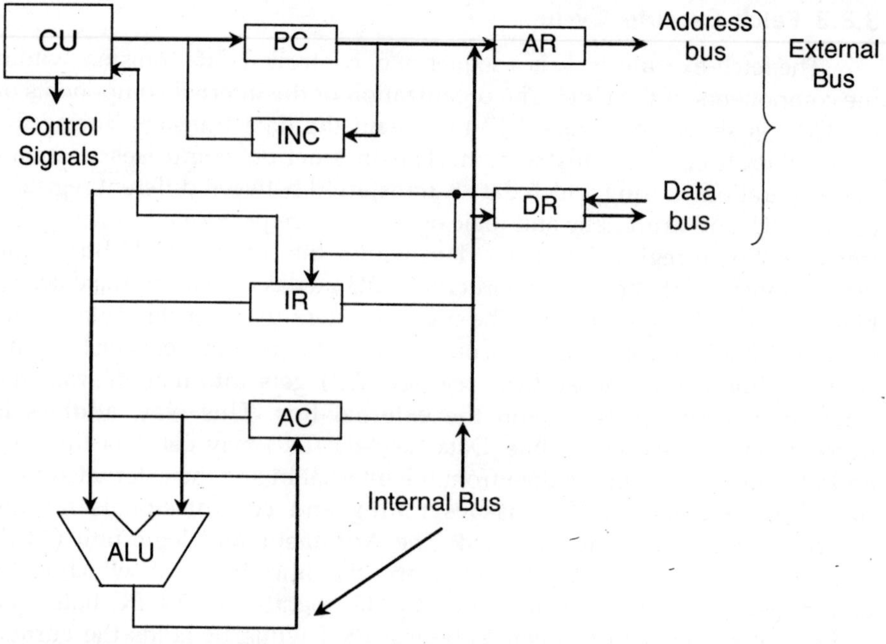

FIGURE 3.17 : Internal Block Diagram of CPU

(9) Move the contents of the AC into the ALU.
(10) Move the result from the ALU into the AC.

Each of the ten small operations mentioned above for the fetch-execute cycle, is a microoperation. The first three steps are the Fetch stage and are the same for all instructions. The rest of the steps of the execution phase depend on the particular instruction. The ten instructions of the fetch-execute cycle are represented in the register transfer language (RTL) in Table 3.1. The symbolic representation of these has been explained in the right most column.

From the above discussion of register transfer, it can be seen that the fetch and execution of every instruction can be reduced to a sequence of transfers between the various components of the system. A method is needed to control these transfers, so that not all transfers take place at the same time, rather only the required register transfers should take place at any one time.

3.8.4 Tri-state Logic

Tri-state logic is a device whose output can be disabled wherever data switching is necessary by using a logic gate. In this state, it seems as if its output were disconnected from the rest of the circuit, and, therefore, no signals can pass through it. When a signal should be transferred to a

TABLE 3.1
Register Transfer Language (RTL) for Fetch-Execute Cycle

Sl. No.	*RTL*	*Comments*
1.	[AR] ← [PC]	Send the address of the next instruction to be executed to memory, through the memory address register
2.	INC ← [PC]	Increment the program counter.
3.	[PC] ← INC	
4.	[DR] ← Memory	Load the next instruction from memory, into the data register
5.	[IR] ← [DR]	Move the instruction from the data register to the instruction register
6.	CU ← [IR]	Move the instruction from the instruction register to the control unit for decoding
7.	[AR] ← [IR]	Send the address of the required data to memory, through the address register
8.	[DR] ← Memory	Read the data from memory, into the memory buffer register
9.	ALU ← [DR]	Move the data from the data register to the arithmetic and logic unit
10.	ALU ← [AC]	Move the contents of the accumulator into the arithmetic and logic unit
11.	[AC] ← ALU	Move the result from the arithmetic and logic unit into the accumulator

particular part of the system, the relevant tri-state logic gate is enabled. Each register can also be enabled, allowing data to be written into it.

3.8.5 Control Signals

The CPU of Figure 3.17 is again illustrated in Figure 3.18, with the tri-state logic gates indicated. The various gates and registers are enabled by control wires from the control unit. In this way, the control unit can regulate the transfer of information between the different components. The details of the control signals needed for the Add operation that was discussed earlier will be taken up. The ALU is a combinational circuit and has no internal storage. The arithmetic and logic operations are performed on the two inputs A and B. The input A comes from the external bus (MBR), while input B is from the internal bus (AC). The result produced is temporarily stored in register AC, and then is available on the external bus. Thus, the sequence of operations to add the contents of R1 to contents of R2, and store the result in R3 are the rows 4 to 11 of Table 3.1.

Table 3.2 shows the sequence of gates and registers that must be enabled to execute the sequence of microoperations.

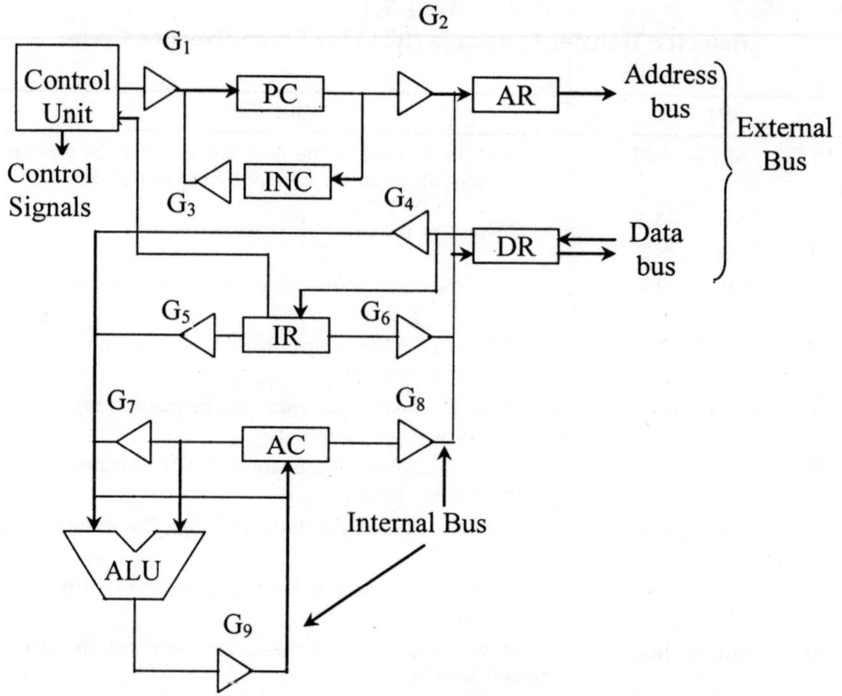

FIGURE 3.18 : Internal Block diagram with tri-state logic

TABLE 3.2
Control Signals and Microoperations

RTL	*Control Signal*
[MAR] ← [PC]	Enable G2, MAR
INC ← [PC]	
[PC] ← INC	Enable G3, PC
[MBR] ← Memory	Enable MS, MBR
[IR] ← [MBR]	Enable IR
CU ← [IR]	
[MAR] ← [IR]	Enable G6, MAR
[MBR] ← Memory	Enable MBR
ALU ← [MBR]	Enable G4, ALU
ALU ← [AC]	
[AC] ← ALU	Enable G9, AC

To control the sequence of register transfers, the control unit uses the regular signal from the clock and a counter so that it can keep track of its position in the sequence.

3.9 MEMORY REFERENCE INSTRUCTIONS

The instruction set of different processors is dissimilar and is designed by its architect. However, the basic instructions performed by most processors are very similar. The fundamental operations can be divided into four categories: arithmetic operations, memory operations, comparisons, and control operations. For effective execution of each instruction, it is important that their function be known accurately. The cycles T1, T2, T3 are the instruction fetch phase which is the same for all instructions. The following section explains the more used instructions.

Memory Reference Instructions

The functions of the memory-reference instructions are described below:

ADD AC

ADD to AC instruction is used to add the contents of the memory word specified by the effective address of MAR to the value of AC. The sum is transferred to AC. The output carry is transformed to the carry Flag. The register transfers are:

T_4: MBR ← M[AR]
T_5: AC ← AC + MBR, SC ← 0

AND AC

AND to AC instruction is used to perform the logical operation on the pair of bits in AC, and memory word specified by the address of MAR. The result of operation is transferred to AC. The register transfer microoperations are:

T_4: M[AR] ← PC
T_5: AC ← AC . MBR, SC ← 0

The result of the operation is transferred to AC.

LDA AC

Load to AC instruction transfers the memory word specified by the effective address to AC. The register transfers to implement the instruction are:

T_4: MBR ← M[AR]
T_5: AC ← MBR, SC ← 0

The memory word is read from the location specified by MAR to MBR directly. After this, the contents of MBR are transferred to AC.

STA AC

Store to AC instruction stores the contents of AC into memory word specified by the address of MAR. The register transfer microoperation is:

T_4: M[AR] ← AC

It can be seen from Figure 3.17 that the output of AC is applied to the bus, and the data input of memory is also connected to the bus. Therefore, the instruction is executed in one clock cycle.

BRN

BRN instruction is for Unconditional Branch. It transfers program to the instruction specified by the effective address. PC is incremented at time T_1, and holds the address of the next instruction to be executed. The microoperations for the register transfer are:

T_4: PC ← AR, SC ← 0

The effective address from MAR is transferred through the common bus to PC. The control is transferred to T_0 by setting SC to 0. The next instruction is then fetched and executed from the memory address given by the PC.

BSA

BSA instruction is for branching to a subroutine or a procedure. This instruction stores the address of the next instruction in sequence into a memory location specified by the address of MAR. The microoperations for the register transfer are:

T_4: M[AR] ← PC, PC ← EA + 1

This instruction is useful for branching to a subroutine or procedures upon execution,

3.10 INTERRUPT

Many devices attached to the processor have speeds much slower than the processor. Some other devices generate asynchronous events, which occur at times that the processor cannot predict or control. Under these conditions, the processor generates an interrupt signal to perform an operation that takes a long time to complete. But the processor must provide service to these events immediately. 'Interrupt' is a method used by processors to handle these types of events. The basic purpose is to allow devices to request the processor stop what it is currently doing and execute software to process the request of the interrupting device. This is similar to the procedure call that is initiated by an external device, rather by the program running on the processor.

3.10.1 Implementing Interrupts

Interrupts are implemented by using certain signals. The processor assigns a signal known as an 'interrupt enable' to each device that can issue an interrupt. 'Interrupt acknowledge' line is also assigned to that device by the processor, to be used to signal the device that it has received and begun to process the interrupt request. When the interrupt occurs, the 'interrupt handler' is brought to service the interrupt request. 'Interrupt vector' is a set of memory locations that contain the addresses of routines of interrupt handler. In the following example, the interrupt vector for a processor has two interrupts. The interrupt vector contains two words of memory, one for each interrupt. User program stores the addresses of the interrupt handler for each one. This is done before the device is attached to the interrupt lines that can be used.

Word 0	Word 1
Address for interrupt 0	Address for interrupt 1

FIGURE 3.19 : An Interrupt Vector

To interrupt the processor, device keeps sending an interrupt signal on the interrupt line till the processor acknowledges the interrupt. The processor sends an interrupt acknowledge signal on the appropriate line, and then the appropriate location in the interrupt vector starts the routine to service the interrupt. A context switch is used to start execution of the interrupt handler. The context switch ensures that the program running on the processor, when the interrupt occurs, is able to resume execution after the interrupt completes.

3.10.2 Interrupt Priorities

It is quite possible that more than one device may interrupt the processor at the same time, or many other interrupts occur while one is being serviced. The decision about which interrupt has to be handled first is based on setting priorities to different interrupts. These priorities might be assigned numbers, and the processor might service higher priority interrupts first, or the lower priorities first.

An alternative to using interrupts is 'polling'. In polling, processor continuously checks each I/O device whether it needs to be handled or not. This method can be useful only if the processor has no other work to handle; otherwise polling requires software running continuously.

In programmed control transfer, the computer keeps checking the flag bit, and when it finds it set, it initiates an information transfer. The difference of rates of information flow between the computer and that of I/O device makes this type of transfer inefficient.

3.11 SUMMARY

The organization of a computer involves three main functional units: processor, memory and input-output, which are interconnected through a bus. The internal organization of the CPU is structured to meet these needs of instruction implementation. The processing of an instruction requires that instruction be fetched from the main memory by the control unit. The operands are fetched in the internal registers of the CPU. The ALU does the processing on the data and results are stored in the memory locations. The memory of a computer is of various kinds depending on the storage space and speed, which are inversely proportional to each other. The third unit, the Input/Output system consists of a range of I/O modules to provide a systematic interaction with the outside world. There are various kinds of registers in the CPU to hold temporary data during the processing of instructions. Buses are needed to provide a path of communication between different components of the CPU. Data Bus, Address Bus and Control Bus are three main buses used to send and receive data between different modules of the computer. The timing and control of the bus is managed by the system bus. Synchronous bus is used to synchronize the operations of the system. Asynchronous operations require no clock and are used in the I/O operations. The instruction implementation involves a fetch cycle followed by the execute cycle. The fetch cycle is the same for all instructions whereas execute cycle depends on the type of instruction. An interrupt signal changes the normal processing of the processor. The construction of the processor may be hardwired or microprogrammed. Whereas the former gains on speed, the latter gains on flexibility and cost. An instruction contains different fields required by the CPU for its execution. The instruction is represented as a sequence of binary digits and divided into different fields containing the opcode and the operands. Microoperation is the smallest operation that can be performed by the CPU. Each instruction is composed of many such microoperations. Register transfer language (RTL) is a symbolic representation of the transfer of data between registers. The microoperations and RTL of the fetch-execute cycle shows the transfer of data within the CPU during the execution of the instruction. Tri-state logic allows a signal to be transferred to a particular part of the system. The control signals, emanated from the control unit, enable the registers and gates to regulate the transfer of data between the different components of the computer. The interrupt cycle is similar to the procedure call initiated by an external device. If more than one device interrupts the system, then interrupt priorities are provided.

References

Patterson, D.A. and J.L. Hennessey, Computer Architecture: A Quantitative Approach, San Mateo, CA: Morgan Kaufmann Publishers, 1990.

John, P. Hayes, Computer Architecture and Organization, Third Edition, McGraw-Hill, 1998.

M. Morris Mano, Computer System Architecture, Third Edition, Pearson Education (Singapore), 1993.

Gibson, G.A., Computer Systems: Concepts ND Design, Englewood Cliffs, NJ: Prentice Hall, 1991.

Tanenbaum, Andrew S., Structured Computer Organization, 4th ed., Prentice-Hall of India, New Delhi, 2001.

Write Short Answers

(i) Define instruction cycle of a computer.

(ii) Make a list of steps involved in executing the instruction ADD R1, R2. The instruction adds the contents of registers R1 and R2, and save the result in register R1.

(iii) Give a sequence of instructions for executing ADD M, R1. This instruction adds the contents of memory location M to contents of register R1.

(iv) What is a microoperation?

(v) What do address register and data register hold?

(vi) What is Program Counter?

(vii) What is the function of registers in a control unit?

(viii) What is the function of ALU in the control unit?

(ix) Explain the functioning of instruction register.

(x) Explain the functioning of data bus.

(xi) How is computer arithmetic performed within a CPU?

(xii) What is the difference between PROM and ROM?

(xiii) How control signals are used for data transfer within the CPU? Draw the organization.

(xiv) How is cycle time related with write time?

CHAPTER

4

Microprogrammed Control

4. INTRODUCTION

Microprogramming is a technique used to construct the control unit of a computer by breaking the instruction in small parts. Microprogramming does not mean programming a microcomputer. Rather, it is a form of stored program logic that substitutes for sequential logic control circuit. There are mainly two approaches to control unit design: hardwired and microprogrammed. In this chapter, both of these techniques will be studied in detail. When many microoperations are performed in parallel, the speed of computation is increased considerably. Parallelism in microinstructions will be discussed. Horizontal and vertical microinstructions further enhance the performance of the computer. Microoperation timing and pipeline control will also be examined.

4.1 FUNDAMENTALS OF CONTROL LOGIC

The basic elements of the CPU are ALU, Registers, Internal and External data paths and control unit. The control unit is the part of the CPU that issues control signals to different parts of the CPU and to external devices to start execution of the instructions at predetermined times. Inputs to this CPU are from instruction register, flags and interrupt signals. The output of the control unit is the microcontrol signals or microoperations, each doing a small task like transfer a data from one register to another, initialize a flag, shift output of address to a register, etc. They are also called atomic operations. The actions of the control unit of a processor are specified by its microoperations. The clock cycle of the processor is determined by the performance of control unit.

Specifically, the control unit performs two basic tasks:

(i) *Sequencing* : The control unit causes the processor to move through a series of microoperations in the proper sequence. This sequence is based on the program being executed.

(ii) *Execution* : The control unit causes each microoperation to be executed.

4.1.1 Control Signals

The control unit governs a series of steps taken by the data path during the execution of a user-visible instruction, or macroinstruction such as load, add, store, conditional branch. Each step in the execution of a macroinstruction is a transfer of information within the data path. This may include the transformation of data, address, or instruction bits by the functional units. A step is called a register transfer (discussed in Section 3.8) and is accomplished by sending a copy of the contents onto internal processor busses, selecting the operation of ALUs, registers, etc. At the same time, the control unit is receiving new values for one or more registers, which are known as 'control signals'. These control signals have the purpose of enabling the gates and those signals that control the sending or receiving of data at the register's control points and operation of selection signals. The control signals identify the microoperations required for each register transfer, and are supplied by the control unit. A complete macroinstruction is executed by generating an appropriately timed sequence of groups of control signals (microoperations). Figure 4.1 shows a model of the control unit and its various inputs and outputs.

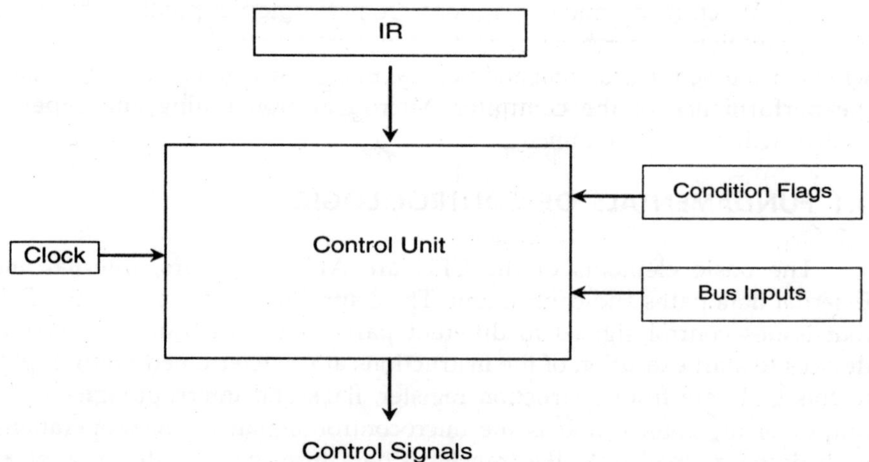

FIGURE 4.1 : A Control Unit with Inputs and Output

4.1.2 Input and Output of Control Unit

The inputs to the control unit are:

(i) Clock

The control unit maintains timing of each microoperation using the clock signal. Each or every group of microoperations is performed for each clock pulse. This time is also referred to as the processor cycle time or the clock cycle time.

(ii) Instruction Register

Instruction register holds the opcode of the current instruction. The microoperations needed to execute the instruction are determined from this opcode.

(iii) Flags

These signals provide the status of the processor and the status of results of the previous execution of the ALU operation.

Control unit can be implemented by hardwired unit or by a microprogram. The decision to choose one of these two design methods is based on optimizing three aspects of control unit design:

1. Complexity of control unit
2. Speed of control unit
3. Cost of the design

When performance cannot be compromised while complexity and higher cost can be accepted, hardware control design is chosen.

4.2 HARDWIRED CONTROL DESIGN

Though hardwired control unit is difficult to design as its cost is high, but these days, the emphasis of computer design is on the performance, therefore, hardwired control is chosen. Thus, almost all processors of today use hardwired control unit.

4.2.1 Fundamental Concepts

The hardwired control unit is considered as a sequential logic circuit that implements microoperations using a combinational circuit. The inputs are from the microoperation counter, instruction register and status register, which are transformed into a set of outputs that are the control signals. Figure 4.2 shows a hardwired control unit.

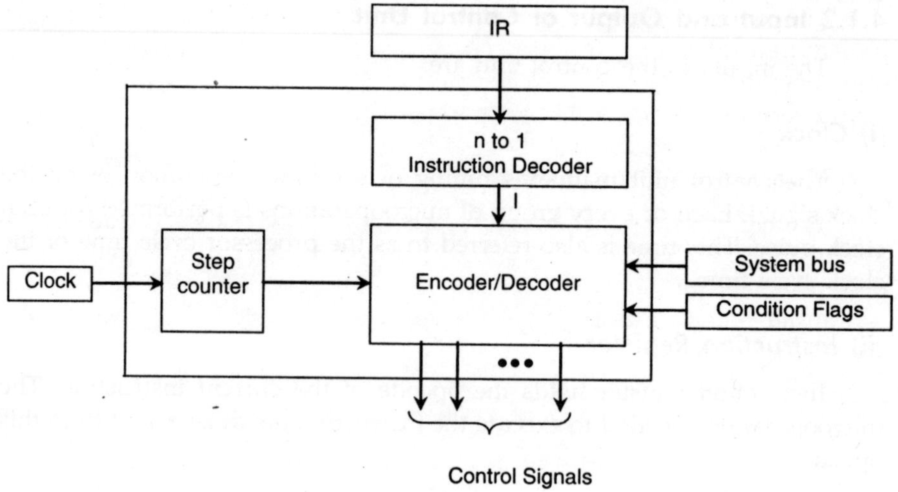

FIGURE 4.2 : Hardwired Control Unit

For the hardwired control unit, the hardware involved is decoder/ encoder circuits, which are combinational circuits that generate the required control signals as output. The input to (n to 1) instruction decoder is from the instruction register IR. When one instruction is selected from n available instructions, that line is set to 1 while all other lines are set to 0. Thus, a separate signal line is provided for each step in the control sequence by the instruction decoder. The output of the instruction decoder consists of a separate line for each machine instruction. The input signals to the encoder are combined to generate the individual control signals.

4.2.2 Design Method

The actions of the control unit are defined. A sequential circuit is constructed whose output signals are the required microoperations based on the actions of the control unit, while the inputs are from the instruction register, control and status flags. It is helpful to construct a state diagram which follows the different states of the control unit to construct a sequential circuit. Some states are driven only by clock and only transition to next state is needed. Various states branch to different states depending on conditions such as condition codes or decoding the opcode. Some of the events that cause transitions are:

event : go to next state
event : go to state 1 or state 2 depends depending on conditions
event : branch to many states by decoding

FIGURE 4.3 : Transitions in State Diagram

The control signals are generated by the control unit for any instruction by sequentially reading the control words of the corresponding microoperation. There are no principles for the design of hardwired control unit. Every case is treated as a separate case.

4.2.3 Design of Control Unit

The control unit implements a program by successively reading the instructions and implementing them. The components involved in the design are various registers that are used in the computation of the program to transfer data to and from the address bus and data bus on way to the

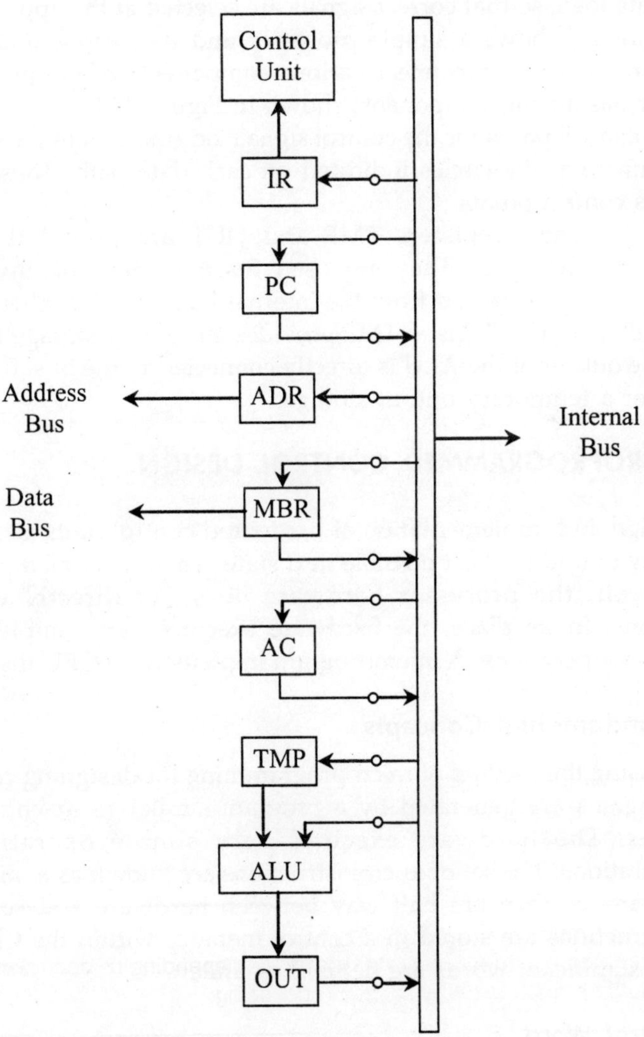

FIGURE 4.4 : Processor with Internal Bus

system bus. The block diagram of a complete control unit is shown in Figure 14.4. The internal bus of the CPU is connected with registers that are utilized for handling processing of ALU. These registers are : Address Data Register (ADR) and Memory Buffer Register (MBR) connected with the system bus. One operand, on which operation has to be performed, is in the ALU while temporary register (TMP) holds the other operand. After the operation in the ALU, results are sent to the OUT register. Program counter (PC) keeps track of the next instruction to be implemented while instruction register (IR) maintains the address of the current instruction. The other inputs to the control unit are the clock, flags, and the control signals from the system bus. All these registers are connected to the internal bus through the tri-state logic so that correct signals are selected at the appropriate time.

Figure 4.4 shows a simple processor and its various data paths. An internal bus is used to connect various components of the processor. This processor has all the components shown in Figure 3.17.

The control paths for the control signals originate from the control unit, and terminate at the circles indicated on each data path. These circles are known as control points.

The two new registers TMP and OUT are provided for proper operation of the ALU. They are used for the operation involving two operands. One is obtained from the internal bus, and the other is obtained from another source. Register TMP provides temporary storage for the other input. The output of the ALU is directly connected to the bus. Register OUT is used for a temporary output storage.

4.3 MICROPROGRAMMED CONTROL DESIGN

Design and implementation of hardwired control units is difficult as it is not easy to find the best possible next state graph. In a microprogrammed control unit, the processor hardware does not directly execute the instructions. In its place, the hardware executes very simple operations called microoperations. A microprogram implements a CPU instruction set.

4.3.1 Fundamental Concepts

By using the method of microprogramming for designing control units, control signals are generated by a program similar to machine language programs. The hardware executes very simple operations called microoperations. The set of microinstructions are known as a microprogram or firmware, as they are half way between hardware and software. The microinstructions are stored in a control memory within the CPU.

The significant words are defined as under:

(i) Control Word

It is a word whose individual bits represent various control signals.

Every control step in the control sequence represents a unique combination of 1's and 0's in the control word.

(ii) Microroutine

A sequence of control words corresponding to the control sequence of a machine instruction represents the microroutine for that instruction.

(iii) Microinstruction

The individual control words in a microroutine are referred to as microinstructions.

(iv) Control Store

The memory in which microinstructions are stored is called a control store. The microroutines for all instructions in the instruction set of a computer are stored in this special memory.

The microcode is written by the CPU engineer during the design phase. Microprograms consist of series of microinstructions. These microinstructions control the CPU at a very fundamental level. For example, a single typical microinstruction might specify the following operations:

Connect Register 1 to the ALU
Connect Register 7 to the ALU
Set the ALU to perform two's-complement addition
Set the ALU's carry input to zero
Store the result value in Register 8
Update the 'condition codes' with the ALU status flags ('Negative', 'Zero', 'Overflow', and 'Carry')

To simultaneously control all of these features, the microinstruction is often very wide, for example, 56 bits or more. Thus, the operation of microprogram is similar to a single high level language statement being compiled to a series of machine instructions like load, store, shift, in a CPU using microcode. Each machine instruction is in turn implemented by a series of microinstructions, sometimes called a microprogram. Microprograms are often referred to as microcode.

The microprogrammed control unit is shown in Figure 4.5 and is divided into several parts, like a microsequencer, address generator, and a decoder. Control signals that are to be simultaneously active at a given time are stored together in a control word. The individual bits of a control word represent the various control signals. A sequence of control words corresponding to a control sequence of a machine instruction makes a microroutine for that instruction. The individual control words in the microroutine are referred to as microinstruction. The collection of control words that implement a macroinstruction is described as a microprogram, and the microprograms are stored in a memory called as the control store.

In short, microprogramming involves a control function that specifies a microoperation, which is a binary variable. When the variable is 1, microoperation, is executed. When it is 0, nothing happens. Control word is string of control variables. Control unit initiates a string of microoperations based on the bits of the control word and these control words are stored in control memory, ROM. Control memory address register specifies microinstruction address. Control data register contains microinstruction read from control memory.

The address sequencing is performed by the sequencer, by incrementing the control address register. Branching is provided by conditional or unconditional branch where mapping process is from instruction bits to an address within control memory.

Microinstruction Counter

The sequence of microoperations needed for execution of a macroinstruction is derived from a series of fetches from the control store. The control unit can generate the control signals for any instruction by sequentially reading the control words of the corresponding microroutine from the control store. To do this, a microprogram counter (μPC) is used. Every time a new instruction is loaded in the IR, the output of the 'starting address generator' is loaded into the μPC. The clock automatically increments the μPC after a clock cycle that causes the successive microinstructions to be read from the control memory. The sequential functioning of the μPC is altered by the change of status and condition codes. In addition to the branch address, these microinstructions specify which of the external inputs or condition codes need to be checked.

Branching

The branching of microinstruction is needed whenever the new microinstruction is not the next sequential instruction. In this case, the output of the control store (control word) is fed back to the starting address generator. In the control unit, the μPC is incremented, every time a new microinstruction is fetched from the control store, except in the following cases: when a new instruction is loaded in the IR, μPC is loaded with the starting address of the microroutine for that microinstruction, when it comes across Branch microinstruction, μPC is loaded with the branch address, or End.

The basic definitions will be discussed more elaborately in the following section:

4.3.2 Microinstructions

Microprogramming language is a language where each line describes a

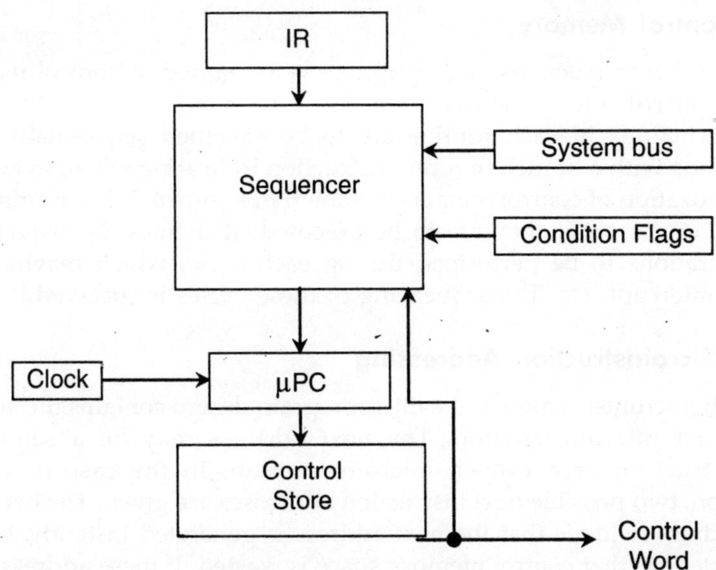

FIGURE 4.5 : Organization of Microprogrammed Control Unit

set of microoperations occurring at the same time. Each line is known as a microinstruction.

The concept of microprogramming can be used to implement control units. For each microoperation, the control unit generates a set of control signals. Thus, for any microoperation, output of each control line is either on or off. This condition can be represented in the form of binary digits for each control line. A control word is a binary word in which each bit represents one control line. As a result, each microoperation would be represented as a different pattern of 1's and 0's in the control word.

Microinstruction Format

A typical microinstruction is presented in Figure 4.6.

F1	F2	F3	BR	AD

FIGURE 4.6 : Microinstruction Format

F1, F2, F3 – Microoperation Address
BR – Branch Address
AD – Address

Symbols are used in microinstructions just as in assembly language.

4.3.3 Control Memory

The microinstructions or control words are stored in control memory called control store, which can be either ROM or RAM. The microinstructions in each routine are to be executed sequentially. Each routine ends with a branch or jump instruction indicating where to go next. The organization of control memory is shown in Figure 4.7. The routines are arranged in the order they are to be executed. It defines the sequence of microoperations to be performed during each cycle, which maybe fetch, execute, interrupt, etc. The sequencing of these cycles is specified.

4.3.4 Microinstruction Addressing

Each microinstruction in the microprogram design contains the address of the next microinstruction. The next address may be a sequential microinstruction or a branch microinstruction. In the case of branch instruction, two possible next instruction addresses are given. The benefit of these address fields is that the next address is generated instantly, but the disadvantage is that control memory space is wasted. If these address fields

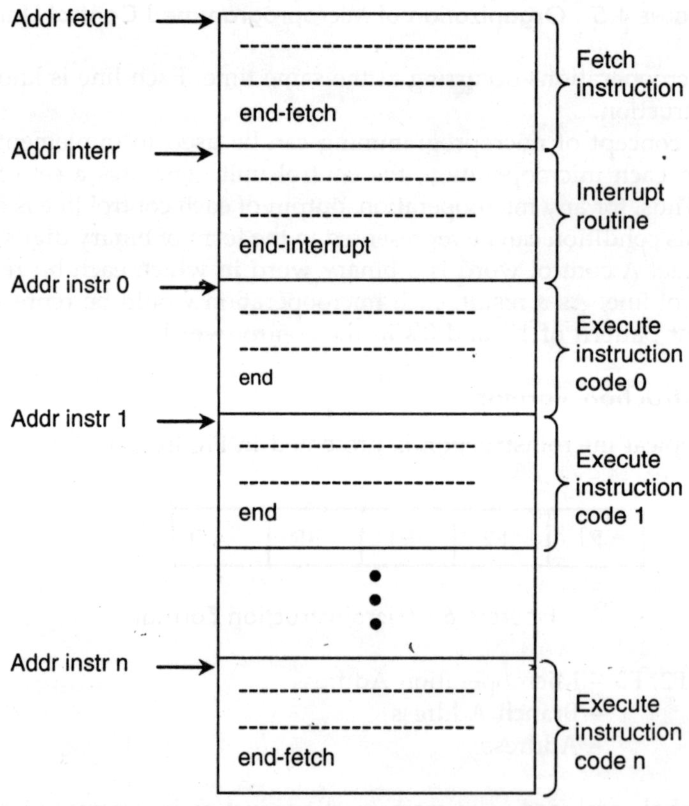

FIGURE 4.7 : Control Store Organization

are removed, then there would be difficulty when branch instruction is to be implemented. The role of microprogram counter is similar to that of a program counter PC. As only one instruction is to be fetched from control memory at a time, microprogram counter is also called control memory address register (CMAR).

4.3.5 Microinstruction Timing

The time during which the microinstruction is active primarily decides the clock time of the processor. The control signals are synchronized by using a single clock signal. The period of this control signal can be made the same as the microinstruction cycle period. For increasing the speed of execution of microinstructions, methods to decrease the cycle time are used. One method to decrease the microinstruction cycle time is by dividing the microinstruction cycle time into several sequential sub-periods or stages. A control signal is generally active during one of the stages. This method of operation in stages permits the microoperation to be executed even for very complex formats. Take the example of a microinstruction that controls the operation of register transfer:

$$R := f(R_1, R_2)$$

This operation of register transfer can be performed in several stages. Some of these stages are as follows:

Stage φ_1 : Fetch the next microinstruction from the control memory.
Stage φ_2 : Transfer the contents of R_1, R_2 to the inputs of the function unit f.
Stage φ_3 : Store results generated by the function f in temporary register.

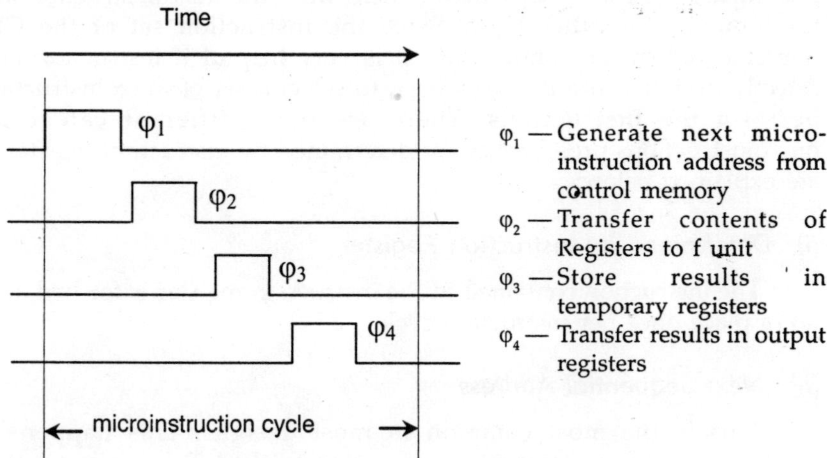

FIGURE 4.8 : Timing Diagram for Four-segment Microinstruction

Stage φ_4 : Transfer contents of temporary register to destination register R.

A microinstruction has control over the process in the stage in which it is active. However, the microinstruction can continue to exercise control on the process until a subsequent microinstruction modifies it. To make this possible, the control field is stored in a register. This control of a short period is known as 'residual control'. The residual control is useful when resources have to be allocated to a system. The timing diagram for a four-segment microinstruction is depicted in Figure 4.8.

4.3.6 Microinstruction Sequencer

The addresses of the control store, for the microprogram to be executed, are generated by a microinstruction sequencer, or sequencer which is part of the control unit. The sequencer generates the starting address and the branch address for the next microinstruction to be executed in the next clock cycle by combination of inputs from IR, system bus and condition flags. Microinstruction sequencer gets the next microinstruction from the control memory. The control signals needed to execute the microinstruction are generated by the execution unit. The tasks are considered together because both affect the format of the microinstruction and its timing.

In this way, the sequencer does the jobs of incrementing the control address register, conditional or unconditional branch and mapping process from instruction bits to an address within control memory. Facility for subroutine call and return is also provided.

4.3.6.1 Microsequencer Design Consideration

Generally a microcounter is used for the selection of the next microinstruction to be executed. A field from the microinstruction is used for jump or for other logic. Since the instruction set of the CPU is implemented in the control unit, it is very helpful if instruction bits are directly decoded into the sequencer, to select a set of microinstructions to perform the instructions. There are three different categories of microinstructions present that are determined by instruction register. They are explained below:

(i) Determined by Instruction Register

The instruction contained in the instruction register is fetched and this takes place once per instruction cycle.

(ii) Next Sequential Address

This is the most common in most designs. This happens most frequently and is a commonly used design method. But this is not the best design technique as branches are necessary.

(iii) Branch

Both conditional and unconditional branches are a necessary part of a microprogram. Microinstruction sequences are generally short, and after every three to four microinstructions, a branch instruction could be present.

The two main factors affecting the design of microinstruction sequencer are the size of microinstruction and the address generation time. The first is needed to minimize the size and cost of memory. The second factor is needed to make the microinstructions execute as fast as possible.

4.3.6.2 Sequencing Techniques

A sequencer is generally a counter, but it may have a separate way to jump to different parts of the control store. Sequencing techniques involve generating the address of the next microinstruction in the control memory. The simplest sequencer is just a register loaded from a few bits of the control store. This decision is based on the current microinstruction, condition flags, and the contents of the instruction register. The format of the addressing techniques should be such that least amount of time is spent to reach the concerned control memory location. A wide variety of addressing techniques are used which are based on the format of the address information in the microinstruction. The three general formats are: two address fields, single address field and variable format.

The explanation of the format to provide two address fields in each microinstruction is explained as follows: Figure 4.9 illustrates how this information is to be used. The two address fields and contents of instruction

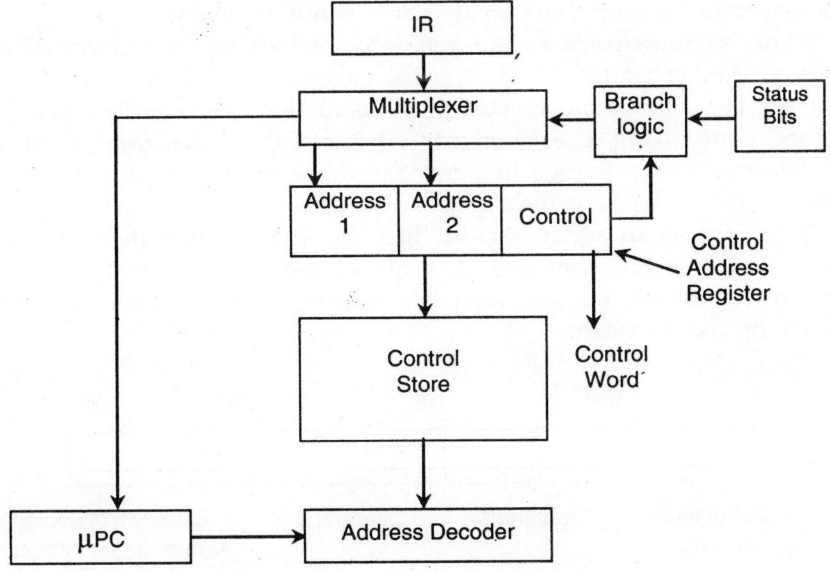

FIGURE 4.9 : Sequencing Technique for Two Address Instruction Fields

register are the two inputs provided to the multiplexer, which selects one of them at a time. The address selection input is affected by flags and the branch logic that makes the multiplexer pass either the opcode or one of the two addresses to the μPC. The contents of the μPC (CAR) are then decoded to produce the next microinstruction address.

4.4 PARALLELISM IN MICROINSTRUCTIONS

The concept of parallelism is that more than one instruction is executed at one time, instead of sequential implementation of instructions that involves executing just one instruction at a time. This obviously increases the speed of execution considerably. Microinstructions are similar to machine instructions because each machine instruction can perform just one operation. Similarly, a single microinstruction can perform just one microoperation. Due to lack of parallelism of microinstructions, more microinstructions are needed to perform a given operation. For parallel execution, the format of microinstruction may have many operations performed at the same time. The common format is of two types : long microinstruction or short microinstruction. Either one of these may be used depending on the number of microoperations it is required to perform. Instructions with long format can perform many microoperations due to parallelism. Microprogrammed processors are known by the maximum number of microoperations that a single microinstruction can perform. This number may range from one to several hundreds. If all the useful combinations of parallel microoperations were specified by a single opcode, the number of opcodes could be enormous. Also, to decode these microoperations, quite complex decoders would be needed.

The microinstructions are generally of two kinds: horizontal and vertical. The horizontal microinstruction controls the CPU elements directly whereas the code of the vertical microinstruction needs further decoding before controlling the elements of the CPU. The format of the microinstruction is divided into two parts. The microoperation part has k disjoint control fields, which specify the value of control-line for a CPU element such as an adder, register, bus, etc. Each control field handles a limited set of microoperations. Any one of these microoperations can be performed simultaneously with the microoperations specified by the remaining control fields.

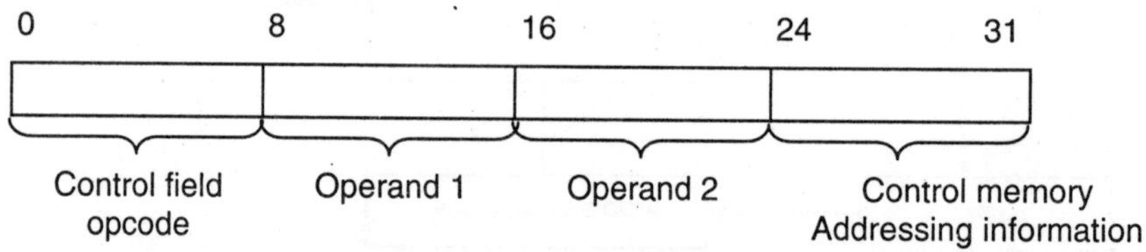

FIGURE 4.10 : A Microinstruction Format

A format of this encoding style is shown in Figure 4.10. This microinstruction consists of 4 bytes (32 bits). The leftmost byte is an opcode that specifies the microoperation to be performed. The operands are specified in the next two bits that are generally the addresses of registers of the CPU. The rightmost byte contains information to construct address of next microinstruction.

Microinstructions may have many other formats depending on the number of bytes allocated to the control fields, which can be different in separate cases. For example, a format might have 90 bits, partitioned into 21 fields to express addressing information, decimal and floating point addition, parity bits to detect errors, next microinstruction address, etc.

4.5 HORIZONTAL AND VERTICAL MICROINSTRUCTIONS

The microinstruction formats are generally of two types, based on the layout used: Horizontal Microinstructions and Vertical Microinstructions. The difference between these two types depends on factors like length of the word, parallelism, and encoding,

4.5.1 Horizontal Microinstructions

Horizontal implies a long microinstruction word. A typical horizontal microprogram control word has a field, a range of bits to control each part in the CPU. For example, one simple arrangement might be as in Figure 4.11.

register source A	register source B	destination register	ALU logic	type of jump	jump addr

FIGURE 4.11 : A Typical Horizontal Microinstruction

Each bit directly controls a microoperation or a control point. These instructions have quite long formats and have the ability to express a high degree of parallelism where many microoperations are performed in one clock cycle. Along with this, they have little encoding of the control information. They can control a variety of components operating in parallel. In other words, a horizontal microinstruction is completely unencoded and each control signal may be assigned to a separate bit position in the microinstruction format. Branching in horizontal microprograms is complicated where each horizontal microinstruction is likely to have at least one branch condition and associated branch address that might include an explicit next-address field.

Horizontal microprogramming is, therefore, less familiar to assembly language programmers and can be more error-prone. However, this form of microprogramming typically provides better performance because of parallelism within the datapath and to have the microprogram branching decisions into the same clock cycle in which the datapath microoperations are active.

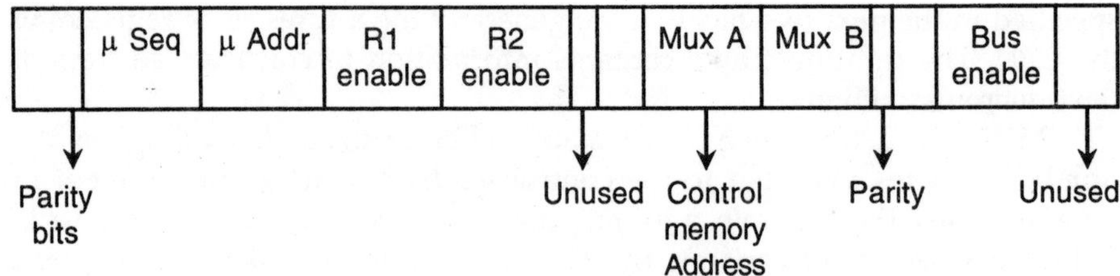

FIGURE 4.12 : A Horizontal Microinstruction Format

Figure 4.12 shows the format of a horizontal microinstruction which is partitioned into many separate control fields. Some fields are used to generate the address of the next microinstruction, and to detect errors by means of parity bits. There are bits that control the sequencer or register inputs of the CPU. Other bits control the multiplexer, inputs to the bus and many are left unused.

4.5.2 Vertical Microinstructions

Vertical microinstructions have a short microinstruction word. The control fields are encoded and they need decoding circuits. The vertical microinstruction can specify just one microoperation. It allows no parallelism.

A vertical microinstruction is highly encoded and looks like a simple macroinstruction that might contain a single opcode field and one or two operand specifiers. Thus, each microinstruction can specify a single datapath operation that, when decoded, activates multiple control signals. Branches within vertical microprograms are handled as separate microinstructions using a 'branch' opcode. This style of microprogramming is more natural to the assembly language programmer, but more number of microinstructions may be needed to accomplish a given task.

Example of a vertical microinstruction is shown in Figure 4.13. This microinstruction consists of fields for source address, destination address, control fields and fields for operands and next states.

Src	Cntrl fields	Dst	Next States	Operand 1	Operand 2

FIGURE 4.13 : A Vertical Microinstruction Format

The characteristics of Horizontal and Vertical Microinstructions are presented in Figure 4.14.

Horizontal mI Format	*Vertical mI Format*
Shows parallelism,	No parallelism, easier to program
Encoding of control information	No encoding
Can specify many microoperations	Can specify only one microoperation (no parallelism)
Long format	Short format

FIGURE 4.14 : Comparison between Vertical and Horizontal Microinstruction Formats

The advantages and disadvantages of the two kinds of microinstructions are mixed. Whereas the long horizontal microinstruction gains on efficient hardware utilization due to the various control fields, the disadvantage is that control word bits are not fully utilized, for the reason to which the control store becomes large. Thus, it makes it costly. The vertical microinstructions have the advantage of very fast execution because of a single microinstruction at a time. The disadvantage is that it needs decoding circuits.

4.6 NANOPROGRAMMING

Nanoprogramming is a method of storing microinstructions that is a combination of vertical and horizontal microinstructions. The decoder circuits in a vertical microprogram storage can be replaced by two-level of storage. First level is control storage having vertical format microprogram and second level is nanostorage having horizontal format nanoprogram. When many of the microinstructions occur several times through the microprogram, the time required to fetch the instruction and interpret it by the microprogram is reduced further by having control memory of these two levels, instead of a single control memory.

In the two-level control, consisting of microcontrol memory in the first level and nanocontrol memory in the second level, the speed of the execution of the control unit increases as number of fetches is decreased by using the nanocontrol memory.

The organization of a two-level control is shown in Figure 4.15. The contents of microcontrol memory are microinstructions. In the lower level nanocontrol memory, nanoinstructions are stored. The nanoinstructions, placed in a small control memory, called nanomemory contain the pointer for the concerned microinstruction in the microcontrol store of the appropriate microinstruction. Nanoinstructions generally have a highly parallel horizontal format. One nanoprogram can interpret many microinstructions.

Usually, the microprogram consists of a large number of short microinstructions, while the nanoprogram contains fewer words with longer nanoinstructions. This two-level control memory is helpful in that it can reduce the total size of control storage, which means smaller chip area for a one chip processor. The reduction in size may be judged by calculating the chip area according to the instructions present in the storage unit. Let the dimensions of microcontrol memory be $A_m \times B_m$, where A_m and B_m are height and width of the microcontrol storage chip respectively, and that of the nanocontrol memory be $A_n \times B_n$, respectively. The total size is reduced to $A_m \times B_m + A_n \times B_n$. This is made possible because the microprograms are encoded in a narrow vertical format in which A_m is large and B_m is small. Nanoinstructions have a highly parallel horizontal format making B_n large. One nanoprogram can interpret many microinstructions. Thus, A_n can be kept relatively small.

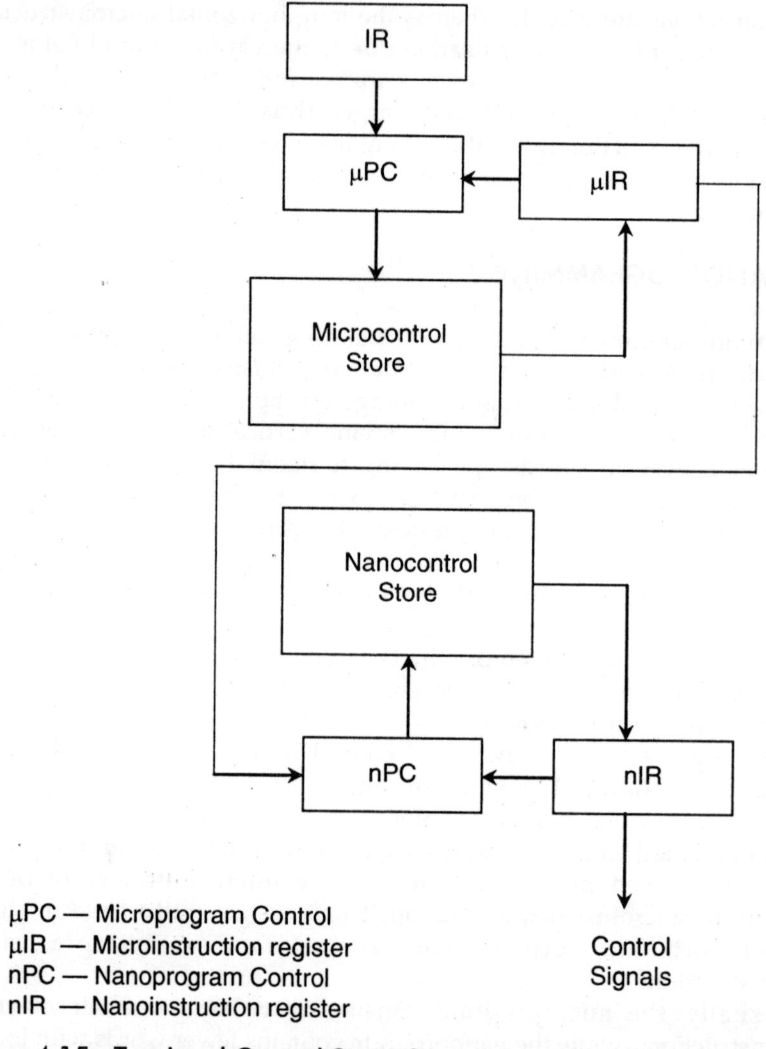

FIGURE 4.15 : Two Level Control Store Organization for Nanoprogramming

Another advantage of nanoprogramming is greater design flexibility. The bonds between instructions and hardware are not fixed because of two levels of memory instead of one. Either microinstructions of level 1 get connected to the hardware or the nanoinstructions of level 2 do the same job. The main disadvantage of the two level control memory is the loss of speed due to extra memory access, and more complex control-unit organization that occurs when none of the required instructions are available in the nanostore.

4.7 SUMMARY

A CPU is partitioned into control unit and data processing unit. The function of the control unit is to issue control signals to the data processing unit for the execution of the program. The control units are of two types: hardwired control and microprogrammed control. A hardwired control unit employs fixed logic circuits to generate control signals. A microprogrammed control unit stores the control signals in sequences of microinstructions in a control memory, where the routines are arranged in the order they are to be executed. It defines the sequence of microoperations to be performed during each cycle. Each microinstruction in the microprogram design contains the address of the next microinstruction. The next address may be a sequential microinstruction or a branch microinstruction. Microinstruction timing is crucial in defining the clock time of the processor. Microinstruction sequencer determines the microinstruction address to be executed in the next clock cycle. The two main factors are the size of microinstruction and the address generation time. A wide variety of addressing techniques are used, based on the format of the address information in the microinstruction. Parallelism of microinstructions can be made possible by choosing a specific format in which many operations can be performed in parallel. Horizontal microinstructions have a long word and have the ability to express a high degree of parallelism. Vertical microinstructions have a short microinstruction word and are encoded. A combination of vertical and horizontal microinstructions in a two-level scheme is called nanoprogramming. In this case, microinstructions are used to access a second control memory called a nanocontrol memory that directly controls hardware.

REFERENCES

John, P. Hayes, Computer Architecture and Organization, Third Edition, McGraw-Hill, 1998.

Hwang, K. and F.A. Briggs, Computer Architecture and Parallel Processing, New York: McGraw-Hill, 1984.

Gibson, G.A., Computer Systems: Concepts and Design, Englewood Cliffs, NJ: Prentice Hall, 1991.

Patterson, D.A. and J.L. Hennessey, Computer Architecture: A Quantitative Approach, San Mateo, CA: Morgan Kaufmann Publishers, 1990.

Tanenbaum, Andrew, S., Structured Computer Organization, 4th ed., Prentice-Hall of India, New Delhi, 2001.

PROBLEMS

1. Define microprogramming.
2. Name ten major atomic operations.
3. Explain the duties of control logic.
4. What happens during each step of execution of a macroinstruction?
5. Give details of the input and output signals of a microprogram.
6. Compare the hardwired control design with a microprogram.
7. Design a hardwired control unit that produces the GCM (Greatest Common Multiple) of two four bit integers.
8. What is the difference between a control path and control points?
9. Define : (i) Control Word, (ii) Control Store, (iii) Microinstruction, and (iv) Microroutine.
10. Explain different units of a microprogrammed control unit.
11. How is a microoperation represented and where is it stored?
12. How is a register transfer performed by using a common bus?
13. Explain the four different categories of microoperations used commonly in digital computers.
14. Discuss the working of a microprogrammed control organization.
15. What is the difference between Program Counter and Microinstruction Counter?
16. Relate branching of microinstructions with the execution of a microgram.
17. What is the basic concept of microprogramming that is used in the microprogram control design? Explain by using the format of a microinstruction.
18. Illustrate the sequencing technique for a three-address instruction.
19. Identify the contents of horizontal and vertical microinstruction control formats.
20. What effect does the microinstruction timing have on the clock cycle time of a processor?
21. How does a microprogram identify the address of the next microinstruction to be executed?
22. How is parallelism of microinstructions used for increasing the speed of execution?
23. What are the essential features of Nanoprogramming that makes it cost-effective?
24. Clearly indicate how the long microinstruction format and the short, encoded format is utilized in the nanoprogram organization.

CHAPTER

5

Instruction Set Architecture

5. INTRODUCTION

The instruction set of a processor decides the architecture of that processor, as the microarchitecture design is based on the microinstructions the processor will execute. Programs that will be executed by the processor will have only those machine instructions as are decided during the design of the processor. This chapter explains the way programs are executed in the computer from the machine instruction point of view. The instructions are brought from the memory to the processor to be executed. The method in which sequence of instructions and data operands are stored will be studied. A close view of different addressing methods used to access operands from memory locations will also be considered.

5.1 CHOICE OF INSTRUCTION SET STRUCTURE

Instruction set architecture (ISA) refers to the design of operations that the processor executes. The choice of the instruction set, the number of registers and decision about how data is accessed is included in this architecture. The feature that distinguishes different processors is based on their instruction set which are a set of basic operations provided by the processor. These basic operations can be divided into four categories: arithmetic operations, memory operations, comparisons, and control operations.

5.1.1 Arithmetic and Logical Operations

Arithmetic and logical operations perform basic computations, such as additions, multiplications, AND, OR, etc., and copying of data from one memory element to another. In general, the data that is used to be read, or write to after results have been computed, is temporarily stored in a set of registers, called register file. Figure 5.1 shows the set of such operations that are used by most modern processors. Some of the instructions have integer and floating-point forms. The amount of memory required by integer and floating point numbers is dissimilar; therefore the hardware determines the inputs of the instruction as integers or floating point quantities and determines which register should be used.

The mnemonics used to express the arithmetic and logical operations presented in Figure 5.1 are relatively self-explanatory. The shift operations SHA and SHL change the position of the bits in one of their inputs. Shift operations take the bits in their first input and move them left by a number of bit positions equal to the value of their second input. Logical shift (SHL) operations are the simpler of the two shift operations. Bits that are shifted out of the word are discarded, and zeroes are shifted into vacant bit positions.

5.1.2 Memory Operations

Memory operations generally used are listed in Figure 5.2. These operations are employed to transfer data between the processor and the memory system. Each of these operations function on an amount of data equal to the word size of the machine.

Operation	*Function*
ADD	Adds its two integer operands.
SUB	Subtracts its second integer operand from its first.
MUL	Multiplies its two integer operands.
DIV	Divides its first integer input by its second.
ADDF	Adds its two floating-point operands.
SUBF	Subtracts its second floating-point operand from its first.
MULF	Multiplies its two floating-point operands.
DIVF	Divides its first floating-point input by its second.
MOV	Copies its input (of any type) to its output, both of which may be of any type.
OR	Performs a logical OR on its two inputs, which can be of any type.
AND	Performs a logical AND on its two inputs, which can be any type.
NOT	Performs logical negation on its input, which can be any type.
SHA	Shifts (arithmetic) first input by number of positions in its second input.
SHL	Shifts (logical) first input by the number of positions in its second input.

FIGURE 5.1 : Arithmetic Operations

Thus, a Load (LDX) reads one word of data from the addresses starting at the address specified by its input and a Store (STX) writes one word of data to the memory starting at the address specified by its address input.

Operation	*Function*
LDA	Load contents of address specified by its input operand into its destination.
STO	Store value contained in its second input into the address specified by its first input.

FIGURE 5.2 : Memory Operations

5.1.3 Comparisons

Comparison operations are utilized very frequently for decision-making in any program. Some commonly used functions are listed in Figure 5.3. These operations compare two or more values so that the program can make decisions. The output of comparison is made available in the status register and exhibited by the flags.

Operation	*Function*
EQL	Tests the two integer operands to see if they are equal.
NEQ	Tests the two integer operands to see if they are not equal.
GEQ	Determines if the first integer operand is greater than its second.
LEQ	Determines if first integer operand is less than or equal to the second.
GTR	Determines if the first integer operand is greater than its second.
LTH	Determines if the first integer operand is less than its second.

FIGURE 5.3 : Comparison Operations

Comparison operations are generally used in combination with control operations to create a 'conditional branch' that executes either one section of a program or another, depending on the result of the comparison.

5.1.4 Control Operations

Control operations are used in the program flow to change the contents of the program counter. Figure 5.4 shows a common set of control operations. The change in ordinary sequential flow may be when a branch operation occurs to a location other than a sequential location. After the branch instruction is executed, the program counter points to the jump address. Thus, when a control operation executes, the program counter is set to the input of the control instruction, causing execution to jump to a different point in the program.

Control operations, which are also called branches, can be divided into two categories: 'unconditional' and 'conditional'. Unconditional branches are also called jumps. They always set the PC equal to their input when they are executed. Conditional branches set the PC equal to their input address if some condition, such as the result of a comparison, is true.

Operation	*Function*
BEQ	Branch if inputs are equal; PC set to value of first operand
BNE	Branch if inputs are not equal; PC set value of its first operand
BLT	Branch if second operand less than or equal to first operand; PC set to value of first operand
BGE	Branch if second operand is greater than or equal to first operand; PC equals value of first operand
JMP	Jump to given address; PC set to value of its input operand, causing the instruction at that address to be executed next

FIGURE 5.4 : Comparison Operations

5.2 TYPES OF INSTRUCTIONS

The instructions available in a processor are executed at the microarchitecture level. At this level, data transfer and operations performed at the register level are taken into account. Register transfer notation is used to express these operations.

5.2.1 Register Transfer Notation

Register transfer was introduced in Section 3.8.2. This method of expression is very close to assembly language notation where the statement such as R2 ← R1 denotes a transfer of contents of register R1 to contents of R2. On performing this operation, the contents of R2 are replaced by contents of R1 while the contents of R1 remain unchanged. This method is very useful to describe the transfer of information from one location in the computer to another. The possible locations that may be involved in such transfers are memory locations, processor registers, or registers in the I/O sub-system. The location is identified by a symbolic name standing for its hardware identity. For example, names for the addresses of memory locations may be A, VAR1, or VAR2. The processor register names may be referred to as R1, R4 and the I/O register names could be PORT1, PORT2, etc. The contents of a location are denoted by placing square brackets around the name of the location. Thus, the expression means that the contents of memory location VAR1 are transferred into processor register RI.

RI ← [VAR1]

The operation that adds the contents of registers R1 and R2, and then places their sum into register R3 can be denoted as:

R3 ← [R1] + [R2]

Note that the right-hand side of Register Transfer Notation (RTN) expression always denotes a value, and the left-hand side is the name of a location where the value is to be placed, overwriting the old contents of that location.

5.2.2 Assembly Language Notation

The machine instructions and programs are denoted in assembly language format. For example, an instruction that causes the transfer described above, from memory location VAR1 to processor register R1, is specified by the statement

MOV VAR1, R1

The contents of VAR1 are unchanged by the execution of this instruction, but the old contents of register R1 are overwritten.

Another example of adding two numbers contained in processor registers R1 and R2, and placing their sum in R3 can be specified by the assembly language statements as:

ADD R1, R2, R3

Here, contents of register R3 are the sum of the contents of register R1 and register R2.

5.2.3 Instruction Types

Different types of instructions are available in the computer to perform various actions. The instruction that is used the most is for copying data from one place to another. Copying means creating an identical bit pattern as the original at the destination location. The data is copied for two reasons. First is the assignment of values to variables, such as X = Y, where the value in memory location Y is copied to memory location X. The second reason is to make the data available at some other memory location where it is more easy to use it. For example, variables are copied from memory locations to registers.

Consider the operation that adds two variables X and Y to produce the third variable Z. The statement Z = X + Y in a high-level language program is a command to the processor to add the current values of the two variables called X and Y, and to assign the sum to a third variable Z. When the program containing this statement is compiled, the three variables X, Y, and Z are assigned to different locations in the memory. The contents of these locations represent the values of the three variables. Hence, the above high-level language statement requires the following action to take place in the computer.

[Z] ← [X] + [Y]

For the execution of this statement, the contents of memory locations X and Y are fetched from the memory into processor registers where their sum is calculated. This result is then stored in location C. This operation can be accomplished in various ways. The address provided by the program to access the memory may be provided in three separate ways. These methods are explained as follows:

Three-address Instruction

Three-address instruction provides three separate addresses for three operands in a single machine instruction. The following instruction is a three address instruction with addresses X, Y and Z. This three-address instruction can be represented symbolically as:

ADD X, Y, Z

Operands X and Y are called the source operands, Z is called the destination operand, and ADD is the operation to be performed on the operands. A general three-address instruction has the format:

Operation Addr 1, Addr 2, Addr 3

Where Addr1 and Addr2 are the source addresses and Addr3 is the destination address.

Two-address Instruction

A two-address instruction has only two operands and has the form

Operation Addr1, Addr2

Where Addr1 and Addr2 are the source and destination addresses respectively.

A two-address ADD instruction is of the type:

ADD X, Y

The above statement performs the operation [Y] ← [X] + [Y]. When the sum is calculated, the result is sent to the memory and stored in location X, replacing the original contents of this location. This means that operand Y is both a source and a destination.

One-address Instruction

One-address instruction specifies only one memory operand. When a second operand is needed, as in the case of an ADD instruction, it is understood implicitly to be a unique location. A processor register, usually called the accumulator, may be used for this purpose. Thus, the one-address instruction is:

ADD X

Which means the following: Add the contents of memory location X to the contents of the accumulator register and place the sum back into the accumulator.

Using only one-address instructions, the operation [Z] ← [X] + [Y] can be performed by executing the sequence of instructions:

```
LDA  X {Load X}
ADD  Y {Add Y to X}
STO  Z {Store Z}
```

The operand specified in the one address instruction may be a source or a destination, depending on the instruction. In the LDA instruction, address X specifies the source operand and the destination operand is accumulator, which is implied. Address Z specifies the destination location in the STO instruction and here the accumulator is the implied source.

Move Instruction

The movement of data between different memory locations is the most used instruction by a programmer. The transfer of data between different locations of memory is achieved with the instruction:

MOV Source, Destination

This instruction places a copy of the contents of Source into Destination. When data are moved to or from a processor register, the MOV instruction can be used rather than the LDA or STO instructions because the order of the source and destination operands determines which operation was intended.

Zero-address Instructions

Zero-address instructions are those in which the locations of all operands are defined implicitly. The execution of these instructions is the fastest as the speed with which a given task is carried out depends on the time it takes to transfer instructions from memory into the processor, and to access the operand. These instructions are generally used for stacks.

5.2.4 Sequential Instruction

The instructions of a program are executed sequentially. In the sequential execution, an instruction is fetched from the memory location and then it is executed. The first step is called instruction fetch. The instruction is fetched from the memory location whose address is in the PC. This instruction is placed in the instruction register (IR) in the processor. At the same time, the PC is incremented to have the address of the next instruction. After determining the operations to be performed for execution of the current instruction, 'instruction execute' phase is completed. This often involves fetching operands from the memory or from processor registers, performing an arithmetic or logic operation, and storing the result in the destination location. When the execute phase of an instruction is completed, the PC contains the address of the next instruction, and a new instruction fetch phase can begin.

The addition of two numbers represented as [Z] ← [X] + [Y] is an example of assembly language representation of instruction execution. The description of memory storage for addition is shown in Figure 5.5. Assume that the word length of the processor is 32 bits and the memory is byte addressable. The three instructions of the program are stored in successive word locations, starting at location I. Since each instruction is 4 bytes long, the second and third instructions start at addresses I + 4 and I + 8.

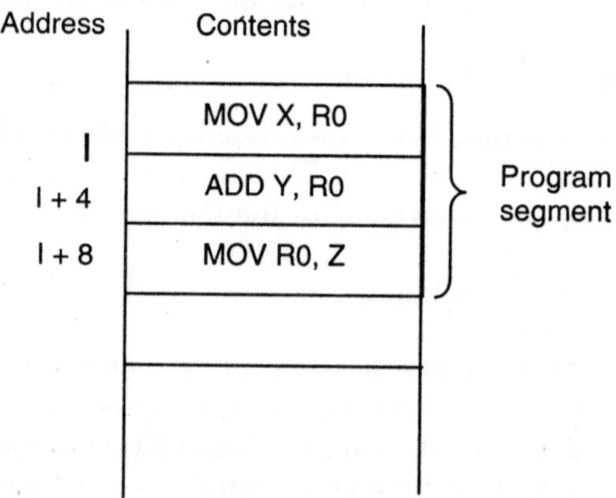

FIGURE 5.5 : Memory Array for Program [Z] ← [X] + [Y]

5.2.5 Branching

When a list of n numbers needs to be added, the sequential program will have ADD instruction repeated n times, which will take a long time.

Instead of using a long list of ADD instructions, it is possible to place a single ADD instruction in a program loop which is repeated n times, as shown in Figure 5.6. The loop is a straight-line sequence of instructions executed as many times as needed. It starts at location LOOP and ends at the instruction BRANCH > 0. During each pass through this loop, the address of the next item to be added is determined, and that item is fetched and added to the register holding the count of loops.

The creation and control of a program loop is as follows: Assume that the number of items in the list, n, is stored in memory location N, as shown. Register R1 is used as a counter to determine the number of times the loop is executed. The contents of location N are loaded into register R1 at the beginning of the program. The contents of R1 are decremented by 1 each time through the loop by the instruction

DECREMENT R1

Execution of the loop is repeated as long as the result of the decrement operation is greater than zero.

The BRANCH instruction loads a new value into the PC. As a result, the processor fetches and executes the instruction at this new address, called the BRANCH ADDR, instead of the sequential instruction at the location that follows the branch instruction.

In the program below, the instruction, BRANCH > 0 LOOP, will allow the Branch to take place only if the condition BRANCH GREATER THAN 0 is true. Here, branch instruction will cause a branch to location LOOP if the result of the immediately preceding instruction is true. The loop is repeated as long as there are items in the list that are yet to be added to R0.

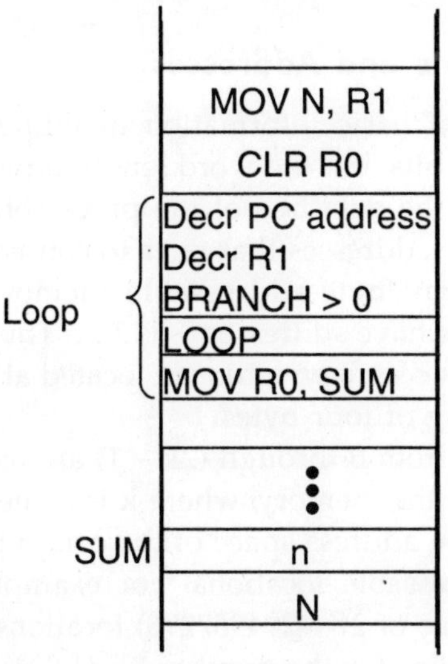

FIGURE 5.6 : A Loop for Addition of n Numbers

At the end of the nth pass through the loop, the Decrement instruction produces a value of zero. In this case, branching does not occur. Instead, the MOV instruction is fetched and executed. It moves the final result from R0 into memory location SUM.

5.2.6 Condition Codes

Condition codes or flags are individual bits of registers in the CPU that are affected by the results of various operations. The result of conditional branch instructions is affected by the outcome of these flags. These flags are usually grouped together in a special processor register called the 'condition code register' or 'status register'. Individual condition code flags are set to 1 or cleared to 0, depending on the outcome of the operation performed.

5.3 INSTRUCTION WORD FORMATS

Though information in the computer is in the form of bits, but size of retrieval of information depends on the type of data that is required. Generally, single bits are used to represent a condition which is either true or false. Other than this requirement, a single bit is a very small amount of information and is rarely used. Therefore, bits are used in groups of fixed size. For this purpose, the memory is organized in such a way so that a group of n bits can be stored or retrieved in a single, basic operation. Each group of n bits is referred to as a 'word' of information, and 'n' is called the 'word length'. The data can be in the form of numbers, character operands, and instructions. This section describes methods to represent this information and discusses the formats for representation of numerical data.

5.3.1 Memory Locations and Addresses

The storage types of basic information quantities are bit, byte and word. A byte is always 8 bits, but the word length typically ranges from 16 to 64 bits depending on the data bus of the processor. The assignment of addresses is to successive addresses that refer to consecutive byte locations in the memory. The term 'byte-addressable memory' is used for this assignment. Byte locations have addresses 0, 1, 2 .... Thus, if the word length of the machine is 4 bits, successive words are located at addresses 0, 4, 8, ... with each word consisting of four bytes.

Generally, numbers from 0 through (2k – 1) are used as the addresses of successive locations in the memory, where k is some suitable value. The λ^k addresses constitute the address space of the computer, and the memory can have up to α^k addressable locations. For example, a 32-bit address generates an address space of 2^{32} (4294967296) locations. Notations that are commonly used are K (kilo) for the number 2^{10} (1,024), M is Mega for the number 2^{20} (1,048,576), G is Giga which is 2^{30} and T (tera) for the number 2^{40}.

5.3.2 Basic Formats

The information within the computer is of two types: instruction, or data. Data is sub-divided into numerical and non-numerical form. Numerical data is further of two types: fixed point, and floating point.

Fixed Point Numbers

Integers are fixed point numbers which have an implied binary point at the right hand side. The binary fixed point number can be represented as:

$b_a b_b b_c \ldots\ldots b_k$

where each b_i is either 0 or 1 and binary point is present on the right side of the number.

Floating Point Representation

Floating point numbers are used to represent fractions. A floating point number consists of two parts: Mantissa M and Exponent E, which denote the number $M \times B^E$, where E is the base.

Non-numeric Data

Non-numeric data is a variable-length character string that is encoded in one or several standard codes, such as ASCII code.

Word Length

A 'word' is a unit of information of some fixed length 'n'. A word with n bits can represent information up to 2^n different things. For example, with n=4, the 10 decimal digits can be encoded.

Bytes

Bytes are 8-bit words. They are used to encode alphanumeric characters or symbols, which are generally the standard symbols on the keyboard.

Precision of a number word is determined by its length. Some information formats are: 1 Bit, used for status flags, logic variables; 8 bit known as a Byte, used for addressable memory unit; 16 bits known as Half Word, used for floating point number; 64 bits known as Double Word, used for long instructions.

5.3.3 Storage Order

It is important to identify whether the bits of a word are indexed from left to right or from right to left. Generally, the right most bit is assigned the index 0, and the bits are indexed in increasing order from right to left. Thus the right-most bit becomes the least significant bit (LSB) and the left-most bit becomes the most significant bit (MSB). The opposite order of right-most bit as MSB and left-most bit as LSB is also possible, but it has to be specified accordingly.

Tags

Tags are used to specify whether the stored information is an instruction or data. The type of Word is determined by the way processor interprets it. Same word can be treated as instruction or data at different times. Generally, 'tag bits', which are a special group of bits, are added to identify whether a word format is instruction or data.

5.3.4 Big-Endian and Little-Endian Assignments

'Endian' is the name given to byte ordering of data in memory. The addressing of bytes can be from left to right or from right to left in the computer storage. Simply speaking, this can be known as byte-ordering. Two specific schemes used are Big-Endian and Little-Endian assignments. The representations are shown in Figure 5.7. The name, Big-Endian, is used when more significant bytes (the leftmost bytes) represent lower byte addresses for the word. The name, Little-Endian, is used where the lower byte addresses are used for the less significant bytes (the rightmost bytes) of the word, which is just opposite of Big-Endian representation. The words 'more significant' and 'less significant' are used in relation to the weights (powers of 2) assigned to bits when the word represents a number

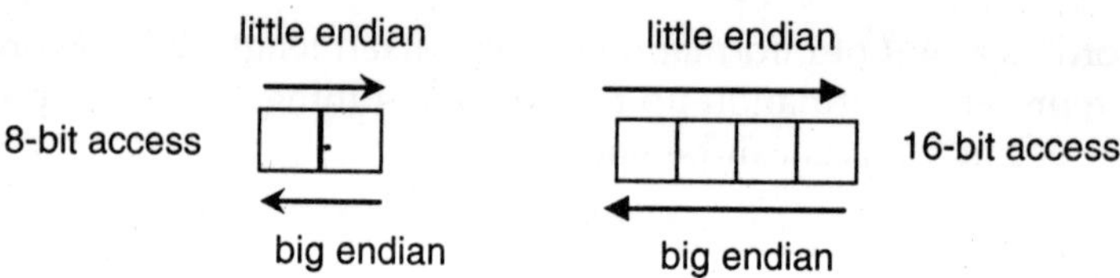

FIGURE 5.7 : Big-Endian and Little-Endian Assignments

Both little-endian and big-endian assignments are used in commercial machines. In both cases, byte addresses 0, 4, 8, . . . are taken as the addresses of successive words in the memory and addresses are used when specifying memory read and write operations for words.

5.4 ADDRESSING MODES

Data used for computation can be organized in various ways, in different locations of the memory. Different addressing modes are used to address the memory to access the required operand(s) stored in various ways in different memory locations. The special way in which the location of an operand is specified in an instruction, is referred to as 'addressing mode'.

The various data types represented in a computer program are constants, variables, pointers, and arrays. In assembly language, a variable is represented by allocating a register or memory location to hold its value. The address field of a typical instruction is relatively small. The memory locations to be addressed may be in the main memory or in the virtual memory. The aim is to reference a large number of memory locations. To achieve this, a variety of addressing methods are employed. Some methods are able to access more number of locations, but to access such a location will involve extra time. Thus, to choose an addressing mode involves trade-offs between address range and number of memory references. Some of the common addressing techniques are as under:

(i) Immediate addressing
(ii) Direct addressing
(iii) Indirect addressing
(iv) Register addressing
(v) Register Indirect addressing
(vi) Displacement addressing
(vii) Stack addressing

The following notations are used for explanation:

(i) M – Contents of address field in the instruction
(ii) R – Contents of address field that refer to a register
(iii) EA – Effective Address of memory location containing the operand
(iv) (X) – Contents of location X

One or more bits in the instruction format are used as the mode field for the control unit to determine which addressing mode is being used. The effective address will either be a main memory address, virtual memory address or a register.

5.4.1 Immediate Addressing

Immediate addressing is the simplest form of addressing. In this form of addressing, the operand is actually present in the instruction.

OPERAND = M

Instruction

	Operand

FIGURE 5.8 : Immediate Addressing

This mode is used to set initial values of variables, or to define constants. The number is set as two's complement and the left-most bit of the operand is used as the sign bit. Advantage of this mode is that only the instruction-fetch is required and no memory reference is needed, thus saving one instruction cycle. Disadvantage is that the size of the number is restricted to the size of the address field.

5.4.2 Direct Addressing

This is also a very simple form of addressing. In direct addressing, the address field contains the effective address of the operand, as shown in Figure 5.9.

$$EA = M$$

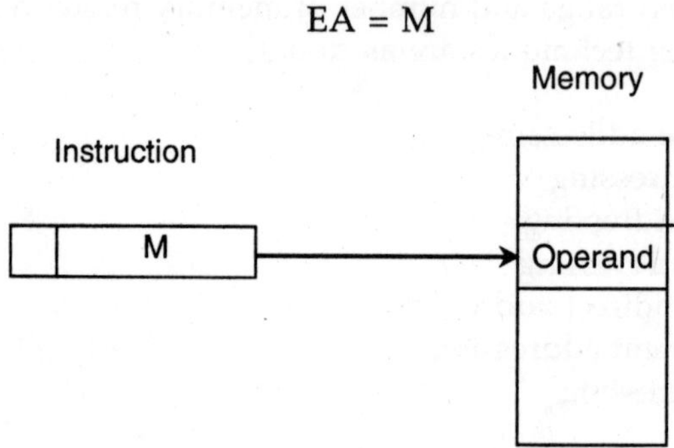

FIGURE 5.9 : Direct Addressing

Only one memory reference is required in this addressing mode. The limitation is that it makes available only limited address spaces and is usually less than the word length.

5.4.3 Indirect Addressing

In indirect addressing, the address field refers to address of a word in memory, which in turn contains the full address of the operand. This is demonstrated in Figure 5.10.

$$EA = [M]$$

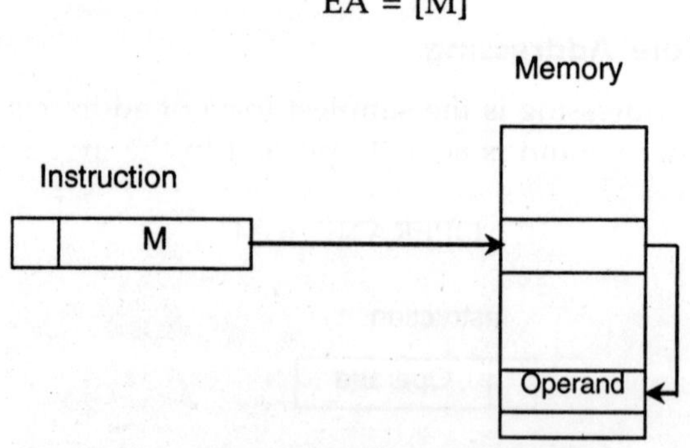

FIGURE 5.10 : Indirect Addressing

The advantage of this mode is that for word length of N, address space of 2^N is available. The disadvantage is that two memory references are needed to fetch the operand. One reference is required to get the address of the operand and the second reference gets its value.

5.4.4 Register Addressing

Register addressing is similar to direct addressing. The difference is that the address field refers to a register rather than a memory location. This form of addressing is exhibit in Figure 5.11.

The advantage of register addressing is that only small address field is needed in the instruction. This means that no memory reference is required. Thus, register addressing is very fast. The disadvantage of this mode is that address space is very limited.

$$EA = R$$

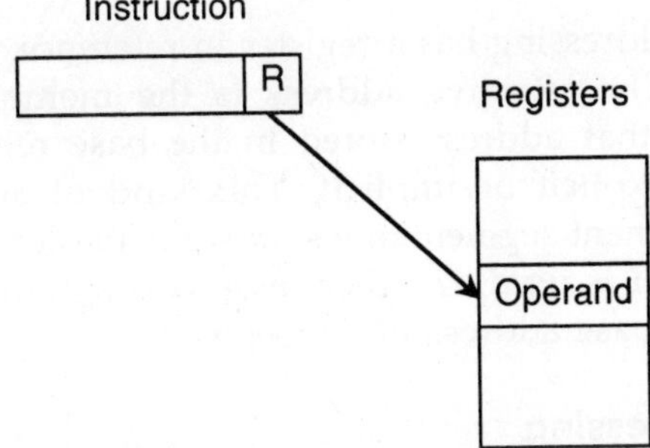

FIGURE 5.11: Register Addressing

5.4.5 Register Indirect Addressing

Register indirect addressing is similar to indirect addressing but address field refers to a register rather than a memory location. Figure 5.12 shows this form of addressing.

$$EA = [R]$$

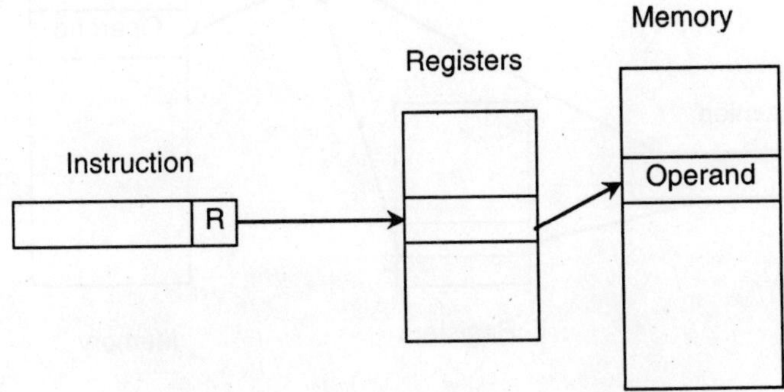

FIGURE 5.12 : Register Indirect Addressing

The advantage of this form of addressing is that though it is the same as indirect addressing, but one less memory reference is used. The disadvantage is that it has to access the registers twice.

5.4.6 Relative Addressing

This form of addressing combines the capabilities of direct addressing and register indirect addressing. The effective address is given as:

$$EA = M + [R]$$

The implied register is the program counter. Current instruction address is added to the address field to produce effective address. The effective address is a displacement relative to the address of the instruction.

5.4.7 Base Register Addressing

Base register addressing has a register in reference which is known as the base register. The effective address is the memory address and a displacement from that address stored in the base register. The register reference may be explicit or implicit. This kind of addressing is quite convenient to implement segmentations. In some implementations, a single segment-base register is used. In other cases, a programmer may choose a register to hold the base address of the segment.

5.4.8 Index Addressing

In this form of memory reference, the address field references a main memory address, and the referenced register contains a positive displacement from that address. Figure 5.13 depicts Index addressing. This method is just the opposite of 'base-register' addressing. Here the address field is considered to be a memory address. The method of calculating the effective address is the same as base register addressing.

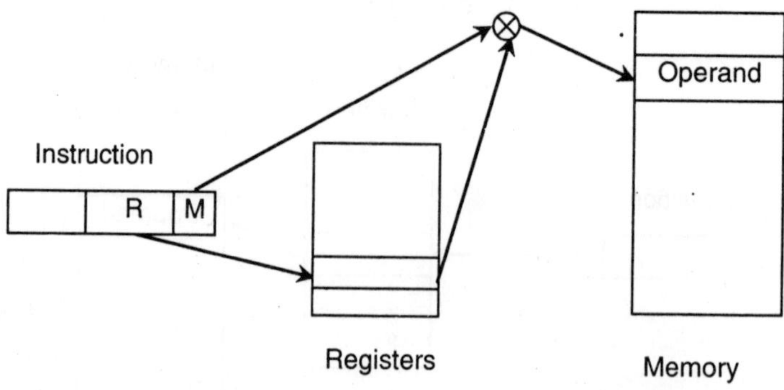

FIGURE 5.13 : Index Addressing

Indexing is used in iterative operations and index registers are used for these operations. Here the index register is just incremented or decremented.

EA = EA + (R)
R ← (R) + 1

First, the contents of the address field are used to access a memory location containing a direct address. The value of the index register is then added to the register value.

5.4.9 Stack Addressing

Stack is a special block of contiguous memory locations. A special register, known as stack pointer, is used to point to the address at one end of these locations, generally known as the top of stack. Stack addressing is similar to register indirect addressing is depicted in Figure 5.14. Stack Pointer maintained in a register

EA = [R]

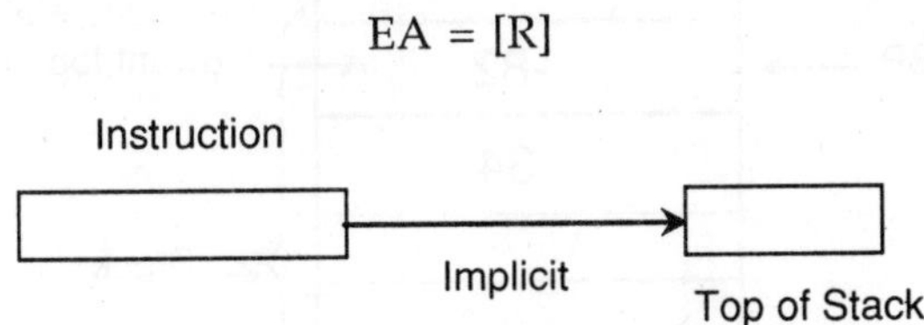

FIGURE 5.14 : Stack Addressing

Stack mode of addressing is a form of implied addressing. The machine instructions do not include a memory reference. The top of the stack is the implied address.

5.5 ARCHITECTURE OF A STACK MACHINE

Stack is a special data structure that is used by the programmers for handling temporary storage of tasks in the main program, called subroutines. While calling a subroutine, current address of the PC needs to be stored so that when the job of the subtask finishes, the program returns back to its original processing. This section will describe stacks, as well as a closely related data structure, called a queue.

5.5.1 Stacks

A 'stack' is a list of data elements, usually words or bytes, that are accessed by using special instructions. The elements can be added or removed at one end of the list only. This end is called the 'top of the stack', and the other end is called the 'bottom of the stack'. A method of organizing the stack is Last-In-First-Out (LIFO) stack where the new element is placed or removed from the top of the stack only. Another way of organization of stack is First-In-First-Out or FIFO, where the new data is placed on the top of the stack and removed from the bottom of the stack.

The location pointed to by a special register, called Stack Pointer register (SP), is termed as the Top-Of-Stack. Figure 5.15 shows a LIFO stack. It contains numerical values, with 66 at the bottom and –82 at the top. A SP register is used to keep track of the address of the element of the stack that is at the top of any given time. It could be one of the general-purpose registers or a register dedicated to this function.

Implicit instructions are used for addressing the stack and the address referred is the address of the top of the stack pointed to by the SP register.

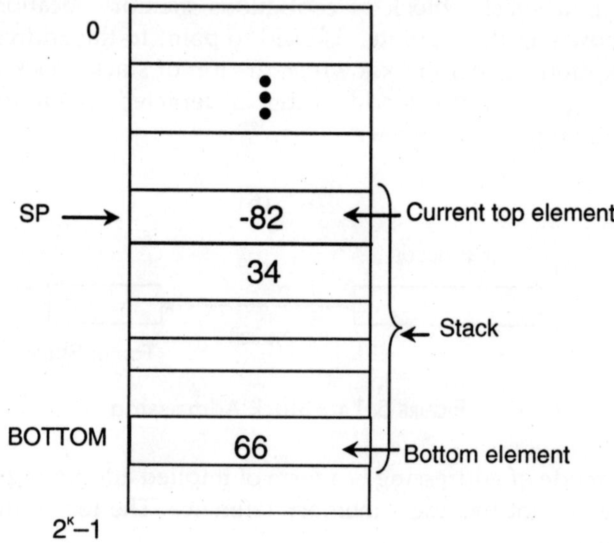

FIGURE 5.15 : A LIFO Stack

Some of the instructions are:

PUSH

POP

MOVE

ADD

SUBTRACT

When a stack is used in a program, it is generally allocated a fixed amount of space in the memory.

5.5.2 Queues

Queue is a data structure that is similar to the stack. Data are stored in and retrieved from a queue on a first-in-first-out (FIFO) basis. Thus, if we assume that the queue grows in the direction of increasing addresses in the memory, new data are added at the back (high-address end) and retrieved from the front (low-address end) of the queue.

A queue would continuously move through the memory of a computer in the direction of higher addresses if no control is exercised. One way to limit the queue to a fixed region in memory is to use a circular buffer.

There is an important difference between how a stack and a queue are implemented. One end of the stack is fixed (the bottom), while the other end rises and falls as data are pushed and popped. A single pointer is needed to point to the top of the stack at any given time. On the other hand, both ends of a queue move to higher addresses as data are added at the back and removed from the front. Thus, two pointers are needed to keep track of the two ends of the queue.

5.5.3 Subroutines

Subroutines are subprograms that perform a small function of the main program many times, and a single program can be built with many subroutines. In a program with subroutines, it is common to have one subroutine call another. This is called 'subroutine nesting'. The return addresses are stored in the stack pointer register. In the case of nesting, the return address of the second call is also stored in the stack pointer register, destroying its previous contents. Hence, it is essential to save the contents of the stack pointer register in some other location before calling another subroutine. Otherwise, the return address of the first subroutine will be lost.

Subroutine nesting can be carried out to any depth. The last subroutine called completes its computations and returns to the subroutine that called it. The return address needed for this first return is the last one generated in the nested call sequence. The return addresses are generated and used in a last-in-first-out order. This suggests that the return addresses associated with subroutine calls should be pushed onto a stack. The Call instruction pushes the contents of the PC onto the processor stack and loads the subroutine address into the PC. The Return instruction pops the return address from the processor stack into the PC. Operands that are used in the subroutine for computation are called Parameters. These parameters must be provided to the subroutine. Later, the subroutine returns the results of the computation. This exchange of information between a calling program and a subroutine is referred to as 'parameter passing'. Parameter passing may be accomplished in several ways. The parameters may be placed in registers or in memory locations, where they can be accessed by the subroutine. Alternatively, the parameters may be placed on the processor stack used for saving the return address.

5.6 LANGUAGE DIRECTED ARCHITECTURE

Language directed architecture is used to execute programs in High-Level-Language (HLL) directly. In the von Neumann computer, instructions are fetched and executed in several steps that form an instruction cycle. The programs, generally written in some HLL, are compiled and the object code comprising of machine language instructions are executed in the CPU. In programming languages, semantics reflects the meaning of programs or functions. The semantic gap means that the objects and operations in a HLL are not closely related to the objects and operations in the architectures that execute the HLL. The semantic gap that separates programming languages from the machines on which programs are run, often results in poor execution efficiency, that has become more of a problem with the development of languages like languages for artificial intelligence programming, Ada and even C-like languages. For increasing the performance of the machine while using such languages, the need was felt for the design of special-purpose, high-level-language-directed computer architectures.

The problem of semantic gap can be controlled by managing the flow of the program, making it dependent on the information structure that would help the design of HLL architecture. Digital computers are usually viewed as being composed of a controller and data paths. A program can be thought of as a realization of a function which when supplied with data will yield the desired result. In order to compute the function, the function and data need to be stored in such a way that the access and manipulation is easy.

In this design of language directed digital computer, information structures are defined and are represented by programs and data. These are called program structure and data structure respectively. In addition to these structures, there are information structures used during execution that are neither program nor data structures. These are called execution structures. Execution of a program in an HLL is defined in terms of transformations on information structures.

A digital computer viewed in terms of structures has the following functions:

1. Stores programs, data and execution structures.
2. Transforms programs, data and execution structures.

A digital computer, therefore, must consist of a set of devices for performing transformations on program, data and execution structures.

Design Methodology

Figure 5.16 shows the elements of language directed architecture. The controller design is built in terms of recognition of an HLL. The data path design is dealt with in terms of information structures.

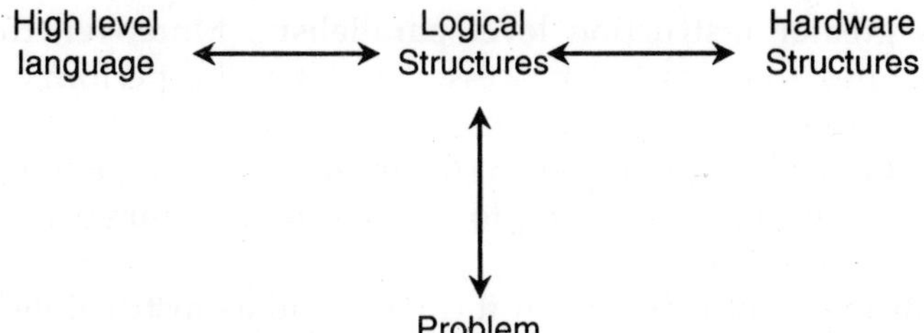

FIGURE 5.16 : Elements of Language Directed Architecture

The controller functions in the following manner:

1. Recognize words of an HLL program.
2. After each word is recognized, a set of control signals is output by the controller that transform information structures in the data path.

The data path consists of:

1. Program, data and execution structures.
2. Devices to move information between structures.

In the language directed architecture, program is considered as a realization of a function operating on data that is supplied to it. The results are obtained after computing of the function in the hardware. For improving performance of such an architecture, the function and data needed are stored in a way that the retrieval and operation is simple.

Information structures are represented by programs and data. These are called program structure and data structure. In addition to these structures, there are information structures used during execution that are neither program nor data structures. These are called execution structures.

A digital computer, therefore, must consist of a set of devices for performing transformations on program, data and execution structures to function as language directed architecture.

5.7 REDUCED INSTRUCTION SET COMPUTING (RISC)

Until mid-80's, the computers that were designed had very large instruction sets, which made the architecture of the CPUs to be very complex. On the other hand, some other architects tried to reverse the trend by building CPUs capable of executing only a very limited set of instructions, which also made the architecture to be quite simple.

Reduced Instruction Set Computer (RISC—Pronounced *risk*) is a type of processor that recognizes a relatively limited number of instructions. The instruction set is reduced both in size and complexity of addressing modes, and allows greater instruction level parallelism. Moreover, these more complex features took several processor cycles to be performed and the performance gap between the processor and main memory was increasing. This led to a number of techniques to streamline processing within the CPU, while at the same time attempting to reduce the total number of memory accesses.

One advantage of RISC is that it can execute its instructions very fast. Another advantage is that RISC chips require fewer transistors, which makes them cheaper to design and faster to produce results. However, RISC also had its drawbacks. Since a series of instructions is needed to complete even simple tasks, the total number of instructions read from memory is larger, and therefore takes longer. The disadvantage is that by making the hardware simpler, RISC architecture puts a greater liability on the software.

Though the individual manufacturers may produce different RISC architectures, the essential features are as under:

- Relatively few instructions and addressing modes
- Reduction of the instruction set
- Fixed length easily decoded instruction format
- Single cycle instruction execution
- Memory access limited to Load/store instructions
- All operations done within registers of CPU
- Hardwired rather than Microprogrammed control
- Instruction pipelining

The earliest RISC computers had less than 40 instructions. The execution structure of an instruction is:

Read instruction from memory
Decode the instruction
Where necessary, fetch operands
Execute instruction
Write back the result

Because of the excessive dependence on software in RISC microprocessors, the CISC microprocessors are also used.

5.8 COMPLEX INSTRUCTION SET COMPUTING (CISC)

A computer with large number of instructions is classified as CISC. They are chips that are easy to program and which make efficient use of memory. Goal is to complete compilation in as few lines as possible. The task of a compiler is to generate sequence of machine instructions for each high-level-language statement. This is achieved by building processor hardware that is capable of understanding and executing a series of operations. Essentially, CISC architecture attempts to provide a single machine instruction for each statement written in high-level-language.

Since the earliest machines were programmed in assembly language and memory was slow and expensive, the CISC philosophy was used in large computers like PDP-11 and DEC systems. The Intel '86 series and Motorola 68 series followed CISC philosophy.

The CISC architecture has following characteristics in the instruction set:

- A 2-operand format
- Variable length instructions
- Instructions that require multiple clock cycles to execute
- Complex instruction-decoding logic
- Small number of general purpose registers
- Several special purpose registers
- A 'condition code' register which is set as a side effect of most instructions
- Microprogramming was used, which is much less expensive than hardwired control.

But CISC has its problems. In the newer generations of the computer, the earlier generations were contained as a subset of instruction set. Thus, the chip hardware became more complex with each generation. Different instructions take different amount of clock time to execute. This slows the overall performance of the machine.

Setting the 'condition codes' of instructions takes extra time. Also, the programmer has to remember to examine the condition code bits before a subsequent instruction changes them.

With time, memory speed increased and high level languages made assembly language disappear. The performance (speed, cost, simplicity of design) needed to be optimized rather than just making the computers fast. Thus, RISC came into existence. These days, CISC and RISC implementations are becoming more and more alike. Today's many RISC machines support many instructions of CISC machines and *vice-versa*.

5.9 COMPARISON OF RISC AND CISC

The comparison between RISC and CISC machines is provided in Figure 5.17.

Basically RISC and CISC are different design methodologies. Neither of them is particularly superior to the other. CISC architectures are capable of coming up to the level of performance of RISC processors. The performance of a microprocessor based computer is a function of more factors than just the microprocessor.

S. No.	RISC	CISC
1.	Simple instructions	complex instructions
2.	Hardwired Control Unit	Microprogrammed control unit
3.	Few addressing schemes for memory operands with only two basic instructions, LOAD and STORE	Extensive addressing capabilities for memory operations
4.	Many symmetric registers which are organized into a register file	Relatively few registers
5.	Emphasis on software	Emphasis on hardware
6.	Small code sizes, high cycles per second sizes	Low cycles per second, large code
7.	Single clock	Multi-clock
8.	Cheaper and faster	Relatively expensive and slow

FIGURE 5.17 : Comparison between RISC and CISC

5.10 EXAMPLE ARCHITECTURE—8085

In this section, the organization and programming of 8-bit microprocessor, the Intel 8085, is described. Only those aspects of the organization are presented that are of significant use to the software designer.

5.10.1 Functional Organization of the 8085

The functional organization of the CPU 8085 is illustrated in Figure 5.18.

5.10.2 Data and Address Busses

The 8085 is an 8-bit microprocessor (μP). As shown in Figure 5.18, the data bus is 8 bits wide. This implies that 8 bits (1 byte) of data can be transferred to or from the 8085 in parallel. There are eight pins dedicated to transmit the most significant 8 bits of the memory address. The least significant 8 bits of the address are transmitted on the eight lines on which data is transmitted. Thus, address multiplexing is performed where data and part of the address are transmitted over a set of shared lines. The data and address (least significant 8 bits) are transmitted at different points in time.

Thus, the 8085 has a 16-bit address transmission capability. This implies that a total of 2^{16} memory locations can be addressed directly by 8085. Each location in a byte has 8 bits of data, which is transferred in parallel between 8085 and the memory. Hence, the 8085 can directly address 64K bytes of memory.

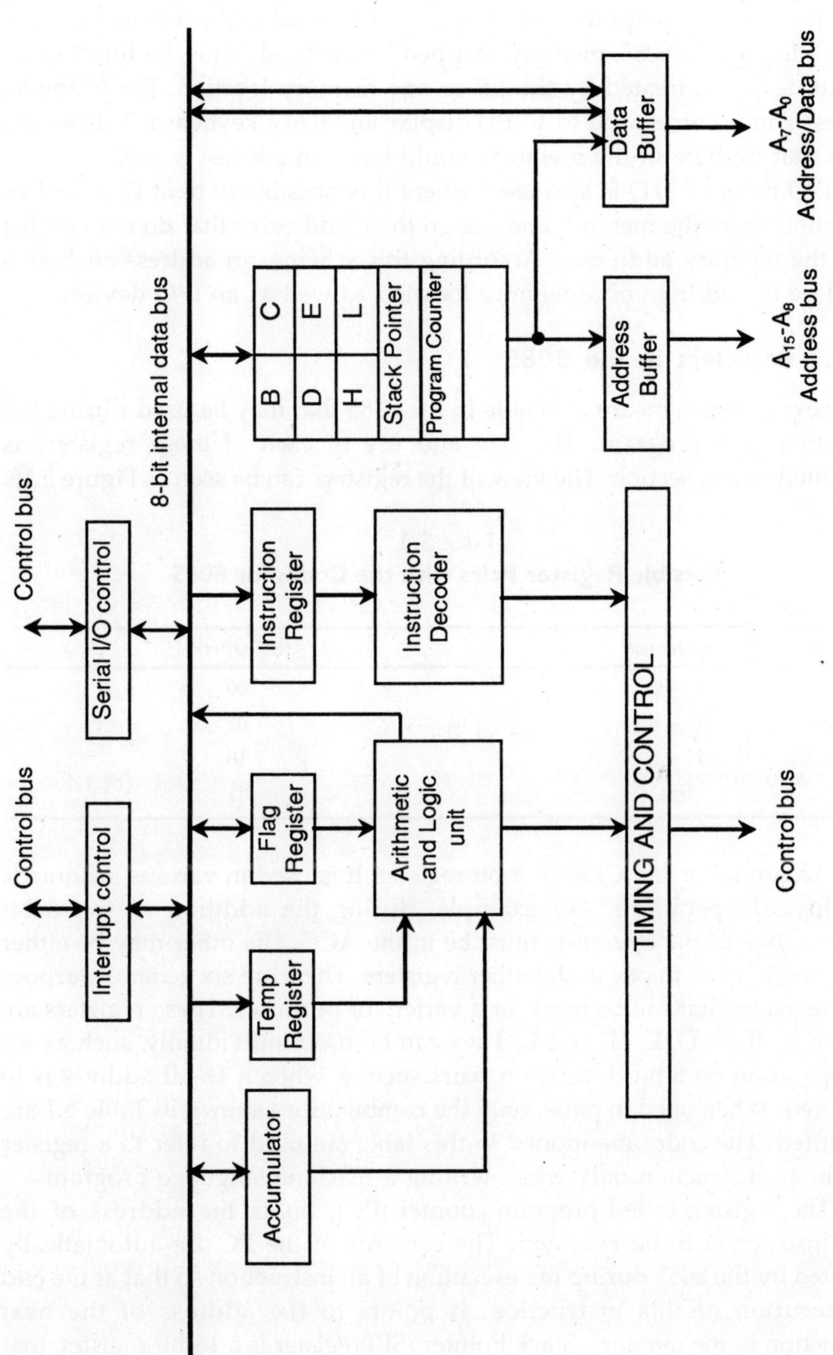

FIGURE 5.18 : Functional Organization of 8085

5.10.3 Addressing the I/O Devices

In any microcomputer, the μP will be connected to the memory as well as I/O devices. In 8085, memory mapped I/O is used. Thus, an input or an output device is treated by the μP as one memory location. For example, address 5 may correspond to a LED display and 6 to a keyboard. This would mean that no byte in the memory would have an address 5 or 6.

I/O mapped I/O is also used where it is possible to treat I/O devices as distinct from the memory and assign them addresses that do not conflict with the memory addresses. According this scheme, an address such as 5 could be the address of a memory location as well as an I/O device.

5.10.4 Registers in the 8085

Several registers are available in the 8085 that may be used during the execution of a program. The size and use of each of these registers is presented in this section. The view of the registers can be seen in Figure 5.18.

TABLE 5.1
Possible Register Pairs with the Codes for 8085

Register pair	*Bit pattern*
B – C	00
D – E	01
H – L	10
Sp1	11

Accumulator (ACC) is an 8-bit register. It is used in various arithmetic and logical operations. For example, during the addition of two-8 bit integers, one of the operands must be in the ACC. The other may be either in the memory or in one of the other registers. There are six general-purpose 8-bit registers that can be used for a variety of purposes. These registers are labeled as B, C, D, E, H, and L. They can be used individually, such as for the operation on 8-bit data, or in pairs such as when a 16-bit address is to be stored. When used in pairs, only the combinations shown in Table 5.1 are permitted. The codes mentioned in this table are used to refer to a register pair in an instruction only when writing a machine language program.

The register, called program counter (PC), holds the address of the next instruction to be executed. The contents of the PC are automatically updated by the 8085 during the execution of an instruction so that at the end of execution of this instruction, it points to the address of the next instruction in the memory. Stack Pointer (SP) register is a 16-bit register, that the programmer uses to maintain a stack in the memory. Flag register is a

TABLE 5.2
General Purpose Register with the Codes for 8085

Register pair	*Bit pattern*
A	111
B	000
C	001
D	010
E	011
H	100
l	101

set of five flip-flops, which are 1-bit registers. They serve as flags. These registers indicate certain conditions such as overflow or carry that arise during arithmetic and logical operations.

5.10.5 Instruction Set of 8085

In this section, the instruction set of the 8085 is presented. A machine or assembly language program is written using suitable combinations of the instructions drawn from this set. The binary operation code and the corresponding mnemonic for each instruction is listed in Appendix A.

Instruction Types

An instruction may be 1, 2, or 3 bytes in length. In any of these three types of instructions, the first byte indicates the operation to be performed. The second and third bytes, if present, contain either the operand or address of the operand on which the operation is to be performed.

Classification of Instructions

The 8085 instructions are classified into the following five groups :

1. Data transfer group
2. Arithmetic group
3. Logical group
4. Branch group
5. Stack I/O and Machine control group

Each instruction specifies an operation to be performed on certain data. In the 8085, the following four addressing modes are used:

(1) Direct addressing
(2) Register addressing
(3) Register indirect addressing

(4) Immediate addressing

The following section explains these addressing modes:

1. Direct Addressing

In this mode, the address of the operand is explicitly specified within the instruction itself. All such instructions are 3 bytes long. The only exception being the IN and OUT instructions each of which is two bytes long. From Appendix A, it can be seen that the LDA (load ACC) and STA (store ACC) are two of the several instructions using direct addressing.

Example

The transfer of the contents of memory location 08A2H to memory location 12FAH may be performed using direct addressing. Assume that the symbolic addresses of these locations are ADDR1 and ADDR2 respectively. The following sequence of instructions are used to transfer the data. The addresses used in the examples given here are in hexadecimal.

```
LDA ADDR1 ;Get contents ADDR1 into ACC
STA ADDR2 ;Transfer contents of ACC to ADDR2
```

When the first of these two instructions is executed, it will cause the contents of ADDR1 (08A2H) to be brought to the ACC. Then, the execution of the second instruction will cause the contents of the ACC to be transferred to the memory location ADDR2 (12FAH).

2. Register Addressing

When the operands for the intended operation are in the general purpose registers, only the registers need be specified as the address of the operands. Such instructions are said to use the register addressing mode, which are one byte instructions. The registers are specified within the byte containing the operation code. For example, the MOV and ADD instructions permit register addressing.

Example

The operation of adding the contents of register B to the contents of register C and transferring the result to register D can be performed using register transfer mode. The following sequence of instructions can be used to perform this task.

```
MOV  A,B  ;Move contents of register B to ACC
ADD  C    ;Add contents of register C to ACC
MOV  D,A  ;Move contents of ACC to register D
```

The two MOV instructions in the example specify two register names and addresses of operands. The ADD instruction specifies only one register as the operand register, the other operand is assumed to be in the ACC. All the three instructions use register addressing.

3. Register Indirect Addressing

In register indirect addressing mode, the contents of the specified register(s) are assumed to be the address of the operand. In this mode of addressing, instead of specifying a register, a register-pair is specified to contain the 16-bit address of the operand. The MOV and ADD, besides others, can use the register indirect addressing mode. These instructions occupy one byte each.

Example

The contents of the register pair H-L refer to a certain memory location. The contents of this location are to be added to the contents of register B, and the sum stored in the memory location OAFFH. The following sequences of instructions perform this task. It has been assumed that the symbolic address of location OAFFH is X.

```
MOV A,M  ;Move contents of memory location pointed
         ;to by H-L to the ACC
ADD B    ;Add contents of register B to ACC
STA  X   ;Store the sum in memory location X
```

It can be seen that the first instruction uses register indirect addressing for the second operand and register addressing for the first operand. The second instruction uses register addressing and the third one uses direct addressing. To specify register indirect addressing, the letter M is used which indicates that the contents of memory location pointed at by the H-L pair are being referenced.

4. Immediate Addressing

With immediate addressing mode, the operand is specified within the instruction itself. In this mode of addressing, the operand address is not specified explicitly as in all the other modes. Instead, one or two bytes within the instruction are used for specifying the data. The MVI, LXI, and ADI are examples of instructions using the immediate addressing mode.

Example

Add the number 5 to the contents of memory location 0AB12H and store the result in location OFAOFH. Z is the symbolic address for location OAB12H. Following instruction sequence may be used to perform this task.

```
LXI  H, OFAOFH ;Load register pair H-L with OFAOFH.
LDA  Z         ;Get value of Z in Acc
ADI  5         ;Add 5 to it
MOV  M,A       ;Store ACC in memory location pointed to by
               ;register pair H-L (location FAOFH)
```

In the above program, first an LXI instruction is used to put the address OFAOPH in register pair H-L. The next three instructions fetch the desired contents, add 5 to it, and store the sum in location OFAOFH using the MOV instruction. The MOV instruction in the program uses register indirect addressing. The instructions using immediate addressing may be 2 or 3 bytes long.

5. *Implicit Addressing*

There are certain instructions that operate only on one operand. Such instructions assume that the operand is in the ACC and, therefore, need not specify any address. Many instructions in the logical group like RLC, RRC, and CMA fall into this category. All these are 1 byte instructions. The instructions that specify the address of one of the operands using one mode or the other, use implicit addressing for the other operand.

Example

Complement the contents of memory location 5992H. This may be done by the following instructions sequence:

```
LXI H, 5992H  ;Set H-L to point to location 5992H.
MOV  A, M     ;Get contents of 5992H in ACC.
CMA           ;Complement ACC
MOV  M, A     ;Store the complement back in location 5992H
```

The different addressing modes help the programmer in specifying operand addresses.

5.10.6 Interrupts

The interrupt process of 8085 is initiated by an external device and is asynchronous in nature. It may begin at any time without reference to the system clock. The response to an interrupt request is directed or controlled by the microprocessor.

The interrupt requests are classified in two categories: maskable interrupt and non-maskable interrupt. A maskable interrupt request can be ignored or delayed by the microprocessor if it is performing some critical task. However, the microprocessor has to respond immediately to a non-maskable request. The interrupt process allows the microprocessor to respond to these external requests for attention or service on a demand basis and leaves the microprocessor free to perform other tasks.

The 8085 interrupt process is controlled by the Interrupt Enable flip-flop, which is internal to the processor and can be set or reset by using software instruction. If the flip-flop is enabled and the input to the interrupt signal INTR goes high, the microprocessor is interrupted. This is a maskable interrupt and can be disabled. The 8085 has a non-maskable and three additional interrupt signals as well.

Enable Interrupt: EI

This is a l-byte instruction. The instruction sets the Interrupt Enable flip-flop and enables the interrupt process.

Disable Interrupt: DI

This is a l-byte instruction. The instruction resets the Interrupt Enable flip-flop and disables the interrupt. It is generally included in a program segment where an interrupt from an outside source cannot be tolerated.

RESTART: RST

The 8085 instruction set includes eight RST instructions. These are 1-byte Call instructions and transfer the program execution to a specific location.

5.10.7 Programming the 8085

Programming of 8085 is done by using its instruction set in assembly language.

The Instruction Format

Each instruction in an assembly program has four fields: a label field, a mnemonic field, an operand field, and a comment field. Furthermore, the comment field is not translated by the assembler during translation of the assembly program into an equivalent machine language program. When it is desired to write only a comment, all other fields may be omitted.

The following are valid assembly language instructions for the 8085.

TABLE 5.3
Insutruction Format of 8085

Label	*Mnemonic*	*Operand(s)*	*Comment*
ADDR1	MOV	A, B	;Move contents of register B to ACC
$NEXT	ADD	M	;Add contents of location pointed at by H-L to ACC

Labels

The label field contains a label. A label could be any character string consisting of lower and upper case letters (A-Z or a-z), digits (0-9) and the $. The first character of the label must be a letter or a $.

Mnemonic

A label is separated from the mnemonic by a colon. Similarly, any operand is separated from mnemonic by at least one space character.

Operands

An explicit operand required by an instruction could be specified in one of the several ways. In the following instructions, there is no operand:

```
CMC        ;This instruction complements the carry flag.
           ;It requires no explicit operand.
MOV A,B    ;Move contents of register B to register A.
```

The above instruction specifies two register operands using a letter to denote each register.

```
LDA  TEMP ;Get the contents of memory location TEMP.
```

A symbolic address can be used as an operand to specify a memory location as in the LDA instruction in the above example. The precise memory address of the label TEMP is determined by the assembler.

In instructions requiring immediate operands, the immediate operand can be specified using a constant, as in the following example:

```
MVI  B,6C       ;Get the constant 6CH into register B.
LXI  D,8ABCH    ;Get the constant 8ABCH into register pair DE.
```

The **comment** field is separated from any operand by a semicolon.

5.11 SUMMARY

The instruction set architecture reflects the method in which sequence of instructions and data operands are stored and executed. The basic operations can be divided into four categories: arithmetic operations, memory operations, comparisons, and control operations. The instructions of data transfers between the memory and the processor registers, arithmetic and logic operations on data, program sequencing and control and I/O transfers are four types of fundamental operations. To facilitate the explanation, register transfer notation and assembly language notations are used. Copying the data from one place to another is an essential feature of a computer. The operation of adding two numbers is also a fundamental capability of a computer. To carry out this action, the contents of memory locations A and B are fetched from the memory and added in the processor. This result is then stored in location C. This operation can be accomplished by using three-address, two-address, one-address or zero-address instructions. After the contents of the current instruction are fetched from the instruction register, the contents of PC are advanced to point to the next instruction. When the execute phase of an instruction is completed, the PC contains the address of the next instruction, and a new instruction fetch phase can begin. This is the sequential execution or straight-line program. If repeated instructions of the same kind are present in a program, a long time is spent to fetch the same instruction from memory. It is possible to place a single instruction in a program loop and use a 'branch' instruction. The information about the results of various operations for use by subsequent conditional branch instructions is kept in individual bits in 'condition code flag register'. The various memory locations are given addresses according to the organization of the memory. The information within the computer is of two types: instruction, or data. The different ways in which the location of an operand is specified in an instruction is referred to as 'addressing modes'. Language Directed Architecture links the objects and operations in a high level language and relates to the objects and operations in the architecture. RISC and CISC are different design methodologies. Neither of them is particularly superior to the other.

References

Hamacher, C., Vranesic, Z., and Zaky, S., Computer Organization, 5th edition, McGraw-Hill, NY, 2002.

Patterson, D.A. and J.L. Hennessey, Computer Architecture: A Quantitative Approach, San Mateo, CA: Morgan Kaufmann Publishers, 1990.

John, P. Hayes, Computer Architecture and Organization, Third Edition, McGraw-Hill, 1998.

A.P. Mathur, An introduction to Microprocessors, Tata McGraw Hill Publishers, 3rd edition, New Delhi.

M. Morris Mano, Computer System Architecture, Third Edition, Pearson Education (Singapore), 1993.

PROBLEMS

1. How is the instruction set architecture of a processor chosen?
2. Explain the following operations:
   (i) SHA
   (ii) SHL
   (iii) STO
   (iv) LTH
   (v) JMP
3. What is the difference between Register Transfer Notation and Assembly Language Notation?
4. Write an algorithm for multiplying two 4-bit positive integers. Assuming that each register transfer is performed in 1 microsecond, how much time will be taken by:
   (i) zero-address instruction
   (ii) one-address instruction
   (iii) two-address instruction
   (iv) three-address instruction.
5. How many references are needed for: (i) direct address instruction, (ii) indirect address instruction.
6. What is the difference between register addressing and register indirect addressing in terms of memory references. Give an example of their use.
7. Explain the difference between Base Register Addressing and Index Addressing.
8. How is Register Stack and Memory Stack implemented?
9. Explain the behavior of a FIFO stack. Write a program to add two numbers A and B stored at two consecutive locations at the top of the stack.
10. What is the difference between a Stack and a Queue in terms of storage and retrieval of data?
11. How is the stack used for subroutine call and return?
12. In which memory space is the return address, parameters and local variables placed?
13. What is subroutine nesting? Explain nesting with an example.
14. What is 'semantic gap' between programming languages and how is it controlled?
15. What is the difference between program structure and data structure?
16. How are the elements of language directed architecture related to von Neumann architecture?
17. Compare the RISC and CISC architectures.
18. Explain how an overflow condition occurs and how it is detected while doing subtraction?
19. How is a floating point number represented in computer memory?

20. What is the significance of decimal point in Big-Endian and Little Endian storage representation.
21. Why are different addressing modes needed for computer architecture?
22. Explain different types of Program Control instructions.
23. Compare Register Addressing with Immediate Addressing.
24. How is relative addressing related to direct addressing and register indirect addressing?
25. How does the High Level Language effect the design of a machine built on language directed architecture?
26. How are information structures represented in a machine built on language architecture?

CHAPTER

6

Memory Systems

6. INTRODUCTION

The memory system of a computer comprises of different kinds of memory units where programs and data are stored. In this chapter, various types of memories used in the computer system will be explained. Ideally, the memory should be fast, large, and inexpensive. But it is not possible to meet all these requirements simultaneously. To solve this problem, many different structures and organizations are used, which will be discussed in the following sections.

6.1 HIERARCHICAL MEMORY STRUCTURE

The basic unit of memory is the binary digit or bit. The bit may contain 0 or 1. The programs and data are stored in the memory, which are transferred to the CPU for the execution. To increase the performance of the computer system, the processor speed has to match with the rate of information transfer from the memory. The aim is to provide high bandwidth of the memory at reasonable cost.

6.1.1 Memory Hierarchy

The different types of memories in the computer have varied speeds and costs, arranged as levels in a hierarchy. The goal in designing an n-level memory hierarchy is to achieve a performance close to that of the fastest memory, and cost per bit of memory should be close to the cheapest memory. The hierarchy is structured so that the memories at level i are 'higher' than the memories at level i+1. The word 'higher' means that the performance attributes should be higher. The speed is inversely proportional to capacity and cost. The hierarchy of memory in a general computer is as shown in Figure 6.1.

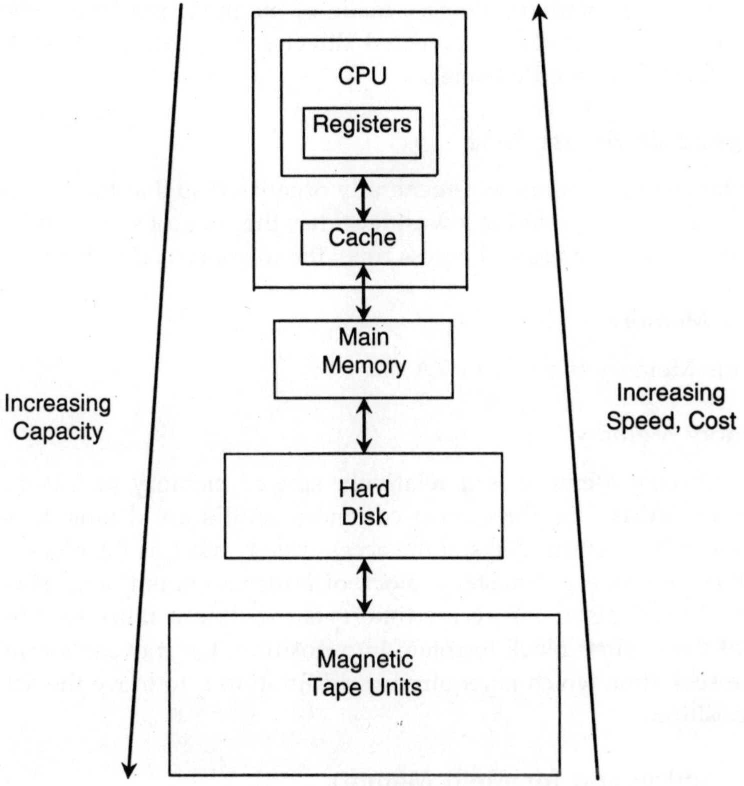

FIGURE **6.1 : Memory Hierarchy**

Memories in a hierarchy can be classified on the basis of method of access and time of access, which are explained below:

(i) Accessing method

The method of access of a memory divides the memories into three basic classes:

Random-Access Memory (RAM)

The access time t_a of a RAM word is independent of its location.

Sequential-Access Memory (SAM)

The information in SAMs is accessed serially or sequentially. Examples are shift register memory like a first-in-first-out (FIFO) buffer, charged-coupled-devices (CCDs) and magnetic bubble memories.

Direct-Access Storage Devices (DASDs)

DASDs are rotational devices made of magnetic materials where any block of information can be accessed directly. They are accessed through special interfaces called channels.

(ii) Speed or Access Time

The memory hierarchy is generally organized so that the highest level has the fastest speed and the lowest level has the slowest speed, as is shown in Figure 6.1. On the basis of access time, the memory is classified as under:

Primary Memory

This Memory is made of RAMs.

Secondary Memory

Secondary Memory is a relatively slower memory and is made of DASDs or SAMs. The three most common DASDs are drums, fixed-head disks and movable-arm disks. If the access rate t_a and t_B is the block transfer time, then the time to transfer a block of information is $t_a + t_B$. For drums and fixed head disks, the access time t_a is the time it takes for the initial word of the desired block to rotate into position. For moveable-arm disks, t_s is the seek-time which is required in addition to t_a to move the arms into track position.

6.1.2 Addressing for Main Memory

Memories consist of a number of locations each of which can store a piece of information. Each location or cell has a number, called an address. If the memory has n cells, they will have addresses 0 – (n–1). The maximum size of the memory that can be used in any computer is determined by the addressing scheme. For example, a 16-bit computer that generates 16-bit addresses can address up to 2^{16} (64K) memory locations. Similarly, with 32-bit addresses, a memory can contain 2^{32} (4G) memory locations. When addresses are 40-bit long, then 2^{40} = 1T (tera) locations can be addressed. The number of locations represent the address space of the computer.

The memory is usually designed to store and retrieve data in terms of word length. The number of bits actually stored or retrieved in one memory access is the word length of a computer.

Figure 6.2 shows the connection of the processor with the memory unit. Data transfer between the memory and the processor takes place through the use of two registers, MAR (memory address register) and MDR

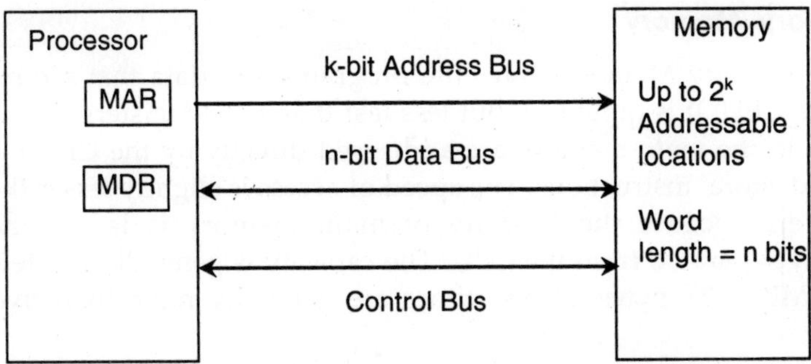

FIGURE 6.2 : Links of the Memory to the Processor

(memory data register), which have been discussed in Chapter 3. If MAR is k-bits long and MDR is n-bits long, then the memory unit may contain up to 2^k addressable locations. The word length is n bits, which means that during a memory cycle, n bits of data is transferred between the memory and the processor. The transfer takes over the processor bus, which has k address lines and n data lines. The bus also contains control lines to carry the control signals of Read and Write.

6.2 MEMORY DEVICE CHARACTERISTICS

A computer may contain several types of memory devices to store the data and instructions. These components have different characteristics and organizations which are used according to the performance needs.

6.2.1 Memory Types

The program and data are stored in the internal and external memories where the CPU accesses them during the processing of the program. The speed of the CPU is the highest, and that of the available memories is lesser. The CPU should have fast access to these memories so that it can operate at its optimum speed. But the memories that are fast are more expensive. The cheaper memories are slower in the access of the information stored in them. The information is distributed over various memory units, and, thus, has different performance and cost. The memory can be broadly divided into four classes, as explained below:

(i) CPU Registers

The registers in the CPU have very high speed. They are used as temporary storage of instructions and data. They form a general purpose register file for storing data as it is processed. The capacity of the register is the word length of the computer. Access to a register is through 'Read' or 'Write' operation which can be performed in one clock cycle.

(ii) Primary Memory

The Primary Memory stores the programs and data that are in active use in the CPU. It is quite fast, but less fast than CPU registers. The storage locations in the main memory are addressed directly by the CPU by using 'load' and 'store' instructions. The speed of access is slightly lesser than that of registers because the capacity of main memory is large, and it is physically separated from the CPU. The capacity is generally in Megabytes (MB). 1 MB is 2^{20} bytes. Access times are generally more than five clock cycles.

(iii) Secondary Memory

Secondary memory has a much larger capacity but is relatively slower. It holds system programs and large data files that are not required continuously by the CPU. The information in the secondary memory is not accessed directly. It is accessed indirectly through input/output programs that transfer information between main memory and secondary memory. Storage capacity of this memory is many Gigabytes (GB). Access times are measured in milliseconds.

(iv) Cache

Cache memory is positioned between CPU registers and main memory. The storage capacity of cache is less than the main memory and the access time is between one to three cycles. Thus, cache is faster than the main memory. Whereas the other three memories can be accessed, caches are transparent to the programmer.

The goal of every memory system is to provide sufficient storage capacity with acceptable level of performance and cost. To achieve this goal, several memory types with different speed, capacity and cost are used. These memories are organized to provide a high average performance at low average cost. The levels of hierarchy are as depicted in Figure 6.1.

6.3 RANDOM ACCESS MEMORIES (RAMs)

In Random Access Memory, the storage locations can be accessed in any order. The access time is independent of the location being accessed.

6.3.1 Static Random Access Memory (SRAM)

Static memories consist of circuits that retain their state as long as power is applied. A method of implementing a static RAM cell is by using a latch to hold the charge temporarily. Figure 6.3 illustrates the cross-connection of two inverters to form a latch which is connected to two bit lines by two transistors T1 and T2. These transistors act as switches that can be opened or closed under the control of a word line. When the word line is at the ground level, the transistors are turned-off and the latch retains its state.

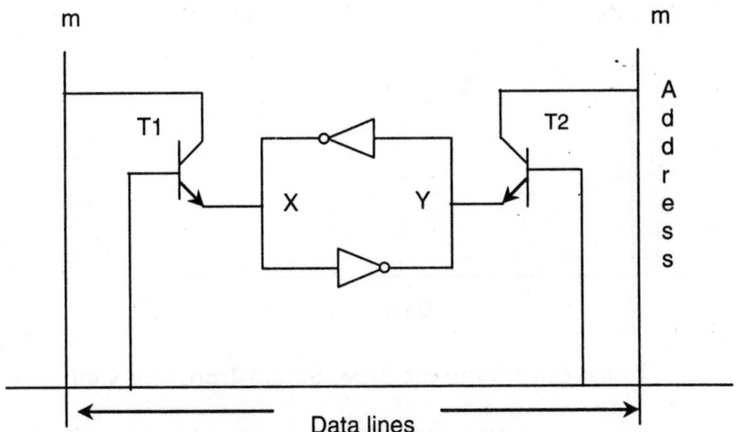

FIGURE 6.3 : A Static RAM Cell

Read Operation

In the read state of SRAM, word line is activated to close switches T1 and T2. If the cell is in state 1, the signal on the bit line b is high and on bit line b′ is low. The opposite is true if the cell is in state 0.

Write Operation

For the write operation, the state of the cell is set by placing either 0 or 1 value on bit line b and b′. After this, the word line is activated. The required signals on the bit lines are generated by the read/write circuit.

Static RAMs are fast and their access time is just a few nanoseconds. But they are very costly as their cells require many transistors. Dynamic RAMs are slightly less expensive RAMs in which the cells do not retain their state indefinitely.

6.3.2 Dynamic RAM

Information is stored in a dynamic memory cell in the form of a charge on a capacitor. This charge can be maintained for only few milliseconds. The contents must be refreshed periodically to store information for a much longer time. This is realized by restoring the capacitor charge to its full charge.

Figure 6.4 shows a single-transistor memory cell having a transistor T and a capacitor C. For storing information in this cell, transistor T is turned on and an appropriate voltage is applied to the bit line. This causes a known amount of charge to be stored in the capacitor.

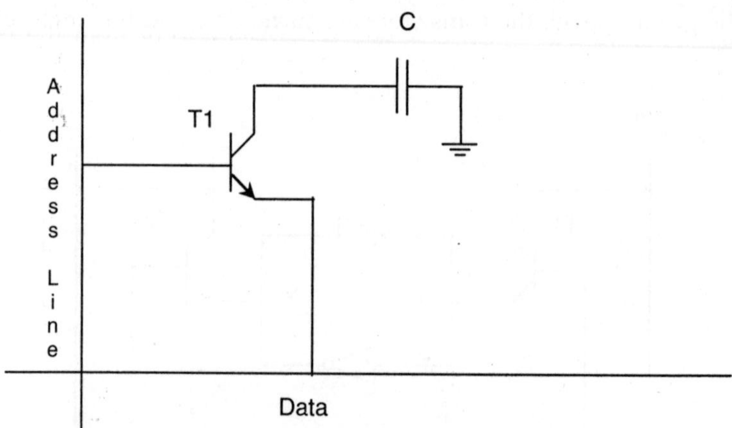

FIGURE 6.4 : Dynamic RAM: Single-Transistor Cell

After the transistor is turned-off, the capacitor begins to discharge. The information stored in the cell can be retrieved correctly only if it is read before the charge in the capacitor drops below the threshold level.

Read Operation

For read operation, transistor in the selected cell is turned on. A sensor connected to the bit line detects whether the charge stored in the capacitor is above the threshold level. If so, it drives the bit line to represent logic 1. The voltage recharges the capacitor to full charge to represent logic 1.

If the sensor detects that the charge in the capacitor is below the threshold value, it pulls the bit line to ground level. This ensures that the capacitor has no charge, which represents a logic 0 level. Thus, reading the contents of the cell automatically recharges its contents.

Write Operation

For write operation, a voltage signal, which is either 0 or 1, is placed on the data line. A signal is then applied to the address line to switch on the transistor T. Thus, a charge to C is transferred if the data line is 1. No charge is transferred to C if the data line is 0.

The advantages of DRAM are its small size and its low price.

6.4 SERIAL-ACCESS MEMORIES (SAM)

In serial-access memories (SAM), the method of access of storage is shared by the storage locations. The stored information is accessed by the read-write head by moving it at different locations at different times, which can be accessed only in a certain predetermined sequence. Examples are magnetic disks, magnetic tapes, and optical memories. Information is stored in a fixed set of tracks. Each track consists of 1-bit storage cells. The information is transferred by the read-write head, to or from the track, by having one or more access points. The storage locations are moved continuously around a closed path or track that can be accessed only when it passes the fixed read-write head. Thus, the time to access a location depends on its position relative to the read-write head when a read request is received.

These memories find their main application in secondary storage because of their low cost per bit and relatively long access time.

6.4.1 Access Method

The SAMs are of two types: the first where each read-write head has one or more fixed heads. The second kind has heads which are shared by different tracks. In some memories, information rotates around a closed track.

A word may be stored along a single track or many tracks may be used to store a word. But it is inefficient to read or write just one word per serial access since the seek time and the time to rotate the head is quite large. Because of this difficulty, words are stored in blocks in consecutive locations so that the time used to access the entire block includes only one seek time and one latency (delay) time. The speed of the data transferred depends on speed of storage information and storage density along the track.

The time t_B to access a block of data in a serial-access memory can be estimated by using the following parameters:

t_S – average seek time
N – fixed average capacity of each track in words
r – speed of each track in revolutions per second
n – number of words per block

Time to access a block of data is:

$$t_B = t_S + 1/2r + n/rN$$

It is assumed that the memory has rotating tracks, each track having a fixed capacity.

6.4.2 Memory Organization

The organization of a serial-memory unit is shown in Figure 6.5. Each word is stored along a single track and a block of words are accessed in each transfer. The address of the data to be accessed is applied to the address decoder which determines the track to be used and the location of the desired block of information within the track. The track address determines the particular read-write head to be selected. The selected head is moved to the position to transfer data from the desired track. A track position indicator generates the address of the block that is currently passing the read-write head. The generated address is compared with the block address produced by the address decoder. When they match, the selected head is enabled and the data transfer between the storage track and the memory data buffer register begins. When the complete block of information has been transferred, the read-write head is disabled.

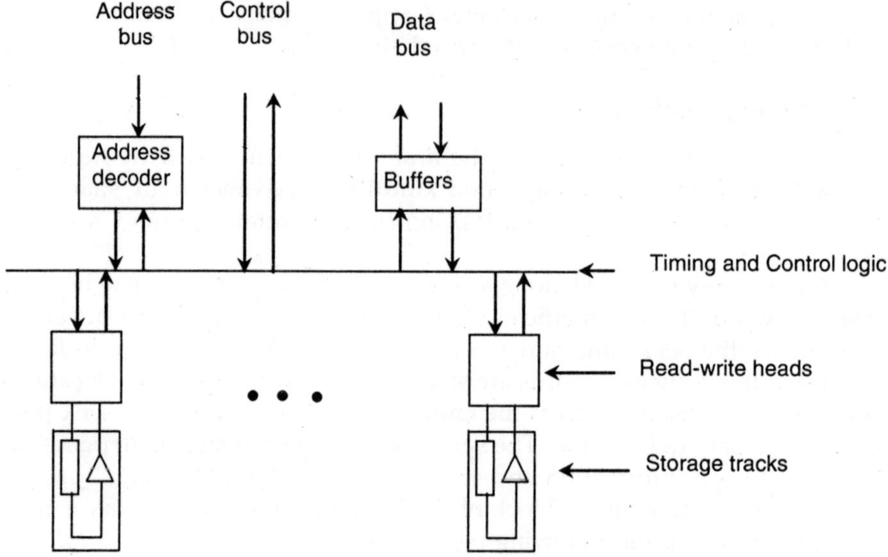

FIGURE 6.5 : Organization of SAM Unit

Comparison with RAM

In RAM, every location has its own access mechanism. Therefore, they tend to be more costly than SAM.

SAMs have a larger access time, and hence, are slower than RAMs.

6.4.3 Magnetic Memories

Secondary memory devices are constructed as magnetic disks and magnetic units. In these memories, electromechanical devices like electric motors are used to perform the access. Some optical memories and CD-ROMs are also used as secondary storage. They may employ laser beams with electromechanical focusing as their read-write heads. Only solid state disks have no moving part.

6.4.3.1 Recording Formats/Methods

Magnetic disks and tape memories store information on the surface of the tracks which are coated with magnetic medium such as ferric oxide. Each cell of a track has two stable magnetic states that represent logical 0 and logical 1. These states are defined by the direction or magnitude of the magnetic flux created in the cell.

Write Operation

The cell which is addressed is moved under the read-write gap. The magnetic field in the ring gap is changed by the current that is transmitted through the write coil. This current changes the magnetization state of the cell under the gap. The direction or magnitude of the write current determines the resulting state of the cell under the gap.

Read Operation

To read a cell, the magnetic field of the cell is influenced by moving it near the read-write head to induce a magnetic flux in the core material of. As the cell is moving, the magnetic field varies and, therefore, induces an electric voltage pulse in the read coil. This voltage is fed to the sense amplifier which identifies the state of the cell.

6.4.3.2 Magnetic Disk/Tape Units

Magnetic disks consist of disks coated with magnetic material on which data can be recorded. One or both surfaces of a disk contain thousands of recording tracks. These tracks are arranged in concentric circles. Several disks are attached to a spindle. These tapes resemble domestic tape cassettes. But instead of storing analog sound, they store binary data. The storage medium is a small plastic tape stored in a cassette.

Construction : The disk head contains an induction coil which floats over the surface. When a positive or negative current passes through the head, it magnetizes the surface just beneath the head. This way the magnetic particles are aligned facing left or facing right depending on the polarity of the current of the drive. When the head passes over a magnetized area, a positive or negative current is induced in the head.

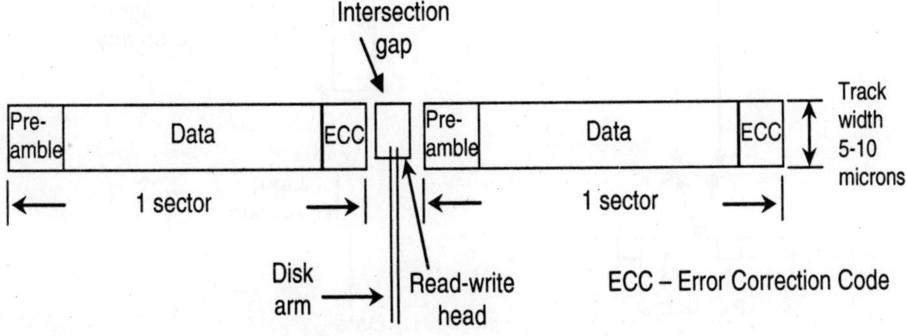

FIGURE 6.6 : A Disk Track

Tracks are in the form of circular disks. When the disk makes a complete rotation, a sequence of bits is read or written, which is called a track. A track is divided into sectors, generally containing 512 data bytes. Preamble bits precede the data and allow the head to be synchronized before reading or writing. Hamming code, which is the error correction code (ECC), follows the data. Two sectors are divided by an intersection gap. Figure 6.6 shows a disk track.

During a memory operation, the disks are rotated at a constant speed by a disk drive unit. A read-write head is supplied to each recording surface, which are connected together with a support (arm) so that all heads can move in union. Thus, a particular set of tracks is selected for reading or writing when the arm moves back and forth. The recording surface is divided into sectors. Part of the track, within the sector, stores a fixed amount of information corresponding to the block of the memory unit.

These days, the magnetic disk memories are decreasing in physical size and increasing in storage density (bits stored per cm). Floppy disks are small, portable, inexpensive, flexible disks. Hard disks are sealed into their drive and have much higher storage capacity and reliability.

6.4.4 Optical Memories

Optical memories provide extremely high storage capacities but their access rates are quite less as compared to magnetic disks. Binary information is stored in optical memories in concentric tracks. The disk is rotated electromechanically while the information is read or written optically with a laser that acts as a read-write head.

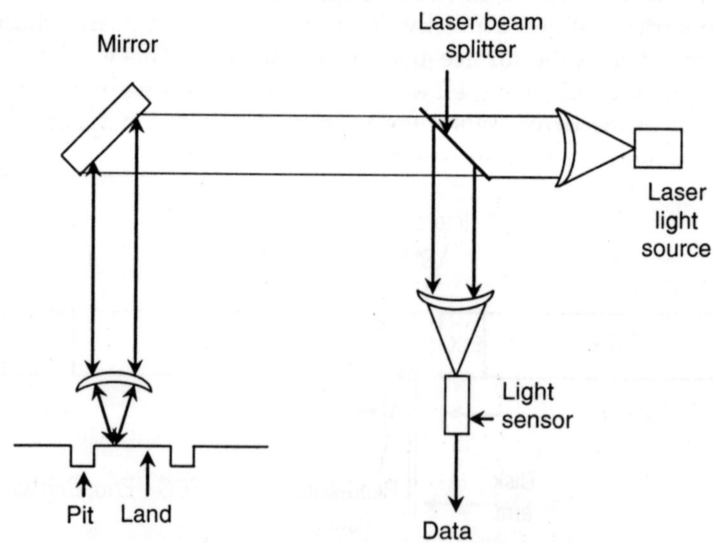

Figure 6.7 : Optical Readout for a CD-ROM

An example of optical memory is CD-ROM. Binary data is stored in the form of 0.1 μm wide pits and lands on circular tracks, on plastic substrate. A laser beam scans the tracks and is reflected differently by lands and pits. The reflected light from the laser is picked up from the sensor and decoded to extract the stored information. This information is converted to binary data for processing. A method for reading data in the form of pits and lands by using laser light source is shown in Figure 6.7. The recording structure is shown in Figure 6.8.

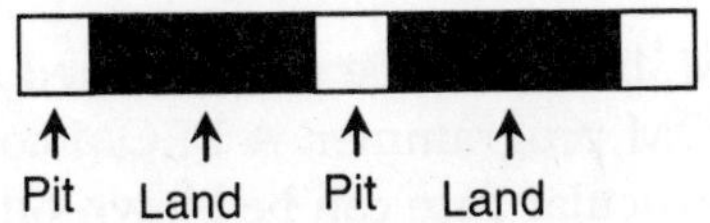

FIGURE 6.8 : Recording Structure of a CD-ROM

A standard 12 cm CD-ROM has a capacity of 600 MB, which stores about 2,40,000 pages of printed text. Access time is about 100 ms and data transfer rate is about 3.6 MB/s. Digital video disk (DVD) is a much denser type of CD having capacity of 16 GB, is also available in read-only or read-write forms.

6.4.5 Magneto-optical Disks

Magneto-optical disk is a combination of magnetic and optical disks. The construction involves the use of rotating disks that store information in magnetic form, but access to the information is by laser beams, similar to that used in the CD-ROM drive.

The surface of the magneto-optic disk is magnetized and this magnetization can be polarized. The level of polarization is either up or down, which corresponds to a 0 or a 1. A slight change in the polarization angle of the reflected laser beam is sensed and decoded by the read mechanism.

Write Operation

Write is performed when the laser beam heats a chosen cell above a specific temperature, making the cell sensitive to external magnetic fields.

6.5 READ-ONLY-MEMORIES

The primary difference between Random Access Memories (RAMs) and Read-Only-Memories (ROMs) is that the information can be read from or written into the memory for RAMs and the stored data is lost when the power is turned-off, whereas for ROMs, data can only be read and the data in it is not lost when the power is turned-off. The information in ROMs cannot be changed or erased by the user without using any special methods.

6.5.1 Read-Only-Memory (ROM)

The data in the ROM is inserted by the designer during the manufacture of the chip. The insertion of data is done by exposing a photosensitive material containing the mask having the desired bit pattern. The unexposed surface is then etched. The data inserted in the ROM cannot be changed, the whole chip has to be replaced.

6.5.2 Programmable-Read-Only-Memory (PROM)

PROM is like a ROM, but it can be programmed to insert the desired information by using PROM programmer. A PROM consists of an array of tiny electronic fuses. A particular fuse can be blown-off by selecting its row and column and then applying a high voltage to a special pin on the chip. They can be programmed only once.

6.5.3 Erasable-Programmable-Read-Only-Memory (EPROM)

Data in EPROMs can be programmed and erased, as desired. EPROM uses a quartz window through which it is exposed to strong ultraviolet light (UV), usually for 10 minutes or more, when the bits are set to 1. Repeated exposures to UV light will wear-off an EPROM and this may typically be repeated about 100 times.

EPROMs are cheaper than PROMs when many changes in data are expected during the design cycle as they can be reused.

6.5.4 Electrically-Erasable-PROM (EEPROM)

The EEPROM has similar semiconductor structure as that of PROM, but allows its entire contents to be electrically erased, and then rewritten electrically, so that they need not be removed from the computer. The data in EEPROMs can be erased by applying electrical pulses to it, generally about 1000 times. They are byte erasable. They can be reprogrammed. But the size of the EEPROM is very small as compared to EPROMs and the speed is also about half of that of an EPROM.

6.5.5 Flash Memories (Pen Drives)

Flash memory is similar to an EEPROM and has come up in recent times. But instead of being byte erasable, it is block erasable and data can be written on it again. It can be erased without removing it from the circuit. The endurance and physical durability has allowed the flash memory to replace magnetic memories. Flash memory is sometimes called flash ROM or flash EEPROM or pen drive. The storage capacity of flash memories can be as high as 16 Giga bytes (as in 2007).

6.6 CACHE MEMORY

The term cache refers to fast intermediate memory within a large memory system that is hidden to the programmer. This memory provides the CPU with fast, single-cycle access to the external memory. Cache acts as a buffer between CPU and main memory.

6.6.1 Characteristics of Cache Memories

In the memory hierarchy, it is seen that the speed of main memory is very less as compared to the speed of the registers of the CPU. The speed of cache is quite close to the speed of the CPU. Thus, by the use of cache memory, the processor does not have to spend much time in waiting to access instructions and data from memory.

The cache is effective because of its property of 'locality of reference'. This principle is based on the fact that instructions in localized areas of the program are executed repeatedly during some time period, and the rest of the program is accessed relatively infrequently. The active program is placed in the cache memory and the total execution time is reduced significantly. The assembly of the cache memory is shown in Figure 6.9.

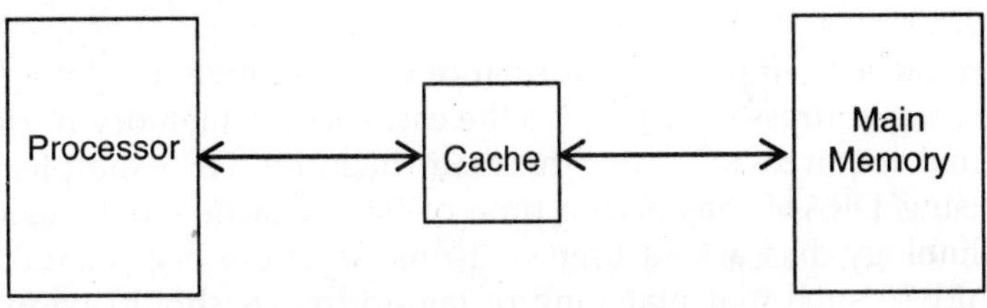

FIGURE 6.9 : Assembly of Cache Memory

'Locality of reference' implies that whenever an information item (instruction or data) is first needed, it should be brought in cache and remain there till it is needed again. Also, instead of fetching just one item from the main memory to the cache, several items that reside at adjacent addresses should be also brought in at the same time. If the required information is available in the cache, it is called a 'cache hit' or simply a 'hit'. In case the information is not present in the cache, it is called a 'cache miss' or simply a 'miss'.

A set of adjacent address locations of same size is referred to by the term 'block' or 'cache lines', which are of the same length. A cache typically contains 4 to 64 consecutive bytes. Lines are numbered consecutively, starting from 0. Thus, with 32 byte line size, line 0 is 0 to 31 bytes; line 1 is bytes 32 to 63 and so on. At any time, some lines are in the cache. When memory is referenced, the cache controller circuit checks if the referenced word is in the cache or not. In case of a hit, the data is transferred from the cache to the CPU. In case of a miss, a replacement policy is used. When a read request is received from the processor, the contents of a block of memory words, containing the location specified, are transferred into the cache one word at a time. After this, when the program references any of the locations in this block, these contents are read directly from the cache. Since the size of the cache memory is small, the number of blocks in the cache is small as compared to the total number of blocks of the main memory. A mapping function is used for the correspondence between the main memory blocks and those in the cache.

6.6.2 Organization of Cache Memories

Cache memory is organized by including cache data memory and cache tag memory. In the former, memory words are stored, while in the latter, addresses of the cache words are stored, called the directory of cache addresses. The main memory is divided into set of blocks and the contents of the data memory are the sets of main memory blocks. The data memory is grouped into small pages called blocks or lines. Each cache block is marked with its block address, which is referred to as tag. The tag specifies to what part of memory space the block belongs. The collection of tag addresses currently assigned to the cache are stored in a special memory called the cache tag memory or directory. The structure of cache is shown in Figure 6.10.

For the cache to improve performance of a computer, the time required to check the tag addresses and access the cache's data memory must be less than the time required to access the main memory. For example, if main memory, using DRAM, has access time of 50 ns, cache's data memory in SRAM technology, has access time of 10 ns, then the organization of the cache should be such that matching of tag addresses should be extremely fast.

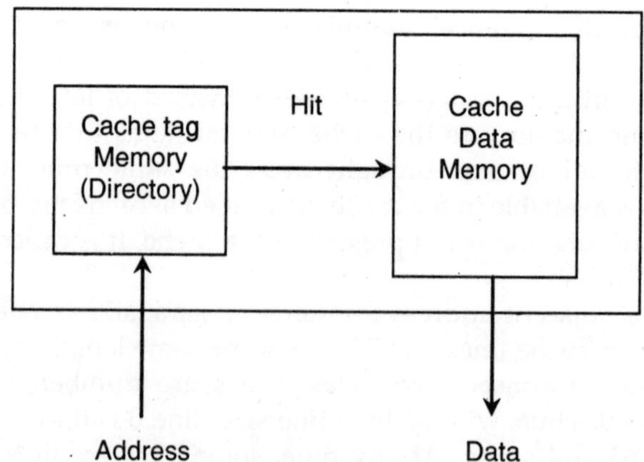

FIGURE 6.10 : Structure of Cache

The cache can be connected to the computer by two methods. The first method is 'look-aside' organization, in which the main memory and cache are directly connected to the system bus. The CPU places the real address on the memory address bus at the start of read or write cycle. The cache immediately compares the tag addresses currently residing in the tag memory. If a match is found, cache hit occurs, otherwise, it is a miss. In the second method, called 'look-through' organization, access to cache is done by the read or write operation to the main memory. The difference in these methods lies in the connection to the CPU, main memory and the system bus.

The organization of a 'look-aside' cache is shown in Figure 6.11.

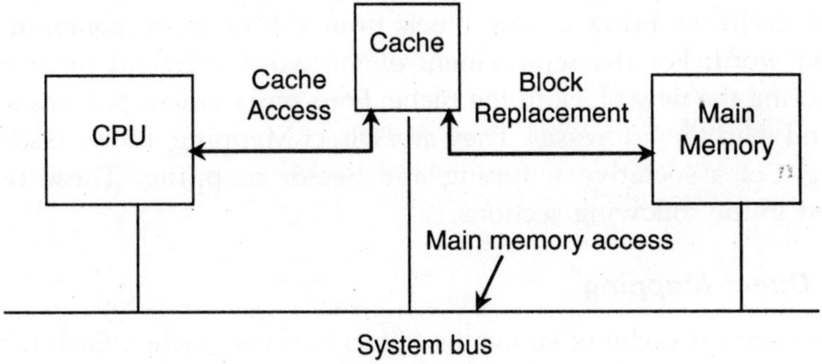

FIGURE 6.11 : Assembly of Look-Aside Cache

A separate bus, which is not connected to the main system bus, is used in the 'look-through' method, for the CPU to communicate with the cache. Therefore, cache access and main memory access can continue simultaneously. Main memory is accessed only in case of a cache miss. The organization of look-through cache is shown in Figure 6.12.

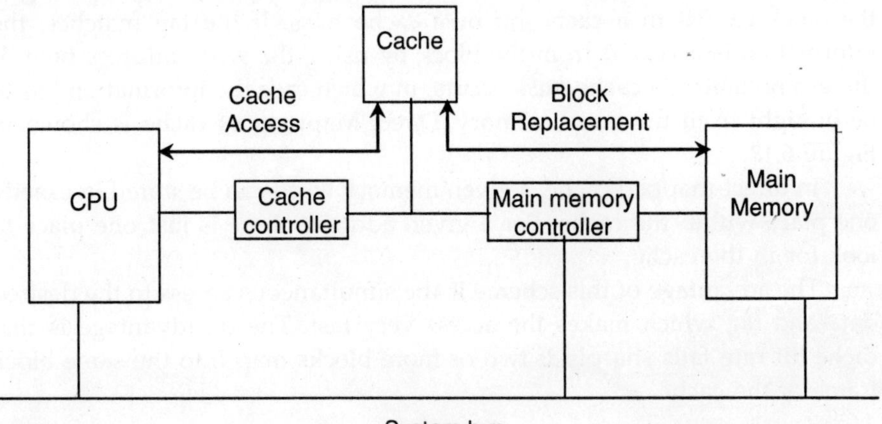

FIGURE 6.12 : Assembly of Look-Through Cache

The disadvantage of look-through cache is that it takes longer for the memory to respond to the CPU when a miss occurs.

6.6.3 Memory Map

Memory map refers to translation of the address of main memory locations to address of the referred locations in the cache. Mapping is needed because when passing address of any memory location, the processor simply issues 'read' or 'write' requests using addresses that refer to locations in the main memory. The cache control circuit determines whether the requested word is currently residing in the cache or not. In case the requested word is not in the cache, a miss occurs and a block is removed from the cache to bring a new block from the memory containing the requested word. For the replacement of the word, different methods are used to bring the new block in the cache. Four replacement policies exist to match and map the addresses. They are: Direct Mapping, Fully Associative mapping, Set associative mapping and Sector mapping. These will be discussed in the following sections.

6.6.3.1 Direct Mapping

The simplest cache is known as 'direct-mapped cache'. Each memory address can be stored in one location in the cache. The memory is divided into regions called blocks whereas the cache is divided into frames. The memory address consists of three fields: the tag, block and word fields. Each block frame has its own tag associated with it. When a block of memory exists in a block frame in the cache, the tag of that frame contains the high order bits of the main memory address of that block. When a physical address is used to refer to memory, the high-order bits of that frame are compared with the tag address of the block. The comparison with the tag of the block results in a cache hit or a cache miss. If the tag matches, the information is accessed from the block by using the word address field. If there is no match, a cache miss occurs, in which case the information has to be brought from the main memory. Direct Mapping of cache is shown in Figure 6.13.

In direct-mapped cache, a given memory word can be stored in exactly one place within the cache. For a given address, there is just one place to look for in the cache.

The advantage of this scheme is the simultaneous access to the desired data and tag which makes the access very fast. The disadvantage is that cache hit rate falls sharply if two or more blocks map into the same block frame of the cache.

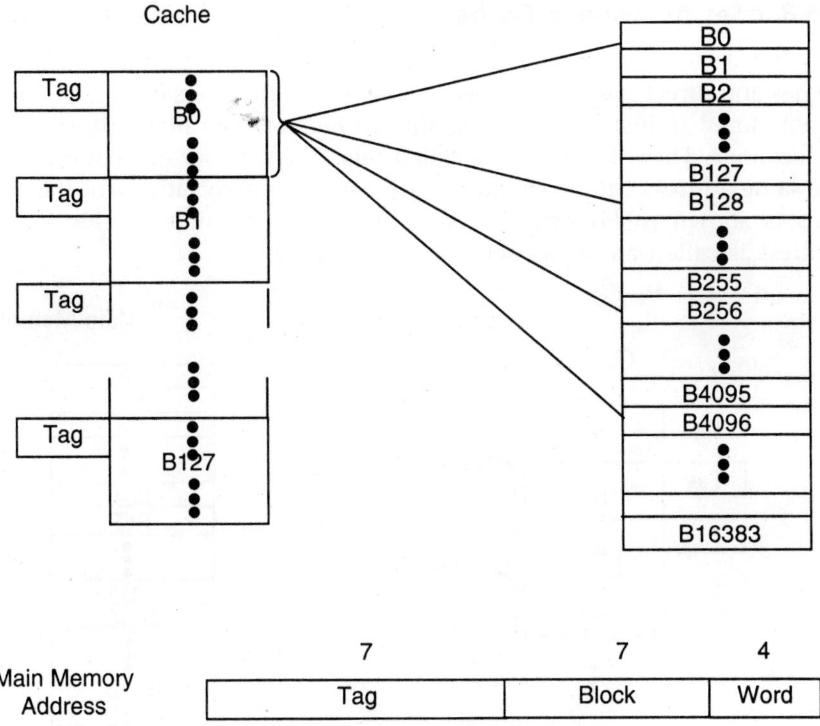

FIGURE 6.13 : Direct Mapped Cache

6.6.3.2 Fully Associative Cache

In fully associative mapping, the mapping is such that any block in memory can be in any block frame. When a request for a block is presented to the cache, all the map entries are compared simultaneously to identify the requested block. The associativity of a cache determines how many locations within the cache may contain a given memory address. Caches with high associativity allow each address to be stored in many locations in the cache, which reduces cache misses. Thus, any address can be stored in any line in the cache. When a read operation is sent to the cache, the address of the request must be compared to each entry in the tag array to determine whether the data referenced by the operation is present in the cache. Figure 6.14 shows the main memory address of fully-associative cache.

This method is rarely used these days.

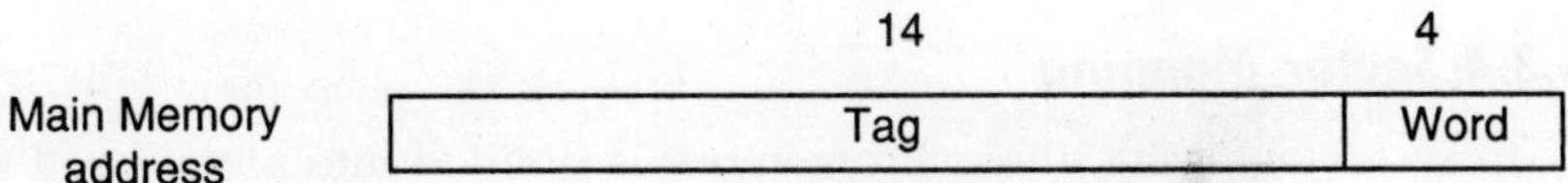

FIGURE 6.14 : Fully Associative Cache

6.6.3.3 Set Associative Cache

Set associative caches are a compromise between fully-associative caches and direct-mapped caches. In a set associative cache, a given address is not stored in just one location, but can be stored in many fixed number of locations. These locations are called sets. The number of locations where the same address can be stored in each set is the associativity of the cache. This is shown in Figure 6.15. A cache with n possible entries for each address is called an n-way set associative cache.

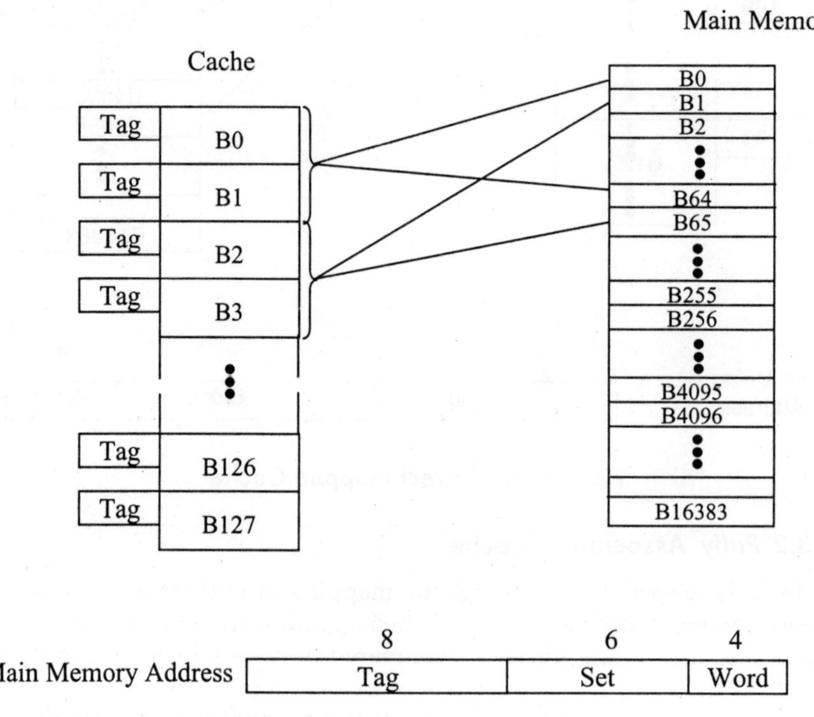

FIGURE 6.15 : Set Associative Cache

Though set-associative cache is more complicated than a direct mapped cache, but the results are much faster. Set-associative caches have a better hit rate than direct-mapped caches but worse hit rates than fully associative caches of the same size. The reason is that storing each address at multiple locations eliminates some redundancy, but not all.

6.6.3.4 Sector Mapping

In sector mapping, the main memory is divided into sectors and each sector is composed of a number of blocks. In the same way, the cache also consists of sector frames, each composed of a set of block frames. The memory request is made for blocks. If a request is put for a block not in cache, the sector to which this block belongs to is brought into the buffer. Only the block that caused the fault is brought into the cache and the remaining block frames in this sector are marked invalid. Figure 6.16 illustrates the sector-cache organization with 16 blocks per sector.

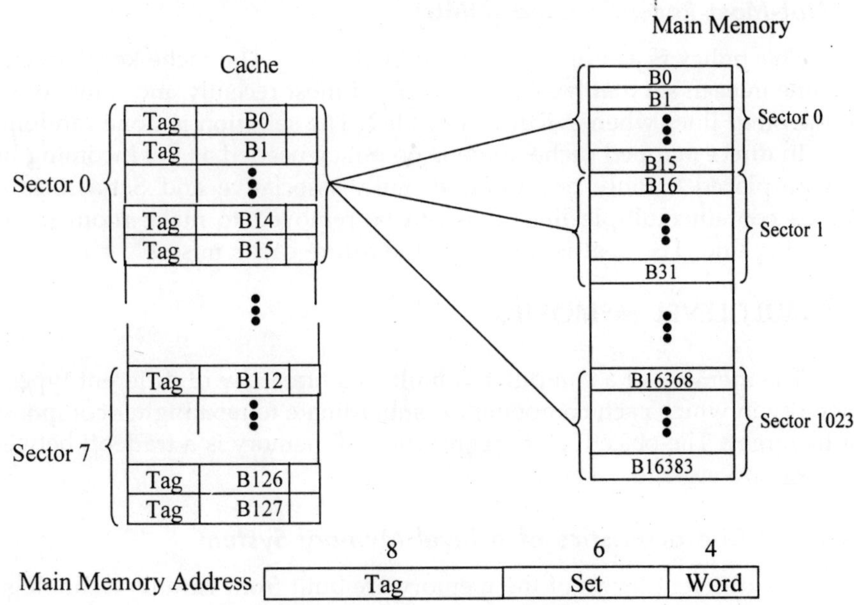

FIGURE 6.16 : Sector Mapping

6.6.4 Block Replacement Policies

The replacement of blocks or cache lines is required because either the cache is full or because of conflicts between requests for a set. The replacement policy is required to determine which line has to be substituted. The replacement policy is perfect if it can estimate the future actions of the program being run and replace it with a one that results in the fewest cache misses. These actions are based on the previous activities of the program. In the design of replacement, the cost of replacement has to be taken into account. Three commonly used replacement policies are discussed below:

1. *Least-Recently-Used (LRU)*

'Least-Recently-Used' (LRU) is the most frequently used replacement policy. In this method, the cache assesses the level of use of each of the lines in the cache memory according to how recently they have been accessed. The least recently used line is removed when replacement is needed. This principle is based on the fact that the lines that have not been referenced in the recent past are unlikely to be referenced in the near future.

2. Random Replacement

Random replacement is also used in many cases and this method also shows good results. A randomly selected line is removed from the related set to make room for the incoming data.

3. Not-Most-Recently-Used (NMU)

This policy is just opposite of the LRU policy. The cache keeps track of the line in each set that has been referenced most recently and removes one of the other lines when eviction is needed. The selection is done randomly.

In direct mapped cache, there is no policy needed as the incoming line can be placed at only one location. Fully-associative and Set-associative caches contain multiple lines that can be removed to make room for the incoming line. The goal is to reduce the future cache misses.

6.7 MULTILEVEL MEMORIES

The memory of a computer is built as a hierarchy of different types of memory in which each component is subordinate to next higher component of hierarchy. The objective of organization of memory is a tradeoff between its cost and storage.

General Characteristics of n-level Memory System

The different levels of the memory are built from various technologies like SRAM, DRAM, magnetic storage, etc. The levels of memory hierarchy are based on the speed and cost of the relevant unit. Consider a n-level

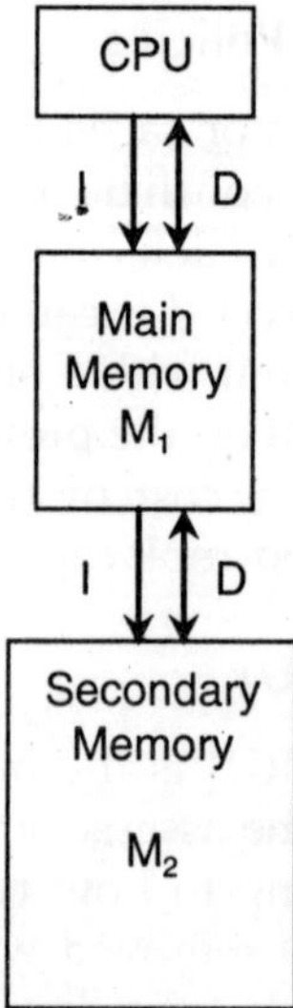

FIGURE 6.17

system of n memory types (M_1, M_2, ... M_n). In this hierarchy, speed of M_1 is higher than speed of M_2 and so on. A two level hierarchy is shown in Figure 6.17, comprising of main memory and secondary memory where I and D are the instruction stream and data stream respectively.

A 3-level memory may include a cache memory, the level lying between main memory and the CPU. The technologies used may be SRAM for cache, DRAM for main memory and secondary storage made from magnetic disks.

Relation between memories M_i and M_{i+1}

The relationship between different levels of memory are based on cost c_i, access time t_i and storage capacity S_i considered at level i. Normally, in adjacent levels M_i and M_{i+1} of the memory hierarchy, cost per bit is $c_i > c_{i+1}$, access time is $t_i < t_{i+1}$ and storage capacity is $S_i < S_{i+1}$. CPU and other processors communicate with M_1 only. M_1 communicates with M_2 and so on.

The factors for evaluation of good performance are address reference statistics, access time t_A of each level relative to CPU, storage capacity S_i of each level, size of the blocks transferred between adjacent levels and the allocation algorithm

6.8 VIRTUAL MEMORY

Virtual memory is a method of memory management that is used to allow slow memory to be used as a level of memory system. It also provides protection between programs running on the same system so that one program cannot modify data of another program. The program being executed by the CPU has to be present in the main memory. Generally, the programs written by programmers are very large that they cannot fit in the main memory for execution. In some cases, the main memory is shared with other users, which may lead to a situation that the space of memory occupied by one user may not be sufficient for the program to execute. To handle these problems, the concept of virtual memory is used.

The idea of virtual memory was developed to reduce the requirements of having a large main memory. The hard disks or other magnetic media form the bottom layer of the memory system. DRAMs or core memory form the main memory. The address space of a program is divided into pages, which are blocks of fixed length that can be assigned to fixed regions of physical memory. Adjacent pages of data are stored on the magnetic media.

When a page of data is referenced, the system copies it into the main memory and is used for the execution of the program. This may require another page of data to be copied from the main memory to the magnetic disk.

Virtual Address Space

Each program has its own virtual address space, which is a set of addresses that programs use for load and store operations.

Physical Address Space

The physical address space is a set of addresses used to reference locations in the main memory.

The terms virtual address and the physical (or real, used synonymously) address are used to describe addresses in the virtual address space and the physical address space respectively.

The arrangement of virtual memory is shown in Figure 6.18.

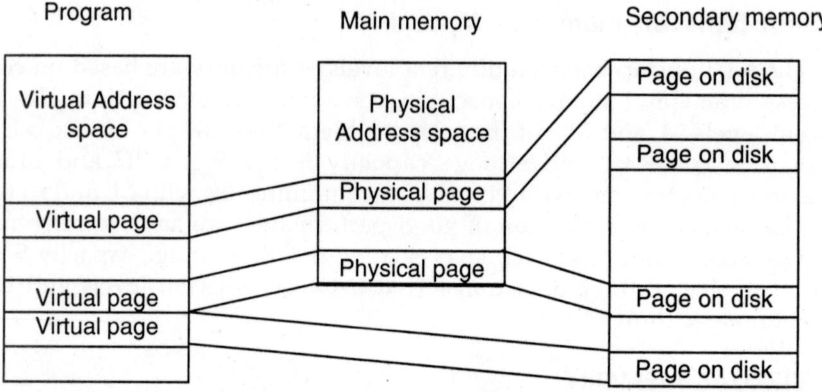

FIGURE 6.18 : Virtual Memory

Virtual memory gives the illusion that the main memory is much larger than it actually is. When a program references a virtual address, it cannot tell whether the virtual address was resident in the main memory of the computer or whether it had to be fetched from the magnetic memory.

6.8.1 Address Translation

All programs are stored in the main memory. The programs that use virtual memory use virtual addresses to load and store instructions. But the main memory uses physical addresses for the memory locations where data is actually stored. When the program uses a memory reference, the virtual address must be converted to equivalent physical address. This conversion is done by a process known as 'address translation', which is a mapping of virtual to physical address. This is done by specialized hardware and software within the computer, which maintains page-table in the memory. This page-table determines whether the virtual page, containing the address that has been referenced by the operation, is currently mapped into a physical page. If it is a valid page, the conversion method in the Memory Management Unit (MMU) determines the physical address corresponding to the virtual address from the page table. If the virtual page is not currently mapped into a physical page, then a page-fault occurs. Then the requested page is fetched from the memory, and the page-table updated.

A table of recently used virtual-to-physical translations, called a Translation Lookaside Buffer (TLB) is used. Translating an address that has an entry in the TLB requires no additional memory reference. However, the TLB can only contain a limited number of mappings between virtual and physical addresses. When the translation for the requested address is not resident in the TLB, the hardware will have to perform the translation and load the result into the TLB.

On some processors, address translation is performed entirely in hardware; the Memory Management Unit (MMU) has to make additional memory references to load the required translations from the translation tables, but no other action is needed. In some cases, operating system may do the translation. An address translation scheme is depicted in Figure 6.19.

Address translation is of two types: Static and Dynamic.. For static address translation, the translation is completed when the program is first loaded for execution. The physical address space is fixed for the duration of its execution. Dynamic translation is needed when the virtual address varies dynamically during the execution of the program.

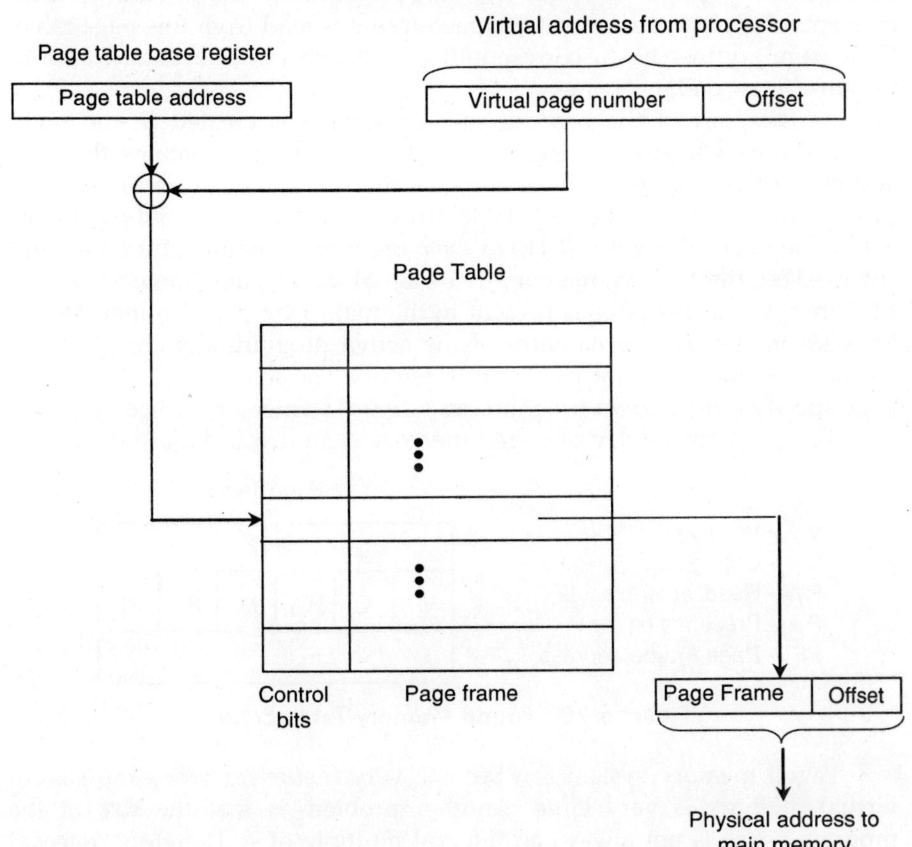

FIGURE 6.19 : Paged Memory Address Translation

Virtual memory gives the illusion that the main memory is much larger than it actually is. When a program references a virtual address, it cannot tell whether the virtual address was residing in the main memory of the computer or whether it had to be fetched from the magnetic memory.

Some common methods of address translation will be discussed below. The first method has blocks of fixed size, called pages. The second method has blocks of arbitrary size, called segments. The third method is a combination of pages and segments.

6.8.2 Paged Memory

A page is a block of addresses of fixed length that can be assigned to fixed regions of physical memory. In paged memory system of address translation, the virtual space is partitioned into pages. These pages are located in matching size blocks, which are called page frames. The virtual address generated by a program consists of two fields: (i) a virtual page number, (ii) displacement of the word within the page. The address map consists of a page-table. If the page exists in the memory, then corresponding base address of the page-frame is read from this page-table. Each page address has a corresponding real address of a page frame in primary or secondary memory.

At the start of the process, one page-table is created in the main memory for each process. The page-table base register contains the base address of the page-table of the process that is currently running on the processor. An index in the page-table array is used to access the page-table entry. The page-table entry (PTE) in the page-table contains V bit for a valid entry, access rights—RW, memory disk bit—M, and a page frame address—PF. When V = 1, the page is present in the main memory. The memory bit M is set to the page table entry of the active program and the PF entry contains the address of the page in the memory. The access rights, RW, of the page specify if the current program can be read, written or is to be executed.

The page table entry of paged memory is shown in Figure 6.20.

Page Table

V - Valid bit
C - Change bit
RW - Read/write/execute
P - Presence bit
PF - Page Frame address

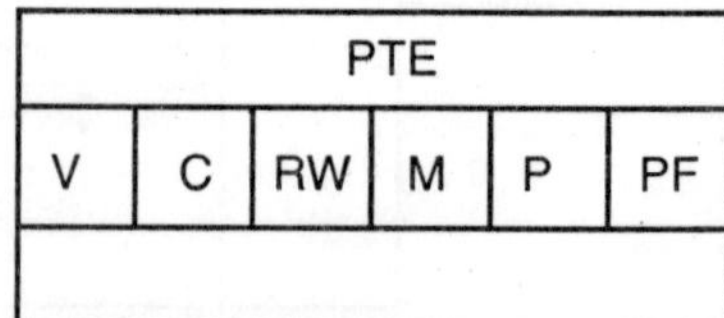

FIGURE 6.20 : Paged Memory Table Entry

Paged memory system can become very inefficient when the size of virtual memory is very large. Another problem is that the size of the program space is not always an integral multiple of 2. Therefore, internal fragmentation occurs in memory because the last part of the last page is wasted. Page-Tables also occupy lot of space in the physical memory.

6.8.3 Segmented Memory

In paged memory system, the pages have a fixed size because of which memory can be wasted or fragmented. Instead of using fixed sized pages, set of logically related adjacent data elements, called segments, are used which are allowed to grow or shrink according to the need of the virtual memory of a program. Segmentation is a technique used for managing the allocation of virtual space, while paging is a concept used to manage the allocation of physical space.

An element in a segment is referenced by a pair of names comprising of segment name and element name. During program execution, the segment name is translated into a segment address by the operating system. While the program is being compiled, the element name maps into a relative address or displacement within the segment.

The mapping of segments is performed as follows: Each process in the system has a segment table—ST pointed to by a segment table base register—SBR, when the process is active. The SBR allows the relocation of the ST, which is a segment itself and is stored in the main memory. The ST consists of segment table entries—STE. The address field contains the absolute base address of the segment in memory. If it is present then segment flag F is set to 1. RW and L fields contain the access rights and length of the segment, respectively. Figure 6.21 shows Segment Table Entry in a segmented system.

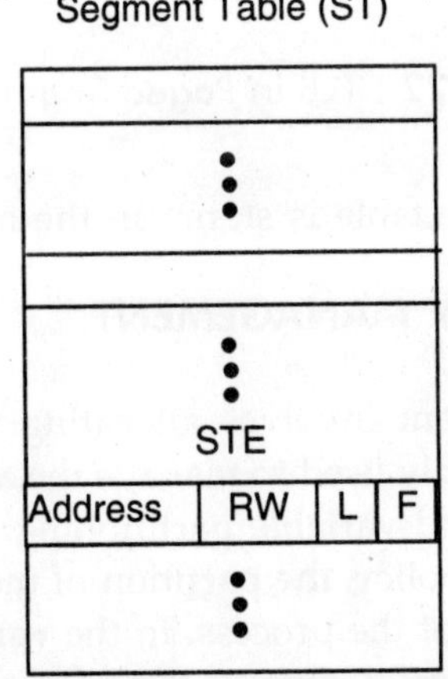

FIGURE 6.21 : Segment Table Entry in a Segmented System

6.8.4 Paged Segments

Paged segment memory system is a combination of paged memory system and segmented memory system to provide the benefits of the two. In this system, each segment is divided into pages and is referenced by a processor through a page table for that segment.

The page table PT contains entry of a segment comprising of address field and presence bit F. If the page is present in the main memory, the address field contains the absolute base address of the page. If the referenced page is absent from the memory, a page fault occurs. In this case, the page-fault-handler retrieves the page from the disk to the memory. Figure 6.22 illustrates the entries in the translation look-ahead buffer used for mapping of the virtual address to the physical address. Using the segment number, the information about the page address is obtained from

Translation look-ahead buffer (TLB)

RW	Seg #	Page #	Main memory page address
⋮	⋮	⋮	⋮

FIGURE 6.22 : TLB in Paged Segment System

the page table. The page table is stored in the main memory.

6.9 VIRTUAL MEMORY MANAGEMENT

Memory management involves allocating pages to active processes. The two policies commonly used to manage the allocation of memory pages are: fixed partitioning and variable partitioning.

In fixed allocation policy, the partition of memory allocated to process is fixed for the life-time of the process. In the variable allocation policy, the partition varies dynamically during the lifetime of the process and the requirements of the process. Various paging algorithms are used for fixed and variable management policies. The following are some common policies used for page-replacement for fixed-space partitioning:

1. Least Recently Used (LRU)

In case of page fault, this algorithm replaces the page with the largest backward distance, where distance is the time of replacement.

2. Least Frequently Used (LFU)

This algorithm replaces the page that has been referenced the least number of times.

3. First-In First-Out (FIFO)

This algorithm replaces the page that has been in memory for the longest time.

4. Last-In First-Out (LIFO)

This algorithm replaces the page that has been in memory for the shortest time.

5. Random (RAND)

This algorithm chooses a page at random for replacement.

LRU is the most popular algorithm. A dynamic list, known as a LRU stack is linked with it. This stack arranges the referenced pages from top to bottom by decreasing order of frequency of reference. At the page replacement time, LRU policy chooses the lowest ranked page in the stack.

6.10 SUMMARY

Memory of a computer system is a hierarchy of memory incorporating various technologies which are organized to provide best performance in terms of speed and cost. The characteristics of memory, which are access time and accessing method are used as benchmarks for constructing primary memory, secondary memory and cache memory. The various kinds of memory devices are used according to their storage capacity and acceptable level of performance. Random-Access-Memories take the same amount of time to access any storage location, and they can be accessed in any order. In serial access memories, access mechanism is shared by the storage locations. Magnetic disks and tape memories store information on the surface of the tracks which are coated with magnetic media. Optical memories provide extremely high storage capacities but their access rates are quite less as compared to magnetic disks. ROMs store information permanently while the chip is being manufactured. Flash memories can be erased without removing it from the circuit. Speed of cache is quite close to the CPU. Four placement policies exist to match and map the addresses: Direct Mapping, Fully Associative mapping, Set associative mapping and Sector mapping. The objective of organization of memory is a tradeoff between cost and required storage of memory. This is the reason to have multilevel memories. Virtual memory is a technique of memory management that is used to allow slow memory to be used as a level of memory system. It also provides protection between programs running on the same system so that one program cannot modify another program's data. The implementations of address translation should be extremely fast as the size of the virtual memory is very large. Two policies are in use for allocating pages to active processes: fixed and variable partitioning.

References

John, P. Hayes, Computer Architecture and Organization, Third Edition, McGraw-Hill, 1998.

Tanenbaum, Andrew, S., Structured Computer Organization, 4th ed., Prentice-Hall of India, New Delhi, 2001.

Patterson, D.A. and J.L. Hennessey, Computer Architecture: A Quantitative, Approach, San Mateo, CA: Morgan Kaufmann Publishers, 1990.

Hamacher, C., Vranesic, Z., and Zaky, S., Computer Organization, 5th edition, McGraw-Hill, NY, 2002.

Hwang, K. and F.A. Briggs, Computer Architecture and Parallel Processing, New York: McGraw-Hill, 1984.

PROBLEMS

1. Illustrate a memory hierarchy of a computer system showing the memory size, type and the access time.
2. What is meant by spatial locality and temporal locality?
3. How will magnetic tape units in the memory hierarchy of Figure 6.1 communicate with the main memory?
4. Arrange the following memories in the order of highest to lowest speed of access: DASDs, RAMs, SAMs.
5. What are the technological reasons for the variation in speed of Registers, Primary and Secondary memories and Cache?
6. Explain the functional organization of DRAM and SRAM.
7. Explain the difference in READ and WRITE mechanisms of SRAM and DRAM.
8. How is READ and WRITE operations performed in SAMs?
9. How are Read/Write heads of secondary memories, employing magnetic media, constructed?
10. Explain the recording and retrieval of information in Optical memories.
11. Draw the block diagram of a RAM and ROM chip and show its function table.
12. Show the constructional features and explain the working of RAM, ROM, PROM, EPROM, EEPROM
13. Give details of methods by which data can be changed in ROMs.
14. What are the fundamental qualities of Cache Memory?
15. What are the advantages of Cache memory? What should be its size?
16. How is Cache memory faster than Main Memory?
17. How is the performance of Cache Memory measured using hit and miss ratios.
18. Explain the operation of cache showing the address of the cache, main memory and the translation.
19. How does cache memory increase the speed of computation? Explain multilevel cache.
20. In 4-way set associative cache of 64M, how many sets exist? How many addresses exist?
21. Suppose main memory has 16 blocks of 4-bytes each and the cache has 8 blocks. Show the placement of block in (i) Direct Mapped cache, (ii) Fully Associative cache, 2-way set associative cache.
22. If a miss occurs, which block should be replaced? Are these replacement policies implemented in Hardware or Software?
23. Explain the difference between:
    (i) Levels of cache
    (ii) Instruction cache (I-cache) and Data cache (D-cache)
    (iii) Unified cache and split cache

24. Explain the address format and the hardware organization of Associative memory.
25. Compare the access time of a memory location using Set Associative Mapping with that using Sector Mapping.
26. What do you understand by virtual memory?
27. Explain the Virtual Address Space and Real Address Space.
28. Which of the following features are implemented directly by virtual memory:
    (a) a larger virtual address space than physical memory
    (b) allow multiple processes to share a physical memory
    (c) higher bandwidth access to disk
    (d) a larger number of interrupts
    (e) protection between processes
    (f) support for memory mapped devices
29. Explain paging memory technique.
30. Write brief note on memory management hardware.

CHAPTER

7

Input-Output

7. INTRODUCTION

In computer systems, Input/Output, or I/O, is the method that different functional units of a computer use to communicate with each other, or the outside world. Inputs are the signals received by the unit, and outputs are the signals sent from it. I/O devices are used to perform different functions, such as keyboards and mouse are considered input devices of a computer, and monitors and printers are considered output devices of a computer. Typical devices for communication between computers are for both input and output, such as modems and network cards. The information is sent through the interfaces which match the speed and other attributes of the I/O devices being used. This chapter provides information about various devices and methods used for I/O.

7.1 INTRODUCTION TO BUS ARCHITECTURE

A computer bus is used for transmitting data from one part of the computer to another and connects all devices to the computer CPU and main memory. The computer bus consists of two parts, the address bus and a data bus. The data bus transfers actual data, whereas the address bus transfers address or memory location of where the data should go. Various components in the organization of the computer system, like the CPU, memory, and peripheral devices are connected by means of buses. The bus provides physical links and the means of controlling the communication exchange of signals over the bus. Figure 7.1 depicts the organization of a single shared bus.

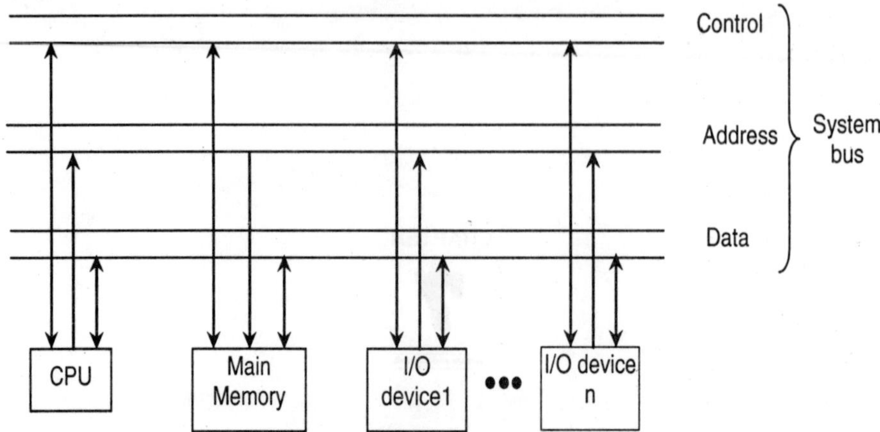

FIGURE 7.1 : Architecture of a Single Shared Bus

New bus architectures are developed to improve bus throughput and reduce bus delay or latency. This is because microprocessor and memory speeds keep increasing and older bus designs cannot manage throughput and delay.

The principle use of the system bus is high-speed data transfer between the CPU and memory. Most I/O devices are slower than the CPU or the memory. The I/O devices are attached to the system bus through external interfaces. For example, magnetic disk storage unit transfers data serially. Therefore, they are connected to the sytem bus through interfaces known as I/O controller. A single I/O controller can interface many I/O devices at the same time to the system bus.

The Input/Output (I/O) ports are used to connect various devices to the computer and, hence, enable communication between the device and the computer. For example, external modem is connected to serial ports while printers are connected to parallel ports. These ports help in transmitting the data from the device to the computer and *vice versa*. Each port has a specific way of communicating and this depends upon the speed and size of the port.

7.2 EFFECT OF BUS WIDTH

The bus width decides how much memory the CPU can address. The more is the bus width, the more memory can be addressed. If the width of the bus is n bits, then 2^n memory locations can be addressed. But memory size cannot be increased beyond a certain limit because having more number of address bits will require additional space and is more expensive.

There are two ways to increase the data bandwidth of the bus. First one is to decrease the bus cycle time, which leads to more transfers per second. The second method is to increase the data bus width, which directs more bits per transfer. Increasing the speed of the bus is possible, but it is difficult as signals on different line travel at slightly different speed. This problem is known as 'bus skew'. The faster the bus, the more serious is the bus skew problem.

When very wide buses are needed, multiplexed buses are used. In this design, instead of having separate address and data lines, these lines are used together. For example, 32 lines are for address and data together. At the start of the bus operation, the lines are used for address, and then later on, they are used for data. Bus designers have to weigh all the options before making a choice.

7.3 BUS STANDARDS

An I/O bus standard defines connectors, signal amplitudes, and clock speeds. A bus standard is necessary so that different manufacturers can produce devices that all communicate properly. There is a number of existing I/O bus standards. This section introduces some of the widely used standards such as ISA, IDE, SCSI, USB and PCI.

7.3.1 ISA Bus

Industry Standard Architecture (ISA) is an internal computer bus that was introduced by IBM. This bus was originally an 8-bit bus that was later expanded to a 16-bit bus in mid-80's. When this bus was originally released, it allowed only IBM to create peripherals and the actual interface. However, later other manufacturers were also creating the bus.

The original ISA bus had 62 signal lines. Of these, 20 lines were for memory address, 8 for data, and one each for control signals of memory read and memory write. The control signals of interrupt and DMA access were present. The bus was etched in the motherboard of the PC and had about 6 connectors in which cards could be inserted.

When PC/AT was introduced, the data bus was extended from 8-bits to 16-bits. Along with this, a second edge connecter containing 36 lines was put on the bottom of the board, adjacent to the main board. On this bus, 31 lines are provided for more address lines, data lines interrupt lines and DMA access channels. The rest of the lines deal with differences between 8-bit and 16-bit transfers.

Later on, the successor to PC and PC/AT was PS/2 series of computers. The architecture of the ISA was started once again, with the bus running at 8.33 MHz. This bus maintains compatibility with existing machine and cards. This bus allowed the computer to automatically detect and setup computer ISA peripherals, such as a modem or sound card. Thus, now the user possesses the capability of connecting a device and not having to configure the device.

7.3.2 Integrated Device Electronics (IDE)

Integrated Device Electronics (IDE) or Advanced Technology Attachment (ATA) external computer bus, developed in mid-80's, is a standard interface for connecting storage devices such as hard disks and CD-ROM drivers inside a PC. IDE is a parallel connector that allows cable lengths up to only 18 inches although cables up to 36 inches are also available. Because of this length limit, the technology normally appears as an internal computer storage interface. It provides the most common and the least expensive interface for this application.

IDE was a 10 MB disk controlled by a disk controller and a plug-in card. The disk had 4 heads, 306 cylinders, and 17 sectors/track. The operating system reads from, and writes to a disk, by placing parameters on CPU registers and then calls the Basic Input Output System (BIOS) located in the ROM. The calling of BIOS addresses the sectors by giving numbers to their head, cylinder, and sectors. The head and cylinder numbers start with 0 and sectors start with 1. For a 528 MB drive having 4 bits for the head, 6 bits for the sector, 10 bit for the cylinder—the drive has 16 heads, 63 sectors, and 1024 cylinders.

Enhanced IDE (EIDE) is an extension to the original IDE standard, again developed by Western Digital. The EIDE supports the drives having a storage capacity larger than 528 MB, up to 8.4 GB. EIDE (Extended IDE) supports a second addressing scheme called 'Logic Block Addressing' (LBA). In this scheme, the sectors are numbered starting from 0 to a maximum of 2^{24}-1. The controller converts the LBA address to head, sector and cylinder addresses.

IDE and EIDE are low priced drives. The interface at first worked only with hard disks, but eventually an extended standard came to work with a variety of other devices like CD-ROM, DVD-ROM drives, tape drives and large capacity floppy drives.

7.3.3 Small Computer System Interface (SCSI)

The requirement of the bus in the computer system should be that it is big enough to support a whole computer, a server or plenty of devices simultaneously. SCSI is a fast bus that can connect a large number of devices to a computer at the same time, including hard drives, scanners, printers, etc. Each SCSI bus can connect up to seven peripherals (8-bit) or fifteen peripherals (16-bit) to a host adapter. SCSI bus is a device independent of system level peripheral interface.

The organization of cylinders, tracks and sectors of SCSI disks are similar to IDE disks. However, they use different interfaces and have much higher transfer rate. SCSI was developed in 1979 and it was modified to SCSI-2 in 1994. Work is going on for developing faster SCSI disks.

Each SCSI device has a unique identification number (ID), from 0 to 7. Wider SCSI disks have an ID of 15. Each device has a connector, one for input and the other one for output. Cables connect the devices in series, from the output of one device to the input of the next one, in a string. The last device in the string must be terminated to prevent reflections from the ends of the SCSI bus from interfering with other data on the bus.

The cable for an 8-bit SCSI has 50 wires, 25 of which are ground wires. These are then paired with the other 25 wires to provide noise immunity needed for high speed operation. Of the 25 wires, 8 wires are used for data, 1 wire for parity and 9 wires for control. The remainder of the wires are used for power or reserved for future use. SCSI controllers can operate as originator or as target of signals. When they act as originator, they issue commands to disks and other peripherals acting as targets. When multiple devices are in use, then bus arbitration is done in phases for issuing commands and responses.

SCSI disks have very high transfer rate. Therefore, they are used as a standard in workstations. On this bus, a SCSI controller and up to seven devices can be attached. These can include one or more SCSI disks, CD-ROMs, CD-recorders, scanners and other SCSI peripherals. Figure 7.2 shows the data rates of various SCSI devices.

Name	*Data bits*	*Capacity MHz*	*Data Rate MB/sec*
SCSI-1	8	5	5
SCSI-2	8	5	5
Fast SCSI-2	8	10	10
Wide SCSI-2	16	10	20
Ultra SCSI	16	20	40

FIGURE 7.2 : Parameters of Various SCSI

Structurally, IDE and SCSI drives are quite similar in their functioning but several factors must be considered when determining whether IDE or SCSI is better in a particular situation. IDE disks are used because they are cheap and they perform well. But to look at performance, one needs to look at the entire drive. The bus structure, not the drive, of SCSI provides performance overhead over IDE. The nature of the SCSI bus allows much better performance when large amount of data is to be transferred in a multi-tasking job. The SCSI bus controller is capable of controlling the drives without any work by the processor. Moreover, all drives on a SCSI chain are capable of operating at the same time. With IDE, only two drives can be used in a chain, and these drives cannot work at the same time. Thus, with multitasking, when several programs are working at once, the SCSI drive is a better choice because the extra capability of the SCSI bus is used. When amount of data to be transferred is limited, and the tasks performed by the CPU are limited, IDE performs properly. Though the SCSI bus is very fast, it generally is not needed in many cases. With the low price of IDE, this drive is good in common cases.

7.3.4 Universal Serial Bus (USB)

Universal Serial Bus (USB), developed by Intel and other technology industry leaders, is a serial bus standard to interface devices. The features of USB that made its use almost universal is that it is designed to allow peripherals to be connected using a single standardized interface socket and to improve plug-and-play capabilities by allowing devices to be connected and disconnected without rebooting the computer. Other favorable features include powering low-consumption devices without the need for an external power supply and allowing some devices to be used without requiring individual device drivers to be installed. USB provides ease of use, expandability, and speed for the end user.

USB is an external bus standard that supports data transfer rates of 12 Mbps. A single USB port can be used to connect up to 127 peripheral devices, such as mouse, modem, and keyboard. USB also supports Plug-and-Play installation (A standard that allows the system to automatically configure adapter-card resources) and Hot-Plugging (The ability to add and remove devices to a computer while the computer is running, and have the operating system automatically recognize the change).

USB was originally released in 1995 at 12 Mbps. USB today operates at 480 Mbps and can be found everywhere in PCs and mobile devices. In addition to high performance and presence everywhere, USB is strongly accepted and is easy to use. Practically, all computers come with one or more USB connectors to which most peripheral devices can be attached.

In the past, connecting devices to computers created problems related to the available ports. Printers need to be connected to low-speed parallel printer ports. High speed drives are needed for connection to the parallel ports. However, most computers had just one parallel port along with one or two serial ports for peripherals like modems and digital cameras. The goal of USB is to end all these problems. The USB provides a single, standardized method to connect up to 127 devices to a computer. Just about every peripheral made now comes in a USB version. They include printers, modems, scanners, mouse, webcams, speakers, video phones, storage drives and the like.

Design of USB

The design of USB was influenced by requirements such as installing new I/O devices without rebooting the system, use of only one kind of cable for connecting all kind of devices, I/O devices should get their power from the cable, system should support real-time devices and up to 127 devices should be attachable to a single computer.

A USB system has an asymmetric design, which consists of a host controller, and multiple devices connected in a tree-like fashion with the use of special hub devices. 127 devices per host controller can be connected. These signals are transmitted on a twisted pair of data cables, labeled D+ and D-, which operate together and are not separate connections. These collectively use half-duplex differential signaling to prevent the effects of electromagnetic noise on longer lines.

USB supports three data rates that can support varied speeds. To connect slow devices like mouse, keyboard etc., the first data rate of 1.5 Mbps is used. The second one has a data rate of 12 Mbps and the devices use the entire bandwidth with this connector. The third one, called the USB 2.0 has a Hi-Speed rate of 480 Mbps. The advantage with USB 2.0 is that it supports low speed USB devices by reducing its bandwidth.

Pin	*Name*	*Description*
1	VCC	+5V DC
2	D-	Data-
3	D+	Data +
4	Ground	Ground

FIGURE 7.3 : Pins of USB

USB Connections

To connect a USB device to a computer, the USB connector is positioned into it. Figure 7.3 lists the pins of USB connector. If it is a new device, the operating system auto-detects it and asks for the driver disk. If the device has already been installed, the computer activates it and starts using it. USB devices can be connected and disconnected at any time.

FIGURE 7.4 : A Typical USB Socket[1]

Many USB devices come with their own built-in cable. These cables are marked as "A" or "B". The USB standard uses "A" and "B" connectors to avoid confusion:

- "**A**" connectors lead "**upstream**" toward the computer.
- "**B**" connectors lead "**downstream**" and connect to individual devices.

By using different connectors on the upstream and downstream end, the use of USB becomes simple.

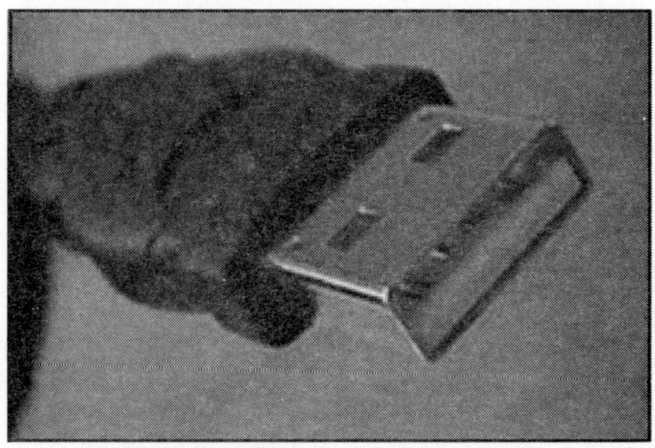

FIGURE 7.5 : USB " A" Connection

FIGURE 7.6 : USB "B " Connection

Features of USB

The main features of USB are that it can connect 127 devices either directly or by way of USB hubs. The cable length can be up to 5 meters long which can be increased up to 30 meters with hubs. Maximum data rate available is 480 Mbps with USB 2.0. The cable has two wires: +5 volts and ground for power, and a twisted pair of wires to carry the data. On the power wires, the computer can supply up to 500 milliamps of power at 5 volts. Low-power devices, like mouse, can draw their power directly from the bus. High-power devices, such as printers, have their own power supplies and draw negligible power from the bus. Hubs can have their own power supplies to provide power to devices connected to the hub. The plug-in devices can be plugged into the bus and unplugged any time. Many USB devices can be put to stand-by by the host computer when the computer enters a power-saving mode.

The USB Functions

The functioning of the USB starts by checking all the devices connected to the bus and assigning each one an address. This process is called 'enumeration'. The host also finds out from each device what type of data transfer it wishes to perform. The various modes available are listed below:

- *Interrupt*—This mode is used by a device like a mouse or a keyboard, which will be sending very little data.
- *Bulk*—This mode is used by devices which receive data in one big packet. Devices like a printer, will use this mode.
- *Isochronous*—This mode is used by devices which use the data-stream in real-time. Example of such a device is a speaker.

The Universal Serial Bus divides the available bandwidth into frames, the control of which is with the host. A frame contains 1,500 bytes, and a new frame starts every millisecond. During a frame, isochronous and interrupt devices get a slot so they are guaranteed the bandwidth they need. Bulk and control transfers use whatever space is left.

7.3.5 Peripheral Component Interconnect (PCI)

The Peripheral Component Interconnect (PCI) Bus is a parallel internal interface. It was originally developed as a local bus expansion for the PC (ISA) bus, and was named the PCI Local Bus. To achieve the speed requirements of various devices, CPU were provided with more than one bus. By using the PCI architecture, very high bandwidth buses are provided.

Electrical requirements for the interface are defined by PCI specifications. The first version of the PCI bus ran at 33MHz with a 32 bit bus, the current version runs at 66MHz with a 64 bit bus. The PCI bus operates either synchronously or asynchronously with the bus rate of the mother board. While operating asynchronously, the bus can operate at any frequency from 66 MHz to 0 Hz. To operate with slower devices, flow control is added. Unlike earlier PC buses, the PCI bus is processor independent.

The Time Multiplexed Address and Data bus may exist as either 0 to 31 bits (32 bits) or 0 to 63 bits (64 bits) using the 64 bit expansion bus. Both the Address and Data line use the same bus, address first then data. 32 bit PCI may also use 64 bit addressing by using two address cycles, termed as Dual Address Cycles (DAC), where the low order address is sent first. When the bus is increased to 64 bits, additional control bits are used. The specification defines both a Reset line and a Clock line. The Clock may be either 33 MHz or 66 MHz.

Ready and Acknowledge lines are used as 'Handshake' lines to allow communication, i.e.. Two Parity lines are made available, one for the 32 bit bus width and an additional one for the 64 bit expansion. For error detection, two error bits, 1 for the LSB 32 bits and one for the upper 32 bits are provided.

The 64 bit-PCI bus is made up of the following major signals as shown in Figure 7.7.

Address/Data Bus	64 bit Address, 64 bit Data, Time Multiplexed .
System Bus	2 bits; Clock/Reset
Interface Control Bus	7 bits; Ready, Acknowledge, Stop
Parity Bus	2 bits, 1 for the 32 LSBs and 1 for the 32 MSB bits
Errors Bus	2 bits, 1 for Parity and 1 for System
Command/Byte Enable	8 bits (0-3 for 32 bit, and 4-7 for 64 bit Bus)
64 MHz Control	6 bits; (2) Enable/Running, (2) Present, (2) Ack/Req
Cache	2 Bits
Interrupt bus	4 bits
Power	+5, +3.3, +12, -12v, GND

FIGURE 7.7 : Major Signals of PCI BUS

Peripheral Component Interface Pinout

Figure 7.8 depicts bus signals of the PCI bus that are essential. The number (#) sign indicates that the signal is asserted when it is at a low voltage while the absence of a # sign indicates that the signal is asserted at a high.

Most modern PCs include a PCI bus in addition to a more general ISA expansion bus. PCI is a 64-bit bus, and may be used as a 32-bit bus. It can run at clock speeds of 33 or 66 MHz. At 32 bits and 33 MHz, it provides a throughput rate of 133 Mbps.

Signal	*Description*
CLK	33 MHz or 66 MHz clock
AD	32 Multiplexed Address or Data bus lines
PAR	Address or Data parity bit
C/BE	Bus command/bit map for bytes enabled, 4 lines
FRAME#	Indicates that AD and C/BE are asserted
IRDY#	Read – master will accept, Write – Data present
TRDY#	Read – Data present, Write – master will accept
PERR#	Data parity error detected by receiver
REQ#	Bus arbitration – request for bus ownership
GNT#	Bus arbitration – grant of bus ownership
RST#	Reset the system and all devices

FIGURE 7.8 : Essential Bus Signals

7.4 INPUT DEVICES

The input to devices such as mice and keyboards, are the physical movement that the human user outputs and converts it into signals that a computer can understand. The output from these devices is treated as input by the computer. Similarly, printers and monitors take as input signals that a computer outputs. These signals are converted into representations that human users can see or read. In the folllowing sections, various Input-Output devices will be examined. The most common input devices used by the computer are the keyboard and the mouse. The keyboard allows the entry of textual information while the mouse allows the selection of a point on the screen by moving a screen cursor to the point and pressing a mouse button. Using the mouse in this way allows the selection from menus on the screen and is the basic method of communicating with many current computing systems. The most common output device is a monitor that can display text and graphics. If hard-copy output is required then some form of printer is used.

Computers and their operating systems cannot control every device. To solve this problem, device drivers are used to translate the functions and provide control to these devices. In theory, a new device, which is controlled in a new manner, should function correctly if a suitable driver is available. Depending on the specific computer architecture, drivers can be 8-bit, 16-bit, 32-bit, or 64-bit. This corresponds directly to the architecture of the operating system for which those drivers were developed. Because of the diversity of modern hardware and operating systems, many ways exist in which drivers can be used. Drivers are used for interfacing with printers, keyboards, storage devices like hard disk, floppy disk, CD-ROM, video adapters, network cards, sound cards, local buses, and I/O buses.

The next section describes some commonly used input devices.

7.4.1 Keyboards

Computer keyboards are the most commonly used input device. Keyboard is a peripheral modeled after the typewriter and is designed for the input of text and characters, and also to control the operation of the computer and other peripherals like mouse. Physically, computer keyboards are an arrangement of rectangular or near-rectangular buttons, or keys. Each button will typically have characters printed on the keys. In most cases, each press of a key corresponds to a single written symbol. However, to produce some symbols requires pressing and holding several keys simultaneously, or in sequence. Some keys do not produce any symbol, but instead affect the operation of the computer, or the keyboard.

The standard keyboard has four groups of keys. The alphanumeric keys and the numeric keys enter text into the computer. The function keys are used by programs as keyboard shortcuts to commands. The cursor is the point on the screen which is active, and where the information that is entered will appear. The cursor-movement keys allow the movement of the cursor to various positions on the screen.

Figure 7.9 depicts the picture of a standard keyboard. A keyboard is also used to type commands in a computer.

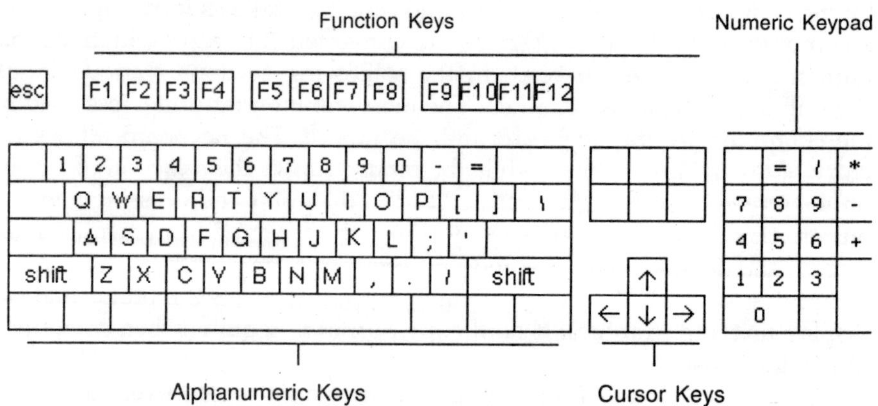

FIGURE 7.9 : **Standard Keyboard**

Working

Membrane keyboards or 'Dome switch' keyboards are generally available as a flat structure consisting of three layers. The top layer of the key is a plasticised material with key positions marked over it. Traces of a conducting material are deposited on the underside of the key. The middle layer is made of rubber, with holes at the key positions. The third layer, which is the bottom layer, is made of metallic material with raised bumps at key positions. When pressure is applied to the top layer of a key, the trace of this key comes in contact with the corresponding bump on the bottom layer. This completes an electrical circuit and current flows which is sensed by the microcontroller that generates a code and sends it over a serial link to the computer. The computer then decides what to do on the basis of the key pressed, e.g. display a character on the screen, or perform some action. Other types of keyboard function in a similar manner, the main differences being how the individual key-switches work.

7.4.2 Mice

Mouse was invented in 1968. It acts as a perfect portable pointing device. Before mice came in existence, text was primarily the only form of information entered in the computer. Mouse made the entry of graphic data quite easy. A mouse allows the movement of the pointer or cursor that is on the screen and selects items by clicking on them. The mouse is a device that fits comfortably in the hands of the operator and can be moved over a flat surface.

Working

A typical PC mouse controlling system has sensors, mouse controller, communication link, data interface, and driver. Sensors are the movement detectors, typically optomechanical, which sense the mouse movement and button switches that signify the button states. Mouse controller reads the state of those sensors and describes the current mouse position. When this information changes, the mouse controller sends a packet of data to the computer data interface controller.

In typical modern PC mouse driver, the actual cursor movement is not linearly related to the mouse movement. There are other ways to change the mouse movement to cursor movement than just simply causing one mouse step to move the cursor by one pixel. It has been found that no particular ratio between mouse movement and cursor movement is best suited for all tasks. Normally, the mouse driver calls mouse cursor moving routines when mouse is moved and sends messages to the software when buttons are pressed.

There are two basic movements in the use of pointing devices: move cursor to desired area and then exactly to desired target. Those two movements have contradictory requirements. Thus, there is a need to monitor the mouse movements and change the counts per inch (CPI) characteristics. When the mouse is moved slowly, it remains 100 CPI and when the mouse is moved fast, it appears to be 400 CPI. This method of adjusting CPI based on its usage has now been adopted by the default drivers.

Kinds of Mice

Mice come in three basic types: mechanical, optomechanical, and optical. The basic design is the mechanical mouse – it has a rubber or plastic ball on its underside that rolls freely in all directions as the mouse is moved. The rotation of the ball is sensed which is linked to the counter taking control of the X and Y axes. The mouse driver in the computer receives that data packet, decodes the information from it and does actions based on the information. A standard mouse driver has the information of the current position and button states of the mouse, and that is passed on to the application or operating system when it asks them. The cursor on the screen is moved as the mechanical sensors within the mouse detect the direction of the rolling ball.

The optomechanical mouse uses optical sensors to detect the motion of the ball. The fully optical mouse uses lasers to detect the movement of the mouse. In optical mice, the optical positioning mechanism that is used instead of the ball, has a red glow and works just like a standard mouse with a track ball on the bottom. However, optical mice are more precise. In addition, they do not need cleaning and can be used without a mouse pad. The only drawback to optical mice is that they will not work on an extremely shiny surface, like glass or mirrors.

The latest addition in the design of types of mice is the cordless mouse, which no longer has to be physically connected to the computer. Two different technologies are used. Some mice operate by an infrared-port, where the mouse must have a clear line of sight to the computer, much like a television remote control. Other mice use radio frequencies for their wireless technology, which allow the mice to roam farther from the computer. Radio frequency mice can transmit to the computer in spite of the pile of papers in between. Both optical and cordless mice are more precise and robust, but are more expensive than other mice.

Buttons

Mice contain at least one button and sometimes as many as three, which can be programmed for different functions. Additional buttons on the side of the mouse are provided that can be used for faster navigation in certain programs. These extra buttons are not needed for ordinary mouse movements. However, for faster navigation, these features can be used. The additional buttons are usually programmable. The most popular use for these extra buttons is to make them work like the Back and Forward buttons on the toolbar of a Web browsing program. Most mice can be customized to control their speed of operation. These customizations might seem minor, but they can add enormous functionality and comfort as well as enhance productivity for any user.

7.4.3 Trackball

A trackball is basically an upside-down mouse with a stationary base. The pointer on the screen is controlled by rollerball, which sits on top of the base. The rollerball can be moved with the hands or fingers.

The operating principles of a trackball are very similar to that of a mechanical mouse. The ball is mounted on a shallow well on the keyboard. The user rotates the ball to indicate the required movement of the curser on the screen.

Trackballs come in a variety of sizes and shapes to meet different needs. Some require a small thumb control on a small rollerball. Others are large enough to be controlled with an entire hand. Software drivers that are available with several others, to provide additional features, such as programming buttons with customized controls that help in double-clicking, scrolling pages and Internet use. Figure 7.10 shows a popular trackball which provides a stable base, large ball and four large, easy to program buttons. The design matches both left and right-handed users.

FIGURE 7.10 : Trackball

7.4.4 Joystick

A joystick is another general control device consisting of a handheld stick that turns about one end and transmits its angle in two or three dimensions to a computer. A joystick can be analog or digital. An analog joystick has continuous states that return an angle measure of the movement in any direction in the plane. Potentiometers are used for measurement. A digital joystick gives only on/off signals for four different directions, and mechanically possible combinations. Some joysticks have one or more 'fire buttons' that are used to trigger some kind of action.

Joysticks are two-dimensional, having two axes of movement. Three-dimensional joysticks are also available. A joystick is generally constructed so that moving the stick left or right signals movement along the X axis, and moving it forward (up) or back (down) signals movement along the Y axis. If joysticks that are arranged for three-dimensional movement twist the stick left (counter-clockwise) or right (clockwise), it signals movement along the Z axis.

Joysticks are often used to control games, and usually have one or more push-buttons whose state can also be read by the computer. But these days the mouse and keyboard are used more. Modern joysticks generally use a USB interface for connection to the PC. The term joystick has become a synonym for game controllers. Apart for controlling games, joysticks are also used for controlling machines such as elevators, trucks, cranes, wheelchairs and other application devices.

7.4.5 Touchscreen

Touchscreens is a very simple device for the interaction with the user. A touchscreen is both an input device and an output device. When the touchscreen is touched, information is passed to the computer acting as an input device. It is an output device as it can read information on the screen. Touchscreens allow a selection to be made from various options displayed on the screen. Different types of sensors can detect which area of the screen has been touched as if the user had used a mouse. Moreover, dust and dirt does not interfere with the input of the computer. They are popular on factory floors and in public areas such as banks and museums.

7.4.6 Speech Input

The eventual aim of input-output required from computers is the ability to converse freely with a machine to understand the production and perception processes involved in human speech communication. The spoken language interfaces to computers are fast becoming a necessity. Improvement in human language technology is needed for the average person to communicate with networks using commonly available devices, such as telephones and televisions.

Speech Input Technologies

The technologies needed for interfacing speech input to computers involves the use of many different technologies and applications. These need to be most natural, flexible, efficient, and economical form of human communication. Primary need is to identity the speaker, or the language being spoken. Speaker recognition can require identifying a specific speaker out of many other users to verify the claimed identity of a user.

Speech recognition concerns with speaking to computers. The acoustic (voice) signal is converted to a stream of words. This is performed by using high performance algorithms and systems. The available speech input capabilities can provide functions like voice dialing, call routing, simple data entry, and the like. First, the various attributes of the digitized signal must be measured. Next, the various speech sounds must be reproduced appropriately.

Several language-based input and output technologies have been developed and integrated for efficient understanding of the speech by the computer. Figure 7.11 shows the major components of a typical conversational system. The spoken input is first processed through the speech recognition component. The natural language component, working along with the recognizer, produces a meaning representation. Finally, the speech recognition and natural language processing techniques are integrated.

For information retrieval applications illustrated in Figure 7.11, the meaning representation can be used to recover the appropriate information in the form of text, tables and graphics. If the information in the utterance is insufficient, the system may choose to query the user for clarification. The methods of natural language generation and speech synthesis can be used to produce spoken responses. Throughout the process, information of the conversation is maintained and fed back to the speech recognition and language understanding components, so that sentences can be properly understood.

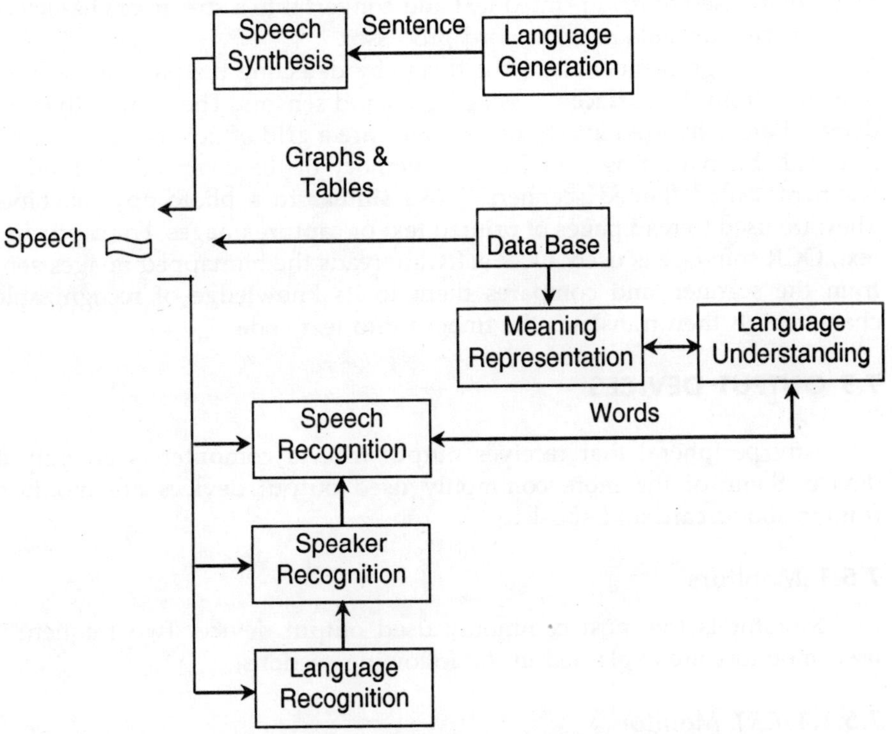

FIGURE 7.11 : Spoken Language Technologies interfaces

Principles of Speaker Recognition

Speaker recognition is the method of automatically recognizing who is speaking on the basis of personal information included in speech waves. The process can be classified into two steps: identification and verification. In the techniques, the voice of the speaker is used to verify their identity and manage access to services such as voice dialing, banking by telephone, voice mail, security control for confidential information areas etc. Another important application of speaker recognition technology is for forensic purposes.

Speaker identification is the method of determining which registered speaker provides a given tone. The process of accepting or rejecting the identity claim of a speaker is known as speaker verification.

7.4.7 Scanner

A scanner is a device that is used to input images into the computer by digitizing them. They are capable of scanning colour or black and white graphics and converting them into data that can be manipulated by the computer. Combined with Optical Character Recognition (OCR) software they can be used to read printed text and convert it to a stream of characters that can be manipulated in a word processor.

The image scanner scans the image by detecting the patterns of light reflecting from the surface by using lights and sensors. The images that are detected are converted into bitmaps which are a grid of dots represented by bits. This bit pattern is stored in the memory of the computer. A kind of scanners, called flatbed scanners, looks similar to a photocopy machine. They are used to read pages of printed text or capture images. For capturing text, OCR software is used. OCR software reads the bitmapped images sent from the scanner, and compares them to its knowledge of recognizable characters. It then translates the images into text code.

7.5 OUTPUT DEVICES

Any peripheral that receives output from a computer is an output device. Some of the more commonly used output devices are monitor, printer, sound card and speakers.

7.5.1 Monitors

Monitor is the most commonly used output device. Two frequently used monitors are explained in the following sections.

7.5.1.1 CRT Monitor

A Cathode Ray Tube (CRT), invented in 1879, is used as a source of electrons to display characters and images by converting the bit pattern. CRT involves an electron gun, which emanates electrons, and a fluorescent tube. Usally the tube has internal or external means to accelerate and deflect the electrons. When electrons strike the fluorescent screen, light is emitted. The entire front area of the tube is scanned systematically in a fixed pattern called a raster. An image is produced by modulating the intensity of the electron beam with the received signals.

In case of monochrome screens, a phosphorescent screen illuminates where the electron beam hits it in the front of the tube. For colour monitors, three electron guns with red, green and blue colors are used. During the horizontal scan, the beam sweeps across the screen, drawing a horizontal line on the display. This is done in about 50 microseconds. After this, a retrace of the line is done to get back to the left edge again to begin the next sweep.

The horizontal deflection plates receive a linearly increasing voltage, which controls the horizontal sweeping. These plates are placed on the left and right of the electron gun. Vertical motion is controlled by linearly increasing voltage applied to the vertical deflection plates, which are placed above and below the gun. The horizontal and vertical sweeps keep taking place, though the vertical sweeps are much slower. After about 400 vertical and 1000 horizontal sweeps, the voltage on the deflection plates are quickly reversed to put the beam on the upper left-hand corner. The screen is repainted about 30 to 60 times per second.

Dots are produced on the screen using a grid inside the CRT. A positive voltage accelerates the electrons which hit the screen and make it glow for a short time. When negative voltage is applied, the electrons are repelled, and they do not pass through the grid, thus the screen does not glow. In this way, the voltage applied to the grid causes the corresponding bit pattern to appear on the screen. Thus, the binary electrical signal is converted to visual display consisting of bright and dark spots.

7.5.1.2 Flat Screen Display

CRT tubes are very bulky and these days Flat Screen Displays have taken their place where instead of an electron gun, Liquid Crystal Display (LCD) technology is used. Flat panel displays include a growing number of technologies allowing video displays that are lighter and much thinner than traditional displays that use CRT, and are usually less than 4 inches (100 mm) thick. They can be divided into two general categories : Volatile or Static.

Volatile displays require constant power output to refresh the image on screen many times a second. The image appears steady because the images are refreshed more often than the human eye can perceive. The examples of volatile flat panel displays include Liquid Crystal Display (LCD) and Light Emitting Diode (LED) display.

Liquid crystals are organic molecules that flow like a vicious liquid, having a spatial structure like a crystal. When all the molecules are lined in the same direction, the optical properties of the crystal depend on the direction and polarization of incoming light. By changing the electric field, and hence the molecular alignment, the display of light can be changed.

The main components of Flat Screen Display are two parallel glass plates between which a liquid crystal is sealed, light source for illuminating the screen, and polarized light provided by Polaroid. Transparent electrodes are attached to both plates while a light illuminates the screen from behind. The electrodes are used to create an electric field in the liquid crystal. The image is displayed by providing different voltages to separate parts of the screen. The light is polarized by using polaroids and at the same time, the twisted crystal structure of the LCD molecules guide the light as it passes through it. While it is passing, it rotates the polarization which makes it come out horizontally. Thus, in the absence of electric field, the LCD screen is uniformly bright while when a voltage is applied to selected parts, the light passing through that part of the crystal is blocked.

Static flat panel displays use materials whose color states are bistable. This means that the image they hold requires no energy to maintain, but instead requires energy to change. This results in a much more energy efficient display, but with a tendency towards slow refresh rates which are undesirable in an interactive display.

7.5.2 Printers

Computers are normally attached to a printer to print the documents or pictures.

The characteristics on which printers can be classified are:

1. Printer image quality – Measured in dots per inch (dpi). Most printers produce 300 – 600 dpi.
2. Speed – Measured in pages per minute (ppm) or characters per second (cps).
3. Initial cost – Consumer printers cost less, but professional printers can be very expensive.
4. Cost of operation – This refers to the cost of supplies used by the printer.

Printer image quality refers to the output quality produced by the printer while speed refers to the printing speed of the printer. There are two main categories of printer technologies available: Impact printer and non-impact printer. Impact Printers have a mechanism that touches the paper in order to create an image. Non-impact Printers do not touch the paper when creating an image. Examples of an impact printer are the dot matrix printer, Daisy wheel printer and Line printer. Examples of Non-impact printers are Laser printers and Inkjet printers. The printers of these two types of technology are further of various kinds. These are illustrated below:

Impact Printers transfer the characters or images against the paper with the help of an inked ribbon and are specially used in environments where low-cost printing is necessary. The specifications of Impact Printers are print speed in cps (characters per second), resolution in dpi (dots per inch), printing width in inches and printing technology.

There are two main impact technologies:

Dot matrix printers use a series of small pins to strike a ribbon coated with ink, causing the ink to transfer to the paper at the point of impact.

Character printers are basically computerized typewriters. They have a ball or series of bars with actual characters, letters and numbers, printed on the surface. The appropriate character is struck against the ink ribbon, transferring the image of the character to the paper. Character printers are fast and abrupt for basic text, but cannot be used for graphics.

The various types of impact printers available are:

(i) Dot-matrix Printer
(ii) Daisy-wheel Printer
(iii) Line printer

7.5.2.1 Dot-matrix Printer

A dot matrix printer is a type of impact printer which has a print head. The main components of the dot-matrix printer are a cylinder coated with rubber and an electromagnetic driver. It prints characters when the print head runs back and forth on the page and strikes an inked ribbon against the paper. These printers are capable of creating carbon and carbonless copies. The pins are arranged in a matrix form which is an arrangement of pins in rows and columns. The speed limit varies from about 50 to over 500 cps.

The working of the dot-matrix is explained as follows:

The paper is pressed against a cylinder coated with rubber and is pulled forward when the printing progresses. The print head is electromagnetically driven to move across the paper and strikes the printer ribbon placed between the paper and print head pin. The impact of the print head on the printer ribbon creates ink dots on the paper. These dots form images or characters on the paper.

The dot-matrix printers have the advantages that they are flexible and can print both graphics and text in different typefaces, they are cheaper and maintenance is easier compared to laser or ink-jet printers. They are also capable of producing multiple copy forms by using a carbon paper. The disadvantages of dot-matrix printers are that are noisy in operation and cannot produce high-quality printing. Also, they have low graphics quality.

7.5.2.2 Daisy-wheel Printer

The daisy-wheel printer is a type of impact printer that has printing characters at the end of a needle on a metal wheel. The daisy-wheel printer has a rotating plastic or metal disk which consists of needles. A type character is available at the end of each needle. The disk is rotated by the printer until the desired letter is made to face the paper. Then a print hammer is made to strike the disk thereby forcing the required characters to strike an ink ribbon, leaving the character impression on the paper.

The advantages of daisy-wheel printers are that printing quality is relatively good. The biggest disadvantage is that graphics cannot be printed. Other disadvantages are that they are slow and capable of printing from 10 to about 75 cps, font size can be changed only if the daisy-wheel is changed and they are very noisy.

7.5.2.3 Line Printer

The line printer is a type of impact printer used to print multiple characters in the same line at one time. The multiple character set is arranged around a horizontally traveling chain. A line is printed by making the correct character pass in front of the paper. At the same moment, the hammer is made to strike the back of the paper. The paper is pressed forward against a ribbon. This makes the ribbon press against the character, thus leaving the character impression on the paper.

Various advantages of line printer are that they are faster in action and are less expensive compared to laser printers. They are used in a large number of business applications. These printers are the fastest impact printers, capable of printing 3000 lines per minute. The disadvantages of line printers are that they are noisy in operation, printing quality in the case of line printer is low and they cannot print graphics.

7.5.2.4 Inkjet Printer

Ink jet printers are non-impact printers. These printers generate an image or text by spraying tiny jets of heated ink on a piece of paper. They are also referred to as thermal inkjet printers, and are used for printing in commercial and industrial applications. The printer uses an electromagnetic field to guide the electrically charged stream of ink through a fine nozzle to create the necessary dots on the paper. A collection of these dots forms meaningful text and images.

The components of inkjet printers are Print head, Print head stepper motor, Belt, Paper tray/feeder, Stabilizer bar, Rollers, Power supply, Control circuitry and Interface port. Many of the contemporary ink jet printers use thermal technology, where the cartridge is surrounded by a series of tiny electrically-heated chambers. These chambers are constructed by using a technique called photolithography. A pulse of current is sent through the heating element to heat the ink. A bubble of air is produced as a result of the steam explosion in the chamber. This bubble pushes a drop of ink onto the surface of the paper. Surplus ink is sucked back from the printing surface when the bubble condenses. When the nozzle cools, ink is again drawn from the cartridge due to the vacuum created by ejected ink. The ink used in thermal ink jet printers is heat resistant. The printing speed of the printer depends on cooling and heating times of the nozzle.

Piezoelectric technology may be used for dropping ink by placing a piezoelectric crystal at the back of the ink reservoir. The method is that when an electric current is applied to the piezoelectric crystal, it bends and forces a drop of ink from the nozzle to fall on the surface of the paper. Minor fluctuations in the crystal result in higher nozzle density due to the small size of the droplets. As there is no need to heat the ink or cool it, the overall printing speed is increased. Also, since the inks are not subjected to high temperatures, inks with better absorption properties can be developed. Inkjet cartridges are either Black and White Cartridges or Color Cartridges.

The speed of inkjet printers are in the range of 2-4 pages per minute (ppm) and resolution 300-600 dots per inch (dpi), comparable to low-end laser printers.

Though the resolution of inkjet printers has greatly improved with the advanced technology, however, the resolution and quality of an ink jet printer cannot be compared to that of a laser printer. Ink jet printers are a cheap alternative to laser printers, especially for color printing.

The advantages of Inkjet Printers are that they operate more quietly compared to the earlier daisywheel and dot matrix printers. Ink jet printers are also less expensive compared to the high-end printers like laser.

The disadvantages of Inkjet Printers are that the operating cost of ink jet printers is more than that of laser printers because of consumables such as ink cartridges increases the operating cost of ink jet printers. Even the smallest drop of water results in severe blurring of the text. Ink bleeding is another common problem in inkjet printers, wherein the ink is scattered sideways due to the capillary effect.

7.5.2.5 Laser Printer

A laser printer works on the principle of static electricity which is created when an electrical charge is built using an insulated object. This happens because atoms that are opposite in charge attract each other, just as the opposites with respect to static electricity have a tendency to stick together.

The basic parts of a laser printer are a photoreceptor drum assembly, toner hopper, corona wire, fuser, developer roller, discharge lamp, and a laser scanning unit. Each part plays an important role in the printing process.

In this type of printer, a laser beam is used to produce an image on a photosensitive drum. The light of the laser alters the electrical charge on the drum wherever it hits. The exposed area of the drum becomes positively charged. The negatively charged powder is picked up and deposited on the paper. The paper is finally heated to fix the toner powder onto the paper. The drum is then rolled through a toner, which is picked up by the charged portions of the drum. Finally, the toner is transferred to the paper through a combination of heat and pressure. An entire page is transmitted to a drum before the toner is applied.

Laser printers are known for their high resolution, 'dots per inch' (dpi) they lay down. The available resolutions range from 300 dpi to 1,200 dpi. Some laser printers attain higher resolutions with special technique known generally as 'resolution enhancement'.

Laser printer may be the standard monochrome that uses a single toner. Color laser printers exist that use four toners to print in full color, and are about five to ten times as expensive as their monochrome counterpart.

These printers produce very high-quality print and are capable of printing an almost unlimited variety of fonts. Most laser printers come with a basic set of fonts, called internal or resident fonts, but additional fonts may be added. One method is using font cartridges. Advantage of font cartridges is that they do not use the memory of the printer. ROM boards on which fonts have been recorded are inserted in these font cartridges. The other method is having 'soft fonts'. The fonts can be copied from a disk to the RAM of the printer which is included in the RAM memory.

In addition to text, laser printers print very high quality graphics. However, a significant amount of memory in the printer is needed to print high-resolution graphics. To print a full-page graphic at 300 dpi, for example, at least 1 MB of printer RAM is needed. For a 600-dpi graphic, at least 4 MB RAM is required.

Another major advantage of laser printers is that they are non-impact printers, their operation does not involve much noise. They are also relatively fast, although not as fast as some dot-matrix printers. The speed of laser printers ranges from about 4 to 20 ppm. However, the disadvantage is they are more expensive.

The next section will explain different methods of exchanging data between memory and I/O devices.

7.6 I/O METHODOLOGY

Input-Output operations generally refer to the data transfer between I/O devices and the memory. Various methods of I/O are differentiated by the extent to which the CPU is involved in their execution. Some operations are completely controlled by the CPU while others execute programs that are initiated by the CPU. Some types of I/O require a little extra hardware. Various kinds of I/O methodology will be discussed in this section.

7.6.1 Programmed I/O

Programmed I/O is a method used in all computers for controlling

I/O operations. It is most useful in small, low-speed systems where the cost of hardware has to be kept minimum. In this method of I/O, all I/O operations are executed under the direct control of the CPU. The data transfer is generally between two programmable registers. The I/O device does not have a direct access to the main memory. A data transfer from an I/O device to main memory requires CPU to execute many I/O instructions.

In programmed I/O, the CPU, the memory and the I/O devices communicate through the system bus. The address lines that are used to select the memory locations can also be used to select the I/O devices which are connected to I/O ports that have addresses. The CPU does not make any difference between the addresses of memory locations and the addresses of I/O ports. Programmed I/O is further of two types: Memory mapped I/O and I/O Mapped I/O

Memory Mapped I/O

In Memory Mapped I/O, the same bus is used to address both memory and I/O devices. A part of the main memory addressable space is assigned to I/O ports. The instructions that are used for addressing the memory and for addressing the I/O ports are the same, except that in the former case, address of memory is referenced whereas in the latter case, address of an I/O port is referenced. The usual load and store instructions are used to transfer data words to or from the I/O ports and no special I/O instructions are needed. Figure 7.12 shows the memory structure for memory-mapped I/O. The control lines READ and WRITE are activated by the CPU while processing the memory instruction.

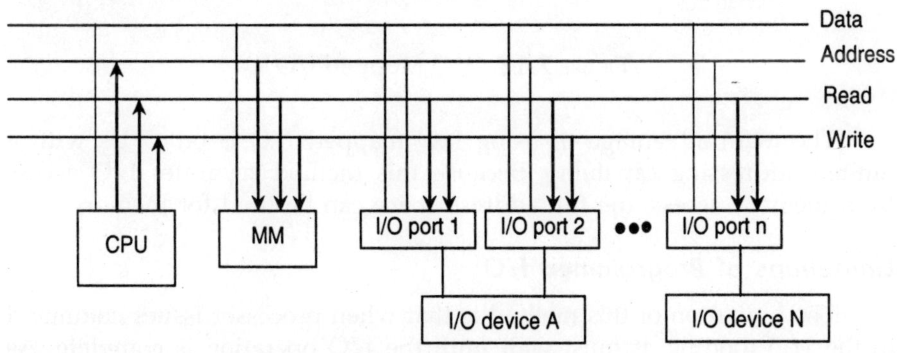

FIGURE 7.12 : Memory-Mapped I/O

I/O mapped I/O

In I/O mapped I/O, special CPU instructions are used for performing I/O. These instructions are IN and OUT instructions which can read and write a single byte to an I/O device. I/O devices have a separate address space from general memory, either provided by an extra I/O pin on the CPUs interface, or an entire bus is dedicated to I/O.

In the I/O mapped I/O, the addresses assigned to memory and I/O ports are separate. In other words, the address spaces of memory and I/O devices are different. The structure is shown in Figure 7.13. The Read M and Write M control lines are activated by memory referencing instruction which does not affect the I/O device. The CPU executes separate I/O instructions to activate Read I/O and Write I/O lines, which causes a word to be transferred between the addressed I/O port and the CPU.

Thus, just two I/O instructions are needed to implement I/O mapped I/O. The instruction IN causes a word to be transferred from the I/O port to one of the registers of the CPU. The instruction OUT transfers a word from a register of the CPU to the I/O port. When the CPU executes the instruction IN or OUT, the I/O port is expected to be ready to respond to the instruction.

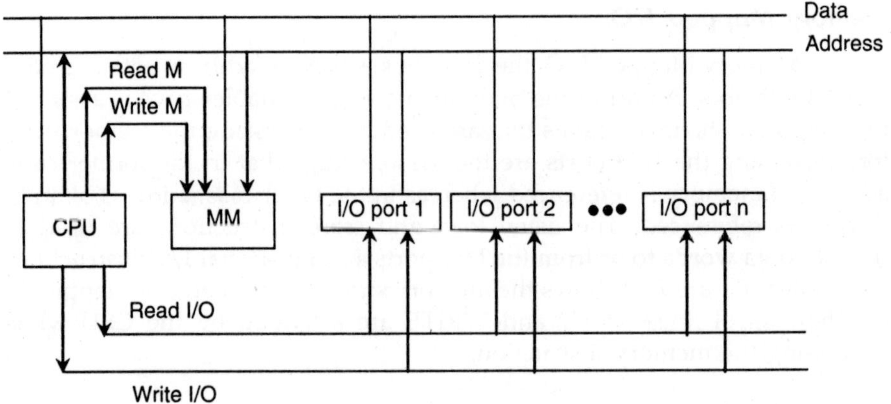

FIGURE 7.13 : I/O Mapped I/O

The main advantage of using I/O mapped I/O is on CPUs with a limited addressing capability. Because this method separates I/O access from memory access, the full address space can be used for memory.

Limitations of Programmed I/O

The limitation of this method is that when processor issues command to the I/O module, it must wait until the I/O operation is complete. As processor is faster than I/O module, lot of time is wasted. The CPU takes time to test and service the I/O device, which limits the speed of data transfer. Thus, the performance of the entire system is affected.

7.6.2 Interrupt Initiated I/O

Interrupts are provided to improve the efficiency of the processor as most external devices are much slower than the processor. Thus, whenever a device requests for I/O, the CPU may initiate an interrupt so that the already executing job can wait for the time till the I/O is completed. An example is the data being transferred by the processor to the printer.

In the methods of I/O discussed above, the processor had to wait for I/O module to start read/write of data. The wait state can be reduced if processor issues an I/O command to a module without introducing a wait state. This may be achieved by interrupting the processor to request service when it is ready to exchange data with the processor. The processor executes the data transfer and then resumes its normal processing. The interrupt signal is generated in case of exceptional events that cause CPU to transfer control temporarily from its current program to another program. This program is known as 'interrupt handler' that performs the program to the event that needs service. Interrupts can be internal or external. I/O interrupts are external interrupts where the CPU initiates or terminates an I/O request. Interrupts are also produced by hardware or software error detection.

The interrupt is provided to the program running in the CPU by activating a control line called 'Interrupt Request', which connects the interrupt source to the CPU. A register in the CPU stores the interrupt indicator that the CPU tests at regular intervals, usually at the end of every instruction cycle. When two or more interrupt requests are present at the same time, priorities must be assigned to the interrupts. The interrupt with the highest priority is selected for handling. If an interrupt is masked, the CPU ignores such interrupts. The techniques used for selection of an interrupt are polling, daisy chaining and independent requests.

Vectored Interrupts

'Vectored interrupt' is the kind of interrupt where the interrupting device supplies the CPU with the starting address or the 'interrupt vector' of the program. In this case, the implementation of the interrupt request

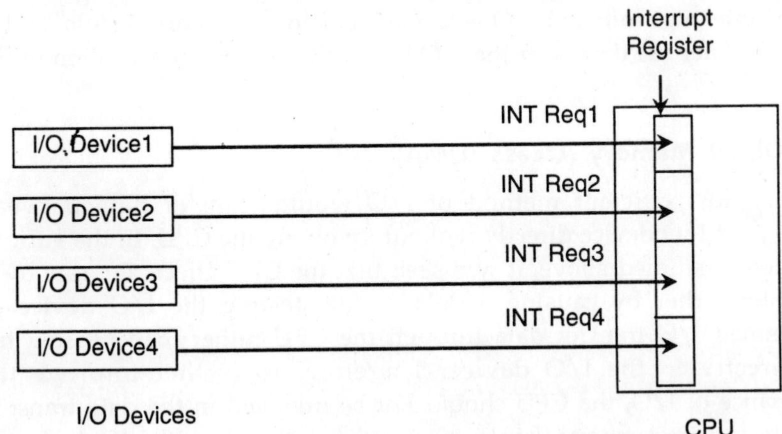

FIGURE 7.14 : Vectored Interrupt Architecture

from a particular device is through a direct hardware of the correct interrupt-handling program. When multiple requests for interrupts are received, each interrupt line generates a unique fixed request. Interrupt requests are received in an interrupt register. These interrupts might be given priorities. Figure 7.14 depicts a multiple-interrupt line organization using Vectored Interrupt. When an interrupt request from I/O port i is accepted then the address is generated from the priority encoder and used by the CPU. As soon as interrupt occurs, many events start both in the hardware and software. Device issues an interrupt signal to the processor which finishes execution of current instruction before responding to the interrupt. At the same time, processor sends an acknowledgement signal to the device that issued the interrupt, and the control is transferred to the interrupt routine after saving information of program status word. The program counter is pushed onto the stack and needed to resume the current program at the point of interrupt. After this, PC is loaded with the interrupt service routine

The process of interrupt initiated I/O is that the I/O module receives a Read command from the processor. Then read the data is in from the concerned peripheral device. This is input in the data register of the module and at the same time an interrupt signal is sent over the control line. The module then waits until the processor requests for the data. When the request is made, module places the data on the data bus, and then is ready for another I/O operation. Thus, for the input operation, the processor just has to issue a Read command. When the interrupt occurs, the status of all the registers is saved and the I/O is processed.

Interrupt I/O is more efficient than programmed I/O because it eliminates the time to wait. But the limitation here is that lot of processor time is wasted as all the data that is written or read from the I/O device or memory has to pass through the processor. A tradeoff between programmed I/O and Interrupt initiated I/O is termed as Direct Memory Access, and is used to transfer the data over the I/O bus with the least intervention of the CPU.

7.6.3 Direct Memory Access (DMA)

The most efficient method of I/O would transfer data between memory and I/O device directly without involving the CPU. In the various I/O schemes studied above, it was seen that the CPU affects the rate of I/O transfer either by causing a delay while testing the I/O device or Programmed I/O transfer data through the CPU rather than passing the data directly to the I/O device. Therefore, to further improve the performance of I/O, the CPU should not be involved in the data transfer; rather the system memory should communicate directly with I/O device. In the method of Direct Memory Access (DMA), transfer of data is directly from the peripheral device to or from memory, without the CPU being required to perform the transfer. Memory can be controlled without using the CPU by using a hardware circuit within a computer.

Principle

DMA allows I/O devices to transfer data without making the CPU to spend time waiting for permission for data transfer. Instead of copying each piece of data from source to destination, a DMA data transfer cycle copies a block of memory from one device to another. CPU only initiates the transfer, it does not execute the transfer itself. The transfer is performed by a hardware element called DMA controller, which is typically part of the motherboard.

The hardware needed to implement DMA is shown in Figure 7.15. The I/O device is connected to the system bus through an interface circuit known as 'DMA Controller'. The organization of DMA controller has special registers such as data buffer register DR, data address register AR and a data count register DC, which are used for the transfer of data over an adjacent memory area. Register AR is used to store the address of the next word to be transferred and is automatically incremented or decremented after each word transfer. The register DC stores the number of words that remain to be transferred and is automatically decremented. When it reaches zero, the transfer stops. The end of data transfer by DMA controller is

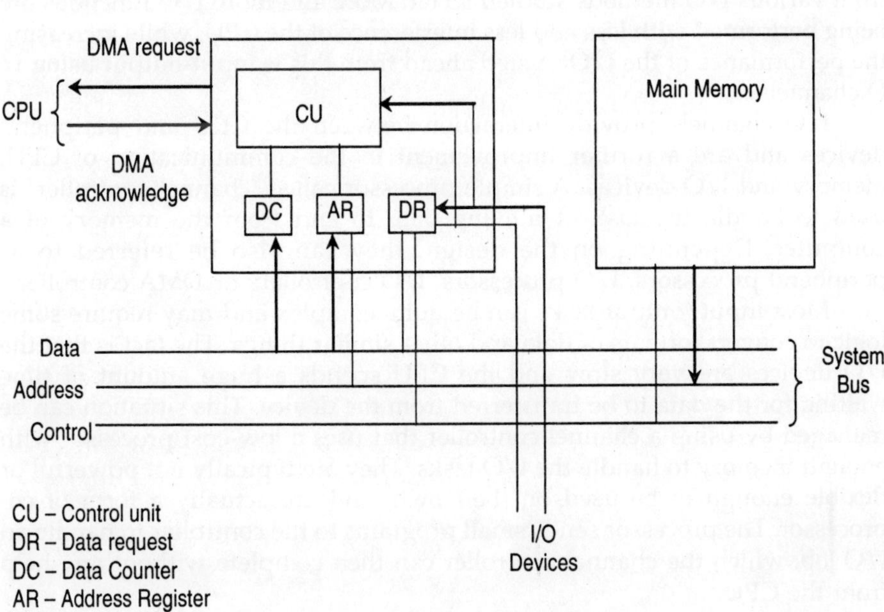

FIGURE 7.15 : DMA Controller

signified to the CPU by sending an interrupt signal. DMA process uses the bus when the processor does not need it, or it suspends operation temporarily. The latter technique is called 'cycle stealing'.

Examples of sub-systems using DMA transfer include disk drive controllers, graphic cards, network cards and sound cards.

Methods of DMA Data Transfer

Different methods are in use to move data under DMA transfer. The first method is of 'block transfer' that makes the DMA controller as the master of the memory bus. This method is generally used by secondary devices like disk drive where a sequence of words of arbitrary length is transferred in a single burst. This is the fastest mode of data transfer, but it can make the CPU inactive for some time.

The second method used is known as 'cycle-stealing', in which the DMA controller uses the system bus to transfer one word after each instruction cycle and the control is returned to the CPU. Cycle-stealing reduces the maximum data transfer rate, but it also reduces the intervention of the CPU in data transfer.

Another method is 'Transparent DMA' in which the interference of the CPU is completely eliminated. The DMA interface is designed so that the bus-cycles are stolen only when the CPU is not using the system bus.

7.6.4 I/O Channel

The functions of I/O are becoming increasingly difficult as is evident from various I/O methods studied so far. More and more I/O functions are being performed with less and less interference of the CPU, while increasing the performance of the I/O. A step ahead from this is input-output using I/O channels.

I/O channels provide interaction between the CPU and peripheral devices and are a further improvement in the communication of CPU, memory and I/O devices. A simple processor called 'channel controller' is used to handle the task of moving data to and from the memory of a computer. Depending on the design, they can also be referred to as peripheral processors, I/O processors, I/O controllers or DMA controllers.

Most input/output tasks can be quite complex and may require some logic to convert formats of data and other similar things. The fact is that the I/O devices are very slow and the CPU spends a huge amount of time waiting for the data to be transferred from the device. This situation can be managed by using a channel controller that uses a low-cost processor with enough memory to handle the I/O tasks. They are typically not powerful or flexible enough to be used on their own, and are actually a form of co-processor. The processor sends small programs to the controller to handle an I/O job, which the channel controller can then complete without any help from the CPU.

In the method of providing I/O through Communication Channels, buses carry both data and control information between the computer and the peripheral devices. This bus provides a path (channel) for the signal to travel. Signals for both monitoring and data are transmitted. Channels may be both input and output, thus providing either simplex or duplex communication. A simplex channel is only capable of communication in one direction. When a peripheral device, such as a mouse, is connected to a simplex circuit, it is only capable of transmitting data. Simplex circuits are seldom used because a return path is generally required for acknowledgement, control information, or error message. Duplex channels provide two paths for the transmission of data. One path is for sending, and the other one is for receiving data.

An I/O channel performs I/O by executing I/O instructions, thus having complete control over I/O operations. These instructions are stored in memory and are executed by special processors in the I/O channels. I/O controller does the entire transfer. The CPU time is used only to give instructions to initiate an I/O transfer which is performed by instructing the I/O channel to execute the program in the memory. The specifications about the device, the memory locations used for storage and actions to be taken under conditions of error are included in the program. In this way, the CPU instructs I/O controller to do transfer and I/O controller does the entire transfer.

The use of I/O channels improves speed as it takes load off the CPU. An example of I/O devices using I/O channels is 3D graphics cards.

Types of I/O Channels

Two types of I/O channels are available. The first kind is 'Selector Channel' that controls multiple high speed devices. The second kind is 'Multiplexer Channel' which handles I/O with multiple devices at the same time.

Figure 7.16 depicts the architecture of Selector I/O Channel. In this arrangement, various I/O devices are connected to the computer through a

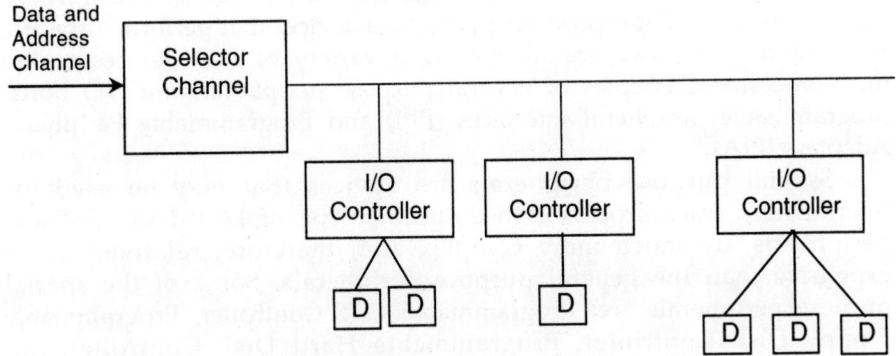

FIGURE 7.16 : I/O Channel Architecture: Selector Channel

number of I/O Controllers. A multiplexer channel is shown in Figure 7.17 that handles I/O with multiple I/O Controllers connected to the devices. The program that handles the I/O resides in the main memory.

Channels can execute a sequence of data-transfer instructions involving different regions of memory without involving the CPU.

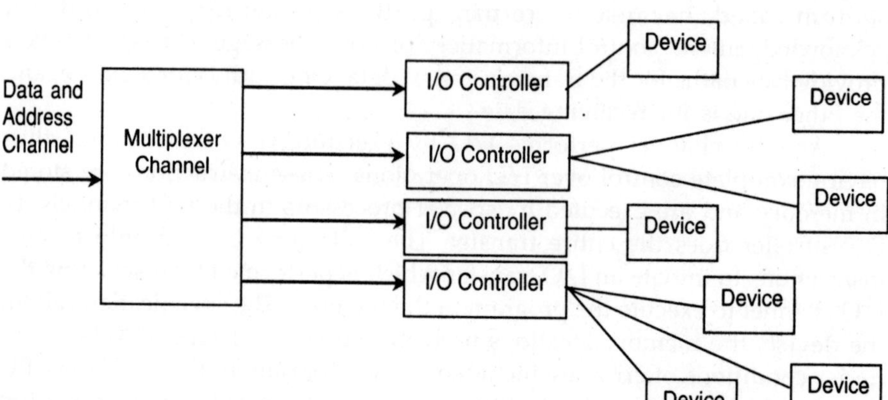

FIGURE 7.17 : I/O Channel Architecture: Multiplexer Channel

7.7 SERIAL/PARALLEL INTERFACES : 8251, 8255

The Input/Output unit of a computer needs to be interfaced with one ore more peripheral devices for the purpose of communication with the outside world. A large number of general and special purpose peripheral devices exist. They can be programmed to fit a variety of configurations.

Types of Interfacing Devices

The interfacing devices may be general purpose or special purpose peripherals. General purpose peripherals are devices that perform a specific task but may be used for interfacing a variety of I/O devices to the microprocessor. Examples of general purpose peripherals are I/O ports, programmable peripheral interfaces (PPI) and Programmable Peripheral Adapters (PIA).

Special purpose peripherals are devices that may be used for interfacing a microprocessor to a specific type of I/O devices. These peripherals are much more complex and, therefore, relatively more expensive than the general purpose peripherals. Some of the special purpose peripherals are: Programmable CRT Controller, Programmable Floppy Disk Controller, Programmable Hard Disk Controller and Programmable Keyboard and Display Interface.

7.7.1 Programmable Peripheral Interface (PPI):8255A

A programmable I/O port has the capability to be programmed using I/O instructions like IN and OUT. In general, a port may be programmed for simple input or output mode, strobed input or output mode, or a control mode. Programmable Peripheral Interface chips have one or more general purpose ports through which data or control signals can be transferred between the microprocessor and the peripheral devices. In this manner, an interfacing peripheral device is connected to the microprocessor for hardware design.

The 8255A Programmable Peripheral Interface (PPI) is a popular chip used for interfacing. The chip provides three 8-bit ports that can be programmed by the microprocessor to obtain a configuration which best suits the needs of interfacing. The characteristics of 8255A and the operating modes are described in the following sections:

Characteristics of 8255A

The 8255A PPI interfaces with the microprocessor on one side and with the peripheral devices on the other side. Figure 7.18 shows the signal diagram of the 8255A. The data is transferred between the microprocessor and the 8255A on the D_0–D_7 bus. The RD and WR signals are control signals that are used for indicating to the 8255A whether a read or a write operation is being performed. The 8255A chip is selected using the CS input before the microprocessor can read or write any data. When CS is high, the D_0–D_7 lines go in tri-state mode.

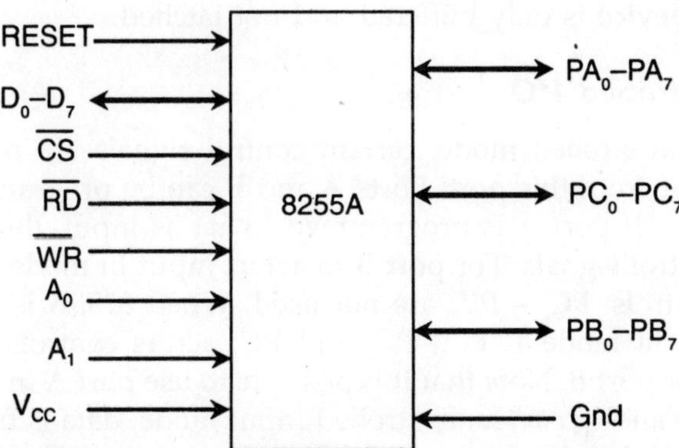

FIGURE 7.18 : PPI 8255A with its I/O Signals

The A_0 and A_1 inputs decide the port to or from which data is to be transferred. For peripheral data transfer, three 8-bit ports A, B and C are provided. For the purpose of programming the 8255A, these ports are grouped as follows:

Group A: port A and most significant 4 bits of port C (PC_4 – PC_7)
Group B: port B and least significant 4 bits of port C (PC_0 – PC_3)
Figure 7.19 lists the basic operations corresponding to A_0 and A_1 inputs.

A0	*A1*	*Read from*	*Write to*
0	0	Port A	Port A
0	1	Port B	Port B
1	0	Port C	Port C
1	1	Not allowed	8255A Control register

FIGURE 7.19 : Basic Operations of 8255A Ports

Operating Modes

The three ports A, B, and C can be programmed to operate in any one of the following three modes:

Mode 0: Basic I/O

In mode 0, the upper four bits of the three Ports A, B, C and lower four bits of port C can be used individually. While in this mode, data can be written or read from the port without any control signals. When a port acts as an output port in mode 0, any data written into the port is latched. However, if the port acts as an input, then the data written into it by the peripheral device is only buffered and not latched.

Mode 1: Strobed I/O

When in strobed mode, certain control signals are required for data transfer to or from this port. Ports A and B can be programmed to operate in this mode. If port A is programmed to act as input, then PC_3 – PC_5 are used as control signals. For port B to act as input in mode 1, PC_0 – PC_2 are used as controls. PC_6 – PC_7 are not used. When 8255A is programmed as output port in mode 1, PC_3, PC_6 and PC_7 act as controls for port A and PC_0 – PC_2 for port B. Note that it is possible to use port A in mode l and port B in mode 0 and *vice-versa*. In strobed input mode, data is transferred to the port by a peripheral device using the strobe signal (STB). In strobed output mode, the device uses the Output Buffer Full (OBF) signal that the write operation is complete.

Mode 2: Bidirectional Data Bus

Mode 2 is known as the 'strobed bidirectional bus input/output mode' and only port A can operate in this mode. PC_3–PC_7 serve as control signals for data transfer in this mode. The port A can be used for both receiving and transmitting data to a peripheral device. The device can strobe data into the port using the STB input.

Bit Set/Reset Pin

Using the bit set/reset pin, the microprocessor can send a command to the 8255A for setting/resetting any one of the 8 bits of port C.

7.7.2 Communication Interface: 8251 USART

Universal Synchronous Asynchronous Receiver Transmitter (USART) 8251 is used to provide data transmission in serial form. This device may be used to transmit or receive serial data in asynchronous or synchronous mode.

Figure 7.20 shows the schematic diagram of 8251. Several pins are provided for transmission and reception of data to be used under different conditions. Some control signals provided in the chip get activated from the CPU. The transmission of serial data is done on the TxD line that goes high after reset to indicate to the 8251 that the microprocessor is ready to accept a data byte. The data is received on the RxD line to make this line to go low on receiving data from the microprocessor. The RxRDY is normally low, but goes high after the 8251 has received serially from an input device. This indicates to the microprocessor that it may fetch the data byte from 8251.

The transmission on the TxD line starts after a data byte has been transferred to the 8251 by the microprocessor. At this time, CTS (clear to send) is low and the transmitter is enabled by a suitable command issued by the microprocessor. The pin TxC controls rate of data transmission. In case

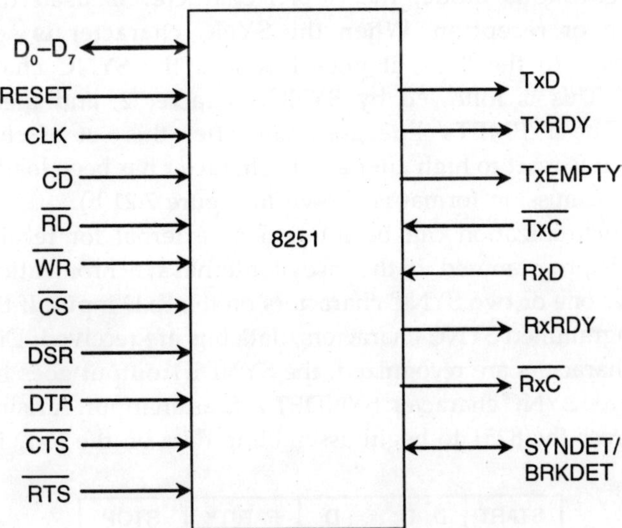

FIGURE 7.20 : Programmable Communication Interface: USART 8251

of synchronous transmission, the baud rate is equal to the clock frequency whereas if asynchronous mode is used, the baud rate is a fraction of the input frequency. Similarly, the rate at which a character is to be received is indicated by the frequency of the clock input to RxC. The baud rate can be at most 64K bits per second. After one byte of data has been transmitted, the TxD line goes high indicating that the transmitter buffer has been emptied. In SYNC mode, a high on TxD indicates that internally generated SYNC characters are either being or about to be transmitted.

Asynchronous Mode

In the asynchronous mode, start and stop bits are used at the beginning and end of data. The transmission format in asynchronous mode is shown in Figure 7.21(a). A start bit 0 is added by the 8251 to the data to be transmitted. This is followed by the 8 data bits. When no data is available, with the 8251 for transmission, the TxD output remains high unless programmed otherwise.

In the receive mode, the start bit is detected by RxD input by checking for a high to low transition and then strobing at the middle of the expected start bit. If found low, a valid start bit is assumed and the subsequent eight bits are treated as data, in which one bit is for parity and one or more stop bits. The stop bit signals the end of the incoming data. After this, the RxRDY line goes high.

Synchronous Mode

In synchronous mode, the SYNC character is used to start the transmission or reception. When the SYNC character is sent by the microprocessor to the 8251, it goes low and the SYNC character 1 is transmitted. This is followed by SYNC character 2, and then the data characters. The TxEMPTY line goes low after this set of characters is transmitted. It is reset to high after a data character has been loaded into the 8251. The transmission format is shown in Figure 7.21(b).

The synchronization can be internal or external for receiving serial data, which is programmed. In the case of internal synchronization, the 8251 first looks for one or two SYNC characters on the RxD input. If these match with the programmed SYNC characters, data bits are received. Directly after the SYNC characters are recognized, the SYNDET output goes high. In the case of external SYNC character, SYNDET acts as an input. A rising input on SYNDET forces the 8251 to begin assembling data on the RxD input.

START BIT	D_0 D_1 . . . D_n	PARITY BIT	STOP BIT

FIGURE 7.21(a) : Asynchronous Mode: Transmit/ Receive Format

SYNC CHAR1	SYNC CHAR2	D_0 D_1 . . . D_n

FIGURE 7.21(b) : Synchronous Mode: Transmit/ Receive Format

The baud rate can be at most 64K.

7.8 SUMMARY

To perform input or output of information from the computer, various functional units are used. The CPU, memory, and peripheral devices are connected by means of buses which provide physical links and the means of controlling signals over the bus. The bus width decides how much memory the CPU can address. I/O bus standards define connectors, signal amplitudes, and clock speeds. ISA, SCSI, USB and PCI are some widely used standards. Keyboard is the most widely used input device. Mouse made the entry of graphic data quite easy. A trackball is an upside-down mouse with a stationary base. Most joysticks are two-dimensional, having two axes of movement. Different types of sensors can detect which area of the screen has been touched as if the user had used a mouse. Touchscreen is both an input device and an output device. Speech input to computers involves the use of many different technologies and applications. Image scanner uses lights and sensors to scan the image and detect the patterns of light reflecting off the surface. Monitors are the commonly used output device. On the CRT monitor, dots are produced on the screen using a grid. Flat Screen Displays use Liquid Crystal Display (LCD) technology. The characteristics of a printer are printer image quality, speed, initial cost and cost of operation. Impact Printers like the dot matrix printer, daisy wheel printer and line printer touch the paper in order to create an image whereas non-impact printers such as laser printers and inkjet printers do not touch the paper when creating an image. Different methods of I/O are differentiated by the extent to which the CPU is involved in their execution. Some operations are completely controlled by the CPU while others execute programs that are initiated by the CPU. With interrupt driven I/O, the I/O module interrupts the processor to request service when it is ready to exchange data with the processor. DMA moves data from a peripheral device directly to or from memory, without the CPU being required to perform the transfer. I/O channels are an extension of DMA. Input/Output unit of a computer maybe interfaced with one ore more peripheral devices. Serial interface 8251 and Parallel interface 8255 can be programmed to fit a variety of configurations.

References

John, P. Hayes, Computer Architecture and Organization, Third Edition, McGraw-Hill, 1998.

M. Morris Mano, Computer System Architecture, Third Edition, Pearson Education (Singapore), 1993.

Patterson, D.A. and J.L. Hennessey, Computer Architecture: A Quantitative Approach, San Mateo, CA: Morgan Kaufmann Publishers, 1990.

Tanenbaum, Andrew S., Structured Computer Organization, 4th ed., Prentice-Hall of India, New Delhi, 2001.

Douglas, V. Half, Microprocessor and Interfacing: Programming and Hardware.

PROBLEMS

1. What is the purpose of Input-Output devices?
2. Give explanation of the use of computer bus to perform I/O.
3. How is the performance of bus architecture measured?
4. Explain the connection between I/O Bus and Interface modules.
5. Explain the problem of 'bus skew'.
6. Why are Bus Standards needed?
7. List internal computer buses with the width of data bus and the speed; external computer buses, their width, speed, cable length and number of devices that can be connected with them.
8. Compare SCSI with IDE.
9. What are the reasons for which USB has become a Universal Standard? Explain its architecture and data rates.
10. Are the following Input devices, Output devices or both? Printer, Mouse, Keyboard, Monitor, hard disk, trackball, CD-ROM, Joysticks, Touchscreen, sound cards, I/O buses, Scanner.
11. On pressing a key on the keyboard, a character is displayed on the screen. Explain the internal process of this action.
12. Describe the technologies and functioning of wireless mouse.
13. Explain the difference between a mouse, a trackball and a joystick.
14. Discuss construction and working of Computers CRT monitors.
15. Justify the use of Touchscreen as an input device and as an output device.
16. Illustrate the fundamentals of speech recognition.
17. How is natural language generation and speech synthesis merged to produce spoken responses?
18. Scanner detects analogue images. How does the computer recognize them?
19. What is Liquid Crystal? Explain their use as data input technology.
20. Name the performance parameters of printers.
21. List the advantages and disadvantages of various impact printers.
22. Explain the structure and working of: (i) Ink-Jet Printers, (ii) Laser Printers.
23. Discuss the working and construction of Laser Printer.
24. Write a detailed note on USB.
25. What is the main difference between various techniques of I/O?
26. Compare the use of CPU for Memory-Mapped I/O with that for I/O mapped I/O, and their limitations.
27. How is interrupt driven I/O more efficient than programmed I/O.
28. What is the difference between I/O program controlled transfer and DMA transfer? Discuss their principles.
29. Explain the working of a DMA controller.
30. Explain, with block diagram, the operation of I/O processor (POP). What is the difference between POP and data communication processor?

CHAPTER

8

Parallel Processing

8. INTRODUCTION

The general digital computers process the instructions sequentially. To improve the performance of these sequential computers, parallel processing is employed. Using this method, more than one instruction can be processed within one clock cycle. This chapter introduces the concept of parallel processing and pipelining. It presents different kinds of pipeline systems and processors. By using more than one processor, the approach of ordinary memory organization may cause problems. New memory organizations are presented to overcome these difficulties. Finally, the difference between control flow computers and data flow computers is discussed.

8.1 CONCEPTS OF PARALLEL PROCESSING

Computer performance can be increased by executing many instructions at the same time by the use of more than one processor simultaneously to execute a program. Ideally, parallel processing makes a program run faster because there are more processors running it. In practice, it is often difficult to divide a program in such a way that separate processors can execute different portions without interfering with each other. Most computers execute programs sequentially and have just one CPU, but some systems have several CPUs where more than one job can be executed at the same time. There are even computers with thousands of processors. Even with single-CPU computers, it is possible to perform parallel processing. It needs to be mentioned that parallel processing differs from computer networks and multiprocessing. The difference lies in sharing of the memory space. Parallel processing is also called parallel computing. Thus, parallel processing or concurrent processing is an efficient form of handling the computer information which utilizes the simultaneous processing of tasks.

8.2 PARALLELISM IN UNIPROCESSOR SYSTEMS

Parallelism in single processor or Uniprocessor systems can be achieved by processing more than one event in the same time period. The basic architecture of systems having a single processor, or the uniprocessor systems, has the same basic architecture. In this section, design of Uniprocessor architecture will be introduced, which will take into account the parallelism in the execution of instructions.

8.2.1 Basic Uniprocessor Architecture

A conventional uniprocessor computer System consists of three major components:

1. Central Processing Unit (CPU)
2. Main Memory
3. Input-Output System

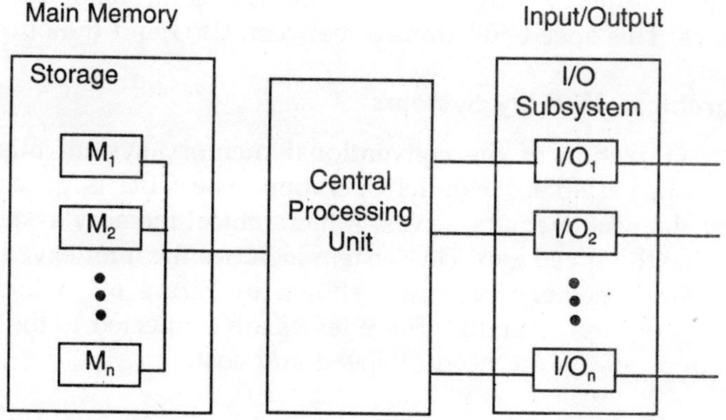

FIGURE 8.1 : System Architecture for a Uniprocessor System

In the architecture of a uniprocessor system as shown in Figure 8.1, the major components are the CPU, main memory and the I/O subsystem. CPU is the master controller of the system and contains the instruction decoding and execution units. It also contains the cache. The main memory is divided into different storage units which are connected to each other like leaves of a book (interleaved). The storage unit provides connections with the CPU Peripherals are connected to the system by using high speed I/O devices.

Parallelism in a uniprocessor system can be provided by hardware or software.

8.2.2 Parallelism through Hardware

(i) Multiple Functional Units

The ALU of a system has to perform many functions. These functions can be distributed in many ALUs, which operate in parallel. An example of multiple functional units is when parallel execution units are provided in the CPU, one for fixed-point arithmetic and the other for floating point arithmetic.

(ii) Parallelism within the CPU

Various phases of instruction execution, i.e. fetch-decode-execute and storage of the results are pipelined to increase the speed of the resultant execution. These various events have an overlapped execution, which means that the next event in the pipeline begins before the event in the previous stage of the pipe has ended.

(iii) Parallelism of CPU and I/O Operations

I/O operations can also be performed simultaneously with the execution within the CPU by using separate I/O controllers, like DMA, or I/O channels. This speeds up transfer between CPU and the output units.

(iv) Hierarchical Memory Systems

The organization of the conventional memory system might cause difficulties when used for parallel operation. The CPU is generally 1000 times faster than the memory access. A hierarchical memory system can be used to bridge the speed gap. This system includes the interleaved memory. The hierarchical memory system is shown in Figure 6.1, which depicts various kinds of memory units. These levels are connected to the CPU, but the access depends on the need of speed and cost.

(v) Bandwidth Balance

Bandwidth of a system is the number of operations performed per unit time. The CPU is the fastest unit in a computer. The processor cycle time is tens of nanoseconds, the cycle time of main memory is hundreds of nanoseconds, while the I/O devices have the slowest cycle time of a few milliseconds. Considering the cycle time, the number of operations performed per unit time by the devices, memory units and the processors are correlated as in the case of cycle time. The main memory has the highest bandwidth as it must be updated by both the CPU and I/O devices. The speed gap between CPU and main memory can be closed by using a cache memory. The speed gap between the slow I/O devices and fast memory can be bridged with the I/O channels.

8.2.3 Parallelism through Software

In a uniprocessor system, many resources can be shared among various user programs. Time sharing and multiprogramming are software techniques to achieve concurrency in uniprocessors. In multiprogramming, there may be multiple programs active in a computer within the same time interval. These programs will be competing for memory, I/O and CPU resources. The total execution time is reduced. Multiprogramming means sharing of CPU by many programs. On the other hand, time sharing of the CPU allows many programs to share the time of the CPU. This is also a method to make the overall execution of the programs faster.

8.3 PARALLELISM TYPES

Various type of parallelism is used for increasing the execution speed of programs. They are explained below:

Pipelining

Parallelism can be achieved by dividing the task to be performed in various stages, instead of executing the process as a whole in a single stage. The input task is subdivided into series of subtasks and a cascade of these stages form a pipeline. Each of these subtasks is executed at the same time by specialized hardware with other stages in the pipeline. A pipeline processor having n stages is shown in Figure 8.2. All the stages are connected to same control unit. The pipelining is at the subtask level. Ideally all stages should have equal processing speed otherwise the speed is restricted by the slowest stage. For the improvement of performance, proper subdivision of input tasks in a correct sequence of subtasks is essential. The improvement in efficiency of the pipeline depends on efficiency and capability of stages, the desired processing speed and cost-effectiveness.

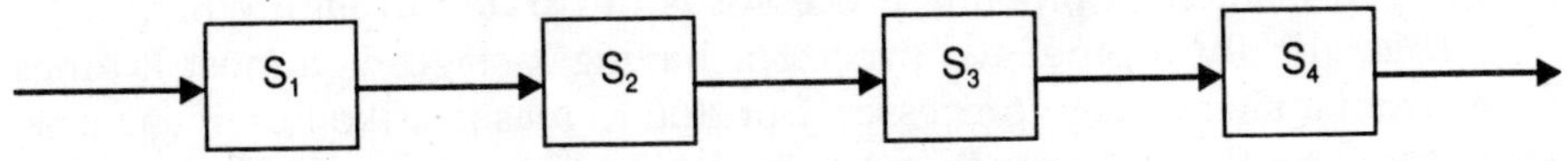

FIGURE 8.2 : Pipelined computer

Different kinds of pipelining can be categorized as follows:

1. Instruction Pipelining

The execution of a stream of instructions with fetch, decode and operand fetch stages can be pipelined by overlapping the execution of the current instruction with the subsequent instruction. The operation of the next stage begins before the current instruction is being executed. Almost all high performance computers have the instruction execution pipelining.

2. *Processor Pipelining*

In this method of pipelining, the time required to fetch data from memory is reduced by fetching the data in the best possible manner. Processors that use the same data stream are pipelined by a cascade of processors each of which processes a specific task. The data stream passes the first processor. The second processor then passes the refined result to the third and so on. But this method is not common in practice.

3. *Arithmetic Pipelining*

Arithmetic operations can be decomposed into sequence of suboperations which take about the same execution time.

8.4 PARALLEL COMPUTER STRUCTURES

Parallel computers are those systems that use different techniques of parallel processing. They are divided in three architectural classes:

- Pipeline Computers
- Array processors
- Multiprocessors System

8.4.1 Pipeline Computers

In a computer that does not use pipelining, the four steps of instruction execution, i.e. instruction fetch from the main memory; instruction decode for identifying the operation to be performed; operand fetch if needed in the execution; and then the execution of the decoded arithmetic logic operation, must be completed before the next instruction can be fetched. But in a computer that supports pipelining, successive instruction are executed in an overlapped fashion. A pipeline processor is illustrated in Figure 8.3.

Theoretically, a pipelined processor having k-stages is almost k times faster from a single stage processor. But due to reasons like nonlinear time spent for execution of instructions, this ideal speedup may not be achieved. Pipeline computers are more suitable for vector processing where the same operations maybe repeated many times. Figure 8.5 shows a typical pipeline computer having 4 processor stages. This pipeline is used in improving the execution time of instructions by having different stages of processors for instruction fetch (IF), instruction decode (ID), operand fetch (OF) and execution (EX) of instruction. These stages maybe overlapped, which means that while the current instruction is being executed in the stage EX, the operand of the next instruction is being fetched in the stage OF, while at the same time—instruction next to current instruction is being decoded in stage ID, and the instruction next to that is being fetched in stage IF.

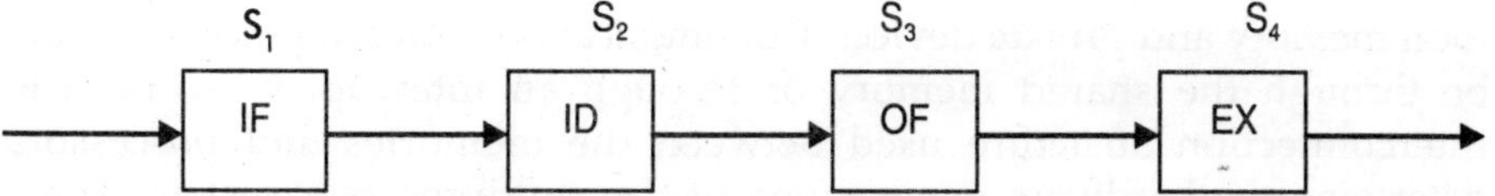

FIGURE 8.3 : Pipelined Computer

8.4.2 Array Computers

An array processor is a synchronous parallel computer having multiple processing elements (PEs). These PEs are multiple arithmetic units that operate in parallel by having many ALUs and are synchronized to perform the same function simultaneously. A typical Array Processor is shown in Figure 8.4. The control unit executes the timing and control instructions. Each PE consists of an ALU with register and a local memory. The PEs are interconnected by an interconnection network, which establishes connection between those PEs which have to do simultaneous execution under the instructions of the program in the control unit. Instruction fetch and decode is done by the control unit. The PEs are passive devices without instruction opcode capabilities.

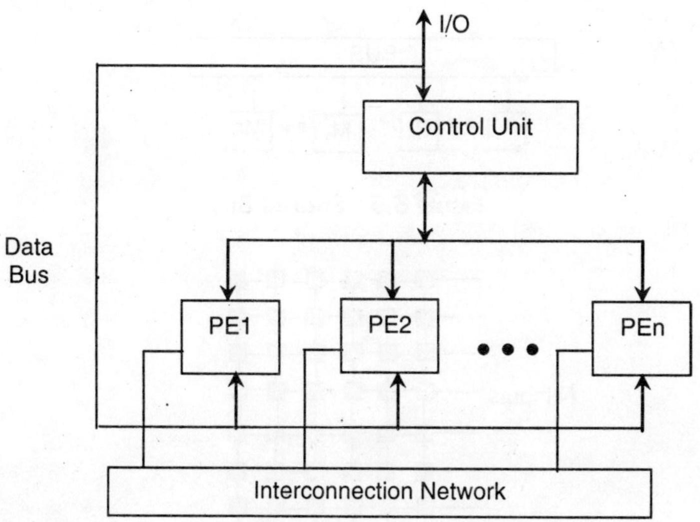

FIGURE 8.4 : Array Processor

8.4.3 Multiprocessor Systems

A multiprocessor system consists of two or more processors of approximately similar capabilities. All the processors share the common memory, I/O devices and peripheral devices. The control of the entire multiprocessor system is by a single operating system which provides interaction between processor and their program at various levels. Beside the shared memories and I/O devices, each processor may have its own local memory and private devices. Communication between processors may be through the shared memory or through an interrupt network. The interconnection structure used between the memories and processors determine the hardware organization of the multiprocessor system. Three different interconnection techniques, namely time shared common bus, crossbar switch and multistage interconnection networks may be used. They are explained below:

Time Shared Common Bus: Each processor and memory module is connected to a common bus as is shown in Figure 8.5.

Crossbar Switch Network: It is a switching network with N inputs and M outputs, where N may be equal to M. Processors and memory modules are connected at the cross-points of the crossbar network with N inputs and M outputs is shown in Figure 8.6.

Multistage Interconnection Network (MIN): This network has different stages between the input and output where processors and memory modules are connected. The organization of the network is such that every input is connected to every output by providing interconnection between different stages. A typical MIN is as shown in Figure 8.7. Different methods to provide concurrency are used to improve the performance of multiprocessors.

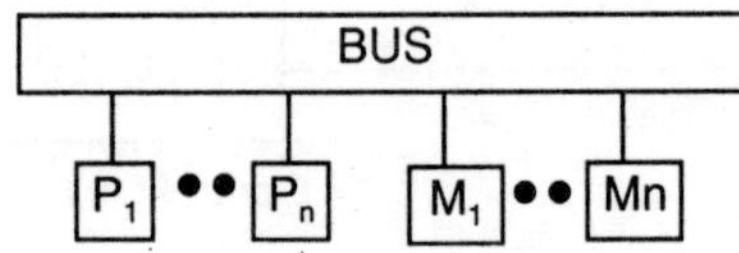

FIGURE 8.5 : Shared Bus

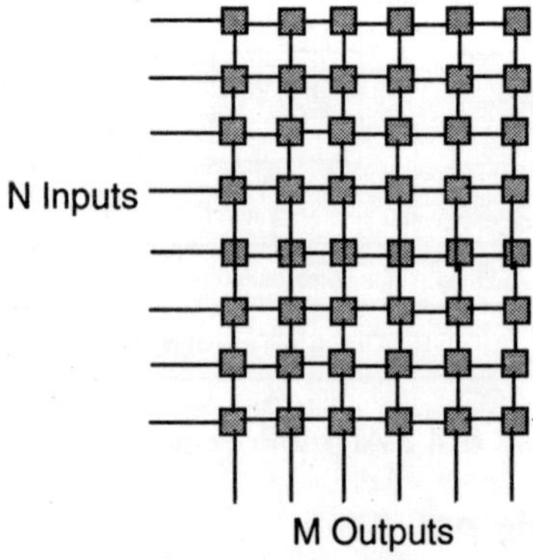

FIGURE 8.6 : N × M Crossbar Network with N inputs, M outputs

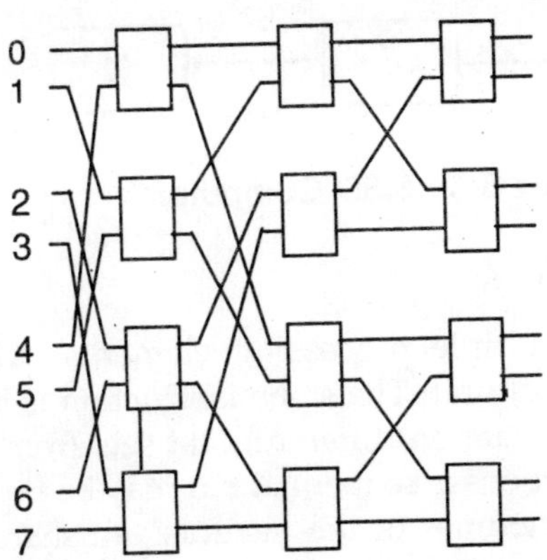

FIGURE 8.7 : 8x8 Multistage Interconnection Network

8.5 FLYNN'S CLASSIFICATION OF COMPUTER ORGANIZATION

In a general digital computer, implementation of an instruction involves fetching the instruction from main memory, executing the instruction and placing the results in memory. The instructions form an instruction stream where a continuous flow of instructions from the memory to the processor are issued to execute a whole program. Similarly, data is used for the execution of a range of instructions and they form a data stream. Thus, the instructions and data streams are being used in a range of instructions and data, which may be used for processor level parallelism.

Flynn's classification is based on the parallelism that might exist because of multiple instructions and multiple data available for processing. The characteristics of this classification are the multiplicity of the hardware provided to execute the instruction and data stream. Based on this, computers may be classified into four categories:

1. Single Instruction stream — Single Data stream (SISD)
2. Single Instruction stream — Multiple Data stream (SIMD)
3. Multiple Instruction stream — Single Data stream (MISD)
4. Multiple Instruction stream — Multiple Data stream (MIMD)

These classes are explained below:

8.5.1 SISD Organization

This organization represents a serial computer. A pipelined computer comprising of various processing elements in a pipeline, functioning under one control unit, constitutes a SISD machine. A general SISD machine with control unit CU, Processing element P and memory unit M is illustrated in Figure 8.8. The execution of sequential instructions but may be overlapped.

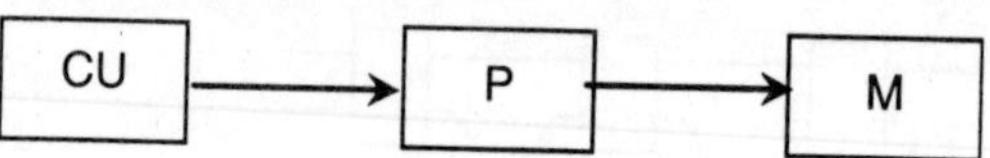

FIGURE 8.8 : SISD Computer

8.5.2 SIMD Organization

SIMD Machine has multiple processing elements. All the PEs are controlled by the same control unit. The same instruction is broadcast from the control unit but they operate on different data sets from different data streams. Execution of instructions is sequential but may be pipelined in their execution stages. Different modules of the memory are shared.

Array Processor, described in Section 8.4.2 is a SIMD machine where a single control unit is used to manage many processors. The PEs can be as simple as 1-bit ALU used for status bits, or can be as complex as for 32-bit addition.

8.5.3 MISD Organization

These machines have multiple processor units, each receiving different instructions operating over the same data stream. Thus, there is parallelism in instructions. But this organization seems infeasible and is not used.

8.5.4 MIMD Organization

MIMD computer are basically N different processors, each controlled by its own respective control unit and private memory. They also share all memory streams that are derived from the same data space shared by all processors and have the same operating system. Most multiprocessors system and multiple computer system can be classified in this category Figures 8.5, 8.6 and 8.7 represents three typical MIMD machines.

8.6 PIPELINE PROCESSORS

Pipeline in the processors may have various characteristics. Different pipelines are classified as under:

8.6.1 Unifunction *vs.* Multifunction Pipeline

Pipelines may be designed to perform a single function or the design may allow different functions to be performed by the same pipeline. Unifunctional pipeline is a pipeline unit which has a fixed and dedicated function, such as floating point adder. A multifunction pipeline may perform different functions either at different times or at the same time.

8.6.2 Static vs. Dynamic Pipeline

The function being executed by the pipeline may or may not change with time of execution. Accordingly, pipelines may have static structure or a dynamic structure. Static pipeline has instructions of the same type executing continuously. The functional design of static pipeline does not change with time. Static pipeline can be either unifunctional or multifunctional.

The design of dynamic pipeline allows many functional configurations to exist simultaneously. Thus, the dynamic pipeline must be multifunctional.

8.6.3 Scalar *vs.* Vector Pipeline

A scalar pipeline is designed for processing a sequence of scalar operands, generally under the control 'DO' loop. The instructions of the DO loop are often prefetched into the instruction buffer and the required scalar operands for the repeated scalar instructions are moved into a data cache for supplying the operands continuously to the pipeline.

Vector pipelines are designed to handle vector instructions over vector operands. Computers having vector instruction are called vector processors. The handling of vector operands in vector pipeline is under the control of firmware and hardware, unlike the software control of scalar pipelines.

According to the levels of processing, the following categorization scheme for the pipeline processors exists:

8.7 LINEAR PROGRAMMING

For a perfect pipeline, all the stages should have equal processing speed. Otherwise, the slowest stage limits the speed of flow in the entire pipe. This problem is called the 'bottle neck' problem. Some stages in the pipe become idle because the result from the previous stage, which might be slower, has not been fully executed and available for the execution in the next stage. Therefore, the sub-division of the input tasks into a proper sequence of sub-tasks becomes an essential factor in determining the performance of the pipeline.

Ideally, all tasks should have equal processing times in all stages in a uniform-delay pipeline. However, in reality, the processing of tasks in different stages may occupy unequal times and, therefore, unequal delays. The optimal division of stages depends on a number of factors including efficiency and capability of the stages, and the desired processing speed.

Assume that the execution of a task T is sub-divided into k sub-tasks, $T_1, T_2, \ldots\ldots\ldots, T_k$ to form k stages of a pipeline.

$[T_1\ T_2, \ldots\ldots\ldots, T_k]$ for a give task T

The tasks have a precedence of execution, which implies that some task. T_j cannot start until some earlier task T_i $(i < j)$ finishes. These sub-tasks are interdependent.

Linear Pipeline

The processing of tasks in a linear pipeline is according in a series of subtasks with a priority. A basic pipeline is shown in Figure 8.9.

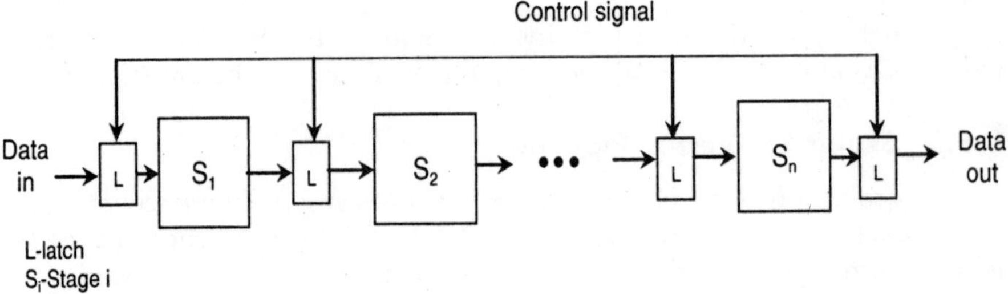

FIGURE 8.9 : Linear Pipeline Processor

The stages are combinational circuits performing arithmetic or logic operation over the data stream flowing through the pipe. The stages are separated by high speed interface latches that are fast registers for holding the intermediate results between the stages. Information that flows between adjacent stages is under the control of common clock applied to all the latches simultaneously. In the beginning, the stage S_1 will complete it's execution in one clock cycle. The results of S_1 are then passed to S_2, which begins its execution. At the end of second clock cycle, execution of both S_1 and S_2 gets completed. Thus, in the first round, the task T will be completed in k clock cycles. Once the pipe is filled up, it will output one result per clock period independent of the number of stages in the pipe. Ideally, a linear pipeline with k stages can process n tasks in $T_k = k + (n-1)$ clock periods, where k cycles are used to fill up the pipeline or to complete execution of the first task, and (n–1) cycles are needed to complete the remaining (n–1) tasks. The same number of tasks can be executed in a non-pipeline processor with an equivalent function in $T_1 = n.k$ time periods.

Speedup that a linear pipeline can achieve is k, where k is the number of stages in the pipe. But maximum speedup is difficult to realize because of many factors such as efficiency of the pipeline and its throughput.

8.8 RESERVATION TABLES

A pipeline with n stages was illustrated in Figure 8.7. Each stage is attached to a latch which acts as a prefetch buffer where data resides after stage i completes its execution and is ready to provide it to stage (i+1), but before stage (i+1) is ready to accept it. The output of the previous stage becomes the input of the next stage. The inputs and outputs of such pipelines are totally independent. This happens in case of a linear pipeline. But it is seen that in many cases, the input to a stage of the pipeline may depend on the outputs of the previous stages. For such a pipeline, the outputs of some stages are fed back as future inputs. These pipelines have a non-linear flow of data. The present state of the pipeline is determined by the outputs of the previous stages of the pipeline. The non-linear data flow depends on the timing of the feedback.

A two dimensional chart, known as the reservation table, is used to recognize how the successive pipeline stages are utilized or reserved for evaluating a specific function in successive pipeline cycles. A reservation table represents the flow of data through the pipeline for one complete evaluation of a given function and shows the state of each stage as a function of time. The rows of the reservation table correspond to pipeline stages and columns to clock time unit. The total number of clock units in the table is called the 'evaluation time' for the given function.

Consider the Instruction fetch pipeline of five stages depicted in Figure 8.10 where the instruction fetch, decode, operation load, execute and storage of the operands are pipelined.

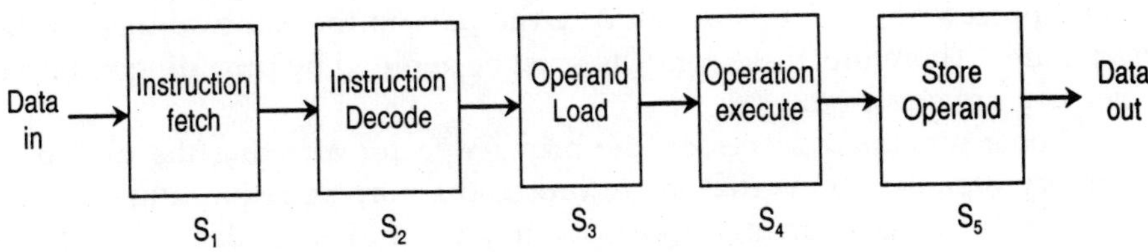

FIGURE 8.10 : Instruction Pipeline of 5 stages

The reservation table of instruction pipeline shown in Figure 8.11 depicts the operation of the pipeline as a function of time. During clock cycle 1, stage S_1 fetches the first instruction from the memory. During cycle 2, S_2 decodes the instruction 1 fetched. At the same time, stage S_1 fetches the

Time

Stage	T_1	T_2	T_3	T_4	T_5	T_6
S_1	1	2	3	4	5	6
S_2		1	2	3	4	5
S_3			1	2	3	4
S_4				1	2	3
S_5					1	2

FIGURE 8.11 : A Reservation table for the Instruction-Fetch Pipeline

instruction 2. During cycle 3, stage S_3 fetches the operands of instruction 1, stage S_2 decodes instruction 2 and stage S_1 fetches the third instruction. During cycle 4, stage S_4 executes the instruction 1, S_3 fetches the operands of instruction 2, S_2 decodes instruction 3, and S_1 fetches instruction 4. During cycle 5, S_5 stores the results of instruction 1, while S_4 executes instruction 2, S_3 loads operands of instruction 3, S_2 decodes instruction 4 and S_1 fetches instruction 5. The reservation table makes the time of events clear.

Thus, the reservation table shows the state of operation related to each stage as a function of time.

8.9 INTERLEAVED MEMORY ORGANIZATION

The ordinary memory organization studied earlier is used effectively for sequential processors. But if the same memory organization is used for pipeline processors, there will be lot of clashes in accessing the memory as many processors may try to read or write data to the same address at the same time. Therefore, these conflicts must be avoided by providing a special memory organization.

For a pipelined processor, the primary factor affecting the design of memory organization is that many processors may be requesting the data from one address, or many processors may want to write data at the same address. The need is that the same address should be accessed by many processors concurrently. Therefore, instead of reading just one data item from an address, multiple numbers of same data item have to be transferred at the same time. The memory design is characterized by the number of memory modules, their addressing structure and bus width. The characteristics of the modules are memory module size, access time and cycle time. The memory bandwidth must match the demand of the processors.

Interleaved memory organization, where memory modules are bound like the leaves of a book, is used to achieve the goals of high performance for pipelined processors. The analogy of this organization is like a book having leaves (pages), and the leaves having data written on them. These characteristics of modules allows the use of memory bandwidth without any conflicts. An example of the need for interleaved memory organization is a pipelined computer having four independent 32 bit floating-point arithmetic pipelines, requiring 32 bit operand and producing 32-bit results with clock cycle of 40 ns. Thus, one 32 bit instruction is fetched for each arithmetic operation. Therefore, demand rate of the four pipelines is to fetch 3×4×32 bits every 40 ns and store 4x32 bits result in the same time.

There are two methods commonly used to organize interleaved memory: S-access memory configuration, where the modules are accessed simultaneously, and C access memory configuration, in which the data is accessed concurrently. The former is explained below:

S-Access Memory Organization

The S in the S-access organization stands for 'simultaneous'. Here all modules are accessed simultaneously. This organization uses low-order interleaving. There are $M = 2^m$ memory modules. The addressing used to access every location is as follows: The higher (n-m) bits of the address are used to access all $M = 2^m$ memory modules simultaneously in one access. The single access returns M consecutive words of information from the M memory modules. Using the low-order m address bits, the information from a particular module can be accessed.

For a fetch operation, the information from each module is transferred to its latch, where the multiplexers are used to direct the desired data to the single-word bus. This design is illustrated in Figure 8.12. S-access configuration is ideal for accessing a vector of data elements or for prefetching a sequential instruction for a pipeline processor.

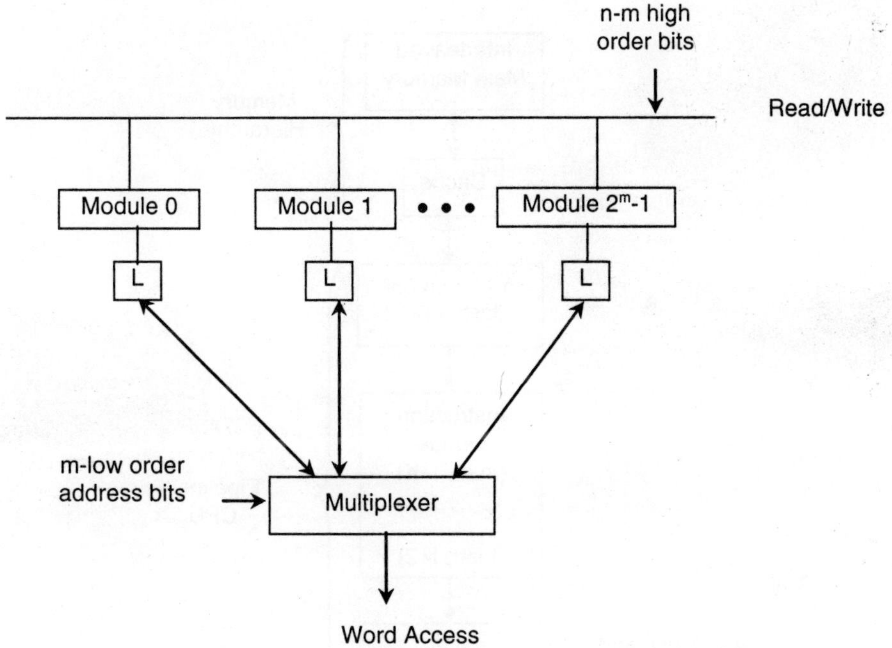

FIGURE 8.12 : S-Access Memory Organization

8.10 PIPELINING IN CPU DESIGN

The concept of pipelining is widely used to improve the performance of a CPU. The execution of an instruction in the Central Processing Unit (CPU) can be partitioned into three sections: The instruction unit, the instruction queue, and the execution unit. Programs and data reside in main memory, consisting of interleaved memory modules. Cache is used to bridge the gap between main memory and CPU. The main pipelined stages are explained in the following section:

1. Instruction Unit

Instruction Unit consists of pipeline stages for instruction fetch, instruction decode, operand address calculation and operand fetch.

2. Instruction Queue

This queue comprises of queue of decoded instructions and fetched operands. It is a first-in, first-out (FIFO) storage area.

3. Execution Unit

It contains multiple pipelines, each for the execution of an arithmetic function.

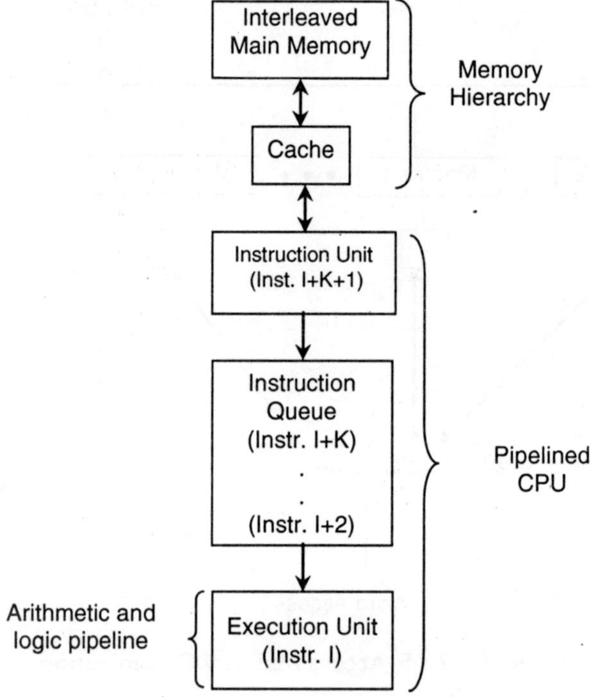

FIGURE 8.13 : Structure of Pipelined CPU

These three units are pipelined for the operation of the CPU. While the instruction unit is fetching the instruction I+K+1, the instruction queue holds instructions I+1, I+2, ..., I+K, and the execution unit executes instruction I. All the units of the linear pipelined CPU are in the process of instruction execution for the current instruction, and parts of instructions following the current instruction. Figure 8.13 shows the structure of the pipelined central processing unit.

8.11 MULTIPROCESSORS

The speed of computing has increased manifold by using many processors in a computer system. The tasks to be performed by a program are sub-divided and are processed by various processors instead of just one processor. This section provides familiarity with basic multiprocessor architectures.

8.11.1 Characteristics of Multiprocessors

Multiprocessors are MIMD machines which have two or more processors that work together on common processing jobs. The performance of the system is improved by having more than one processor, instead of just one processor. These multiple processors might share data paths, memory, I/O devices, program libraries, databases and common operating system. Multiprocessors are different from multicomputers and computer networks. Though the latter two have multiple CPUs, they operate independently using separate memory spaces.

Advantages of Multiprocessors

Multiprocessors improve performance and reliability of the computing system.

1. A large task is distributed among many small tasks performed in parallel among different CPUs.
2. Speed of computation is increased as n processors provide n times faster speed.
3. System cost is reduced by sharing a common memory by n processors.
4. Systems are scalable, which means that system size can be increased by adding processors.
5. Reliability of the system is increased. If one processor fails, it will not bring the system down. The function of the faulty CPU is taken over by a non-faulty CPU.
6. The system allows fault-tolerance.

8.11.2 Functional Structures of Multiprocessors

Multiprocessors are characterized by two attributes:

(i) Multiprocessor is a single computer that has multiple processors.
(ii) These processors communicate at different levels to solve a given problem.

Multiprocessors and multicomputers have the same goal of concurrent processing. The distinction is based on the level of resource sharing and support in problem-solving. The structure of multiprocessors are classified depending on the organization of their memory systems, which relates to their speed, how easily they can interact with each other, and the number of processors they contain. Three commonly used classifications are described below:

1. Shared Memory Systems or Tightly Coupled Systems.
2. Distributed Memory Systems or Loosely Coupled Systems.
3. Massively Parallel Processors.

8.11.3 Tightly Coupled Processors

In the tightly coupled systems, the processors, memory units and I/O devices are connected directly to the bus. These units time-share the bus for transfer of data from memory to processors, which means that only one pair of units can use the bus at a time. Such a memory is known as global memory and can be used by all processors.

Tightly Coupled Systems or Shared memory systems are simple and have low cost. The disadvantage of such an arrangement is that the single bus provides a restricted access for data transfer. The reason is that if two or more units request the use of the bus, contention or conflict in requests occurs, which leads to delay. This brings degradation in performance. Another problem that may occur is of synchronization when multiple requests to the bus are controlled by a semaphore. A shared memory system is shown in Figure 8.15 where a global memory unit and a global I/O unit are attached to the bus, along with various processors.

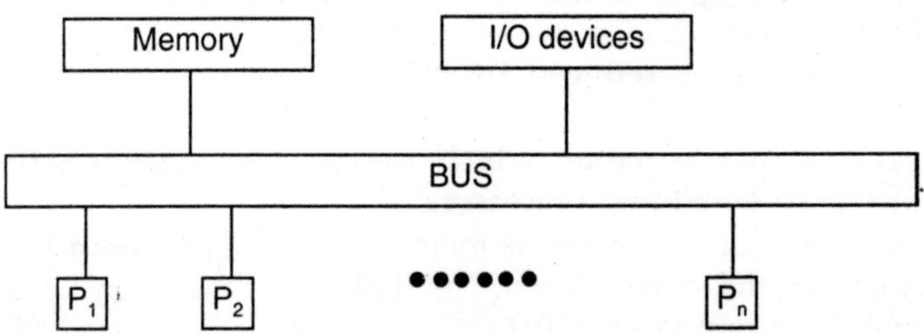

FIGURE 8.14 : Tightly Coupled System

8.11.4 Loosely Coupled Processors

Loosely Coupled or Message-Passing multiprocessor architectures have processors which transfer data by message-passing. The memory conflicts found in these systems is very less as compared to tightly coupled multiprocessors. Each processor has its own local memory and set of input-output devices. Thus, every processor has its own address space and a processor cannot read or write data contained in another processor's address space. This arrangement avoids contention problems of the shared memory system.

A processor, its local memory, and I/O devices constitute a 'computer module'. The communication between the modules is through exchanging messages. To send a message, a processor executes an explicit SEND (data, destination) operation that instructs the hardware to send the specified data to the destination processor. Figure 8.16 shows a computer module and Figure 8.17 shows a loosely coupled system. These computers have very high performance when interaction between tasks is less, but they provide problems in program design.

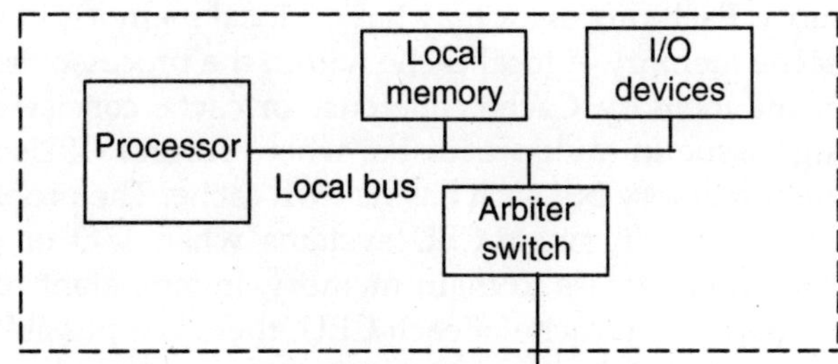

FIGURE 8.15 : A Computer Module (CM)

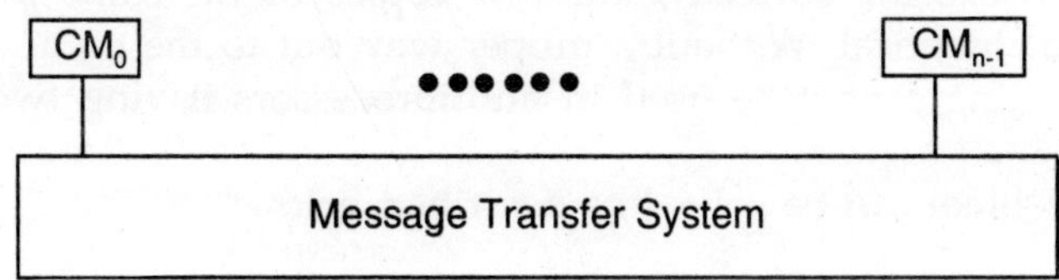

FIGURE 8.16 : Loosely Coupled System

8.11.5 Massively Parallel Machines

With the development of VLSI technology, the architecture of Massively Parallel Processors (MPP) has emerged, which have hundreds or thousands of processors that transfer data by message-passing. Various static and dynamic interconnection structures are present for MPP.

Static structures are hypercubes and trees that can control many processors. Meshes and hypercube structures are also frequently used for MPP. Figure 8.17 shows a 3×4 mesh where the processors are attached to the edges of the mesh.

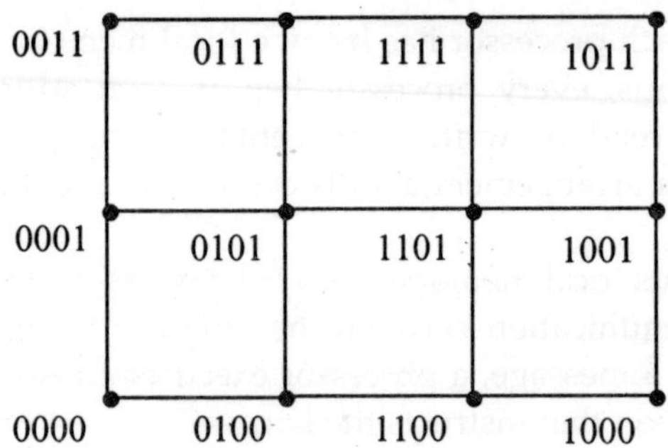

FIGURE 8.17 : A 3×4 Mesh

8.11.6 Cache Coherence Problems

In shared memory multiprocessor systems, all the processors share a common memory. Each processor may have a local memory, in which a part of it may be cache memory. A local cache within the processor saves average access time of the memory. Cache coherence or cache consistency problem is a basic design issue in multiprocessors where several CPUs share access to the same main memory but each has its own cache. The problem of cache consistency also arises in single-CPU systems when I/O or processor is present that has direct access to main memory, independent of the CPU.

With an independent cache of each CPU, there is a possibility that two or more caches may contain different version of the same data at the same time. This is called the cache-coherence problem. To illustrate this problem, consider a system having three processors A, B and C. For the memory operations to exeçute correctly, multiple copies of the same information must be kept identical. Without a proper way out to the cache coherence problem, caching cannot be used in multiprocessors having two or more processors.

This problem can be solved as described below:

(i) When there is a change in the data of module M_1, the data in module M_2 is revised in response to changes made in the corresponding data in another module M_1.

(ii) The problem can be reduced by having memory designs that contain caches that are associated with the main memory.

(iii) A software-based solution to achieve coherence is as follows: Use tag information during the program compilation as either to be stored in the cache (SC) or not stored in the cache (NSC). Thus, all items to be written in the cache are marked as NSC, which means that they can be accessed directly from the main memory only.

(iv) A hardware-based solution to maintain cache coherence is that a process will broadcast its write operations to all caches and the Global memory via the shared bus. Every cache controller then examines its cache. If the broadcast item is presently allocated to it, the cache block in question is either updated or marked as modified. Hardware-based solution provides higher speed and program transparency, but they are expensive.

Cache coherence problem can also be solved by a combination of software and hardware schemes. All caches attached to the bus constantly monitor the network for possible write operations and the cache controller updates or invalidates their own cache copies.

8.12 MULTISTAGE INTERCONNECTION NETWORK

Multistage Interconnection Networks (MINs) provide interconnection in a multiprocessor system through a number of switch stages, where each switch is a basic crossbar network (Figure 8.6). Though a crossbar network is deal for connecting processors and memory modules in a multiprocessor, its cost increases tremendously as the size of the network increases. MINs act as a cost-effective alternative.

8.12.1 2×2 Crossbar Switch

To understand the basic principle of the construction of multistage network, first have a look at the functioning of a 2x2 crossbar switch. Many stages of interconnected switches form a multistage SIMD network. These networks are described by three characteristic features:

(i) Switch box
(ii) Network topology
(iii) Control Structure

The switch box is an interchange device with two inputs and two outputs. The four states of the box are: straight, exchange, upper broadcast and lower broadcast. These states of a 2x2 switch are depicted in Figure 8.18.

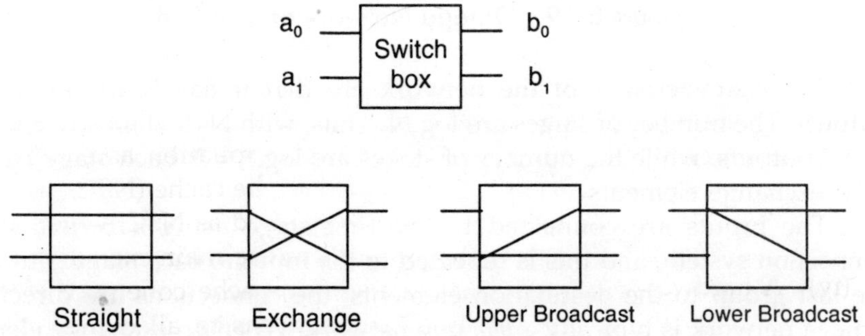

FIGURE 8.18 : Four Possible States of a 2×2 Switch

Many stages of these interconnected switches make a two sided multistage network that has an input side and an output side.

By using this switch to act as a demultiplexer, and constructing an ordered binary graph, a multistage network is constructed. Most of the MINs are usually constructed using 2×2 crossbar switches and have $n = \log_2 N$ stages, every stage consisting of N/2 switching elements (SEs). Total number of switches in the network is $N(\log_2 N)$ for NxN network, as compared to $O(N^2)$ for a crossbar network.

8.12.2 Omega Network

Figure 8.19 shows the layout of Omega network, which is a popular interconnection network used for interconnecting processors and memory modules in a multiprocessor environment. It is an indirect topology that relies on the Perfect Shuffle interconnection.

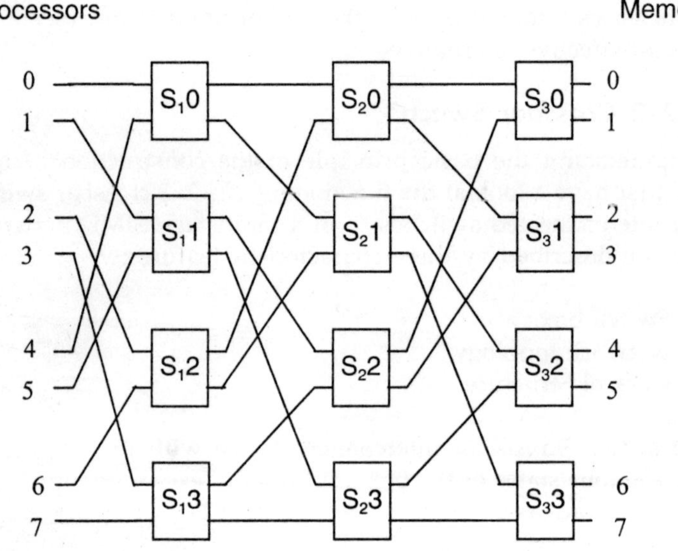

FIGURE 8.19 : Omega Network of Size 8×8

The characteristics of the network are that it has N inputs and N outputs. The number of stages are $\log_2 N$. Thus, with N=8, there are 8 inputs and 8 outputs, while the number of stages are $\log_2 8 = 3$. Each stage has N/2 (4) exchange elements.

The inputs are connected to the first stage using a *perfect shuffle* connection system, and this is repeated to the input to each stage. But from the last group to the destination elements, the connections are direct. An Omega network is typically a *blocking* network. When an exchange element is in use, the next message or data packet that needs this element must wait.

The 2×2 switches are named according to the stage they belong to. The switches in the three stages are named S_1, S_2, and S_3. Within each stage, there are three levels 0, 1, 2, 3. For example, for the interconnection of processor 2 with memory module 7, the connection is through switch $S_1$2 in first stage, $S_2$1 in second stage and $S_3$3 in the third stage. After this, it reaches memory module 7 directly.

8.13 SUMMARY

Instead of using sequential processing, modern day processors use parallel processing to increase by using multiple number of processors to improve the performance of the system. This chapter presents various methods that are being used for parallel processing. Parallelism can be achieved in a speed of computations uniprocessor system through hardware or software. Parallelism through software is achieved during processing of instructions. During execution of instructions, more than one processor may be used to perform different tasks. Multiplicity of data and instructions can be used to design new processor architectures to speedup the computations. Pipeline computers increase the execution speed by overlapping instruction execution. Array processors have multiple processing elements. The interconnection structure between memories and processors of the multiprocessor systems speeds up the processing. Different categories of pipeline processors are used to perform different functions. While using pipelining, the organization of the memory is interleaved to avoid any conflicts in accessing the operands. A reservation table shows the state of operation related to each stage as a function of time. Pipelining in the design of the CPU breaks the whole architecture in different stages to improve the performance. The continuous attempt these days is to improve the performance of computer systems. Multiprocessors increase the speed of computations by allocating different jobs of the same process to more than one processor. The characteristics and functions of processors have to be studied before considering them for the use as a multiprocessor. The sharing of memory is the key consideration for the use in tightly coupled, loosely coupled or a massively parallel computer. Various interconnection techniques such as common bus, multi-bus, crossbar switch, and multistage interconnection networks are used to interconnect various modules of the multiprocessor system. Cache Coherence is needed for proper memory operation of a multiprocessor system.

REFERENCES

Hwang, K. and F.A. Briggs, Computer Architecture and Parallel Processing, New York: McGraw-Hill, 1984.

John, P. Hayes, Computer Architecture and Organization, Third Edition, McGraw-Hill, 1998.

Gibson, G.A., Computer Systems: Concepts and Design, Englewood Cliffs, NJ: Prentice Hall, 1991.

Tanenbaum, Andrew S., Structured Computer Organization, 4th ed., Prentice-Hall of India, New Delhi, 2001.

PROBLEMS

1. What is Parallel Processing? How does parallel processing increase the speed of computation?
2. Explain the difference between Parallel Processing, Compute Networks, Multiprocessing.
3. How is parallelism achieved through software?
4. Compare the performance of parallel processing achieved by a uniprocessor and a multiprocessor in terms of speed and cost.
5. Make clear the design principles of Pipelined Processors.
6. Clarify with the help of a block diagram an example pipeline processor.
7. Give details of the difference between Pipelining and Parallel Processing.
8. Provide examples of various types of pipelining.
9. Define Parallel Computers in terms of hardware and name their different classes.
10. Give explanation of the kind of parallelism provided by pipeline computers, array processors, and multiprocessor systems.
11. Identify the role of different elements of Array Computers.
12. What kinds of memories exist in a multiprocessor system? Explain the different interconnection techniques between memories and processors?
13. Describe the bottleneck problem of a linear pipeline.
14. Is Flynn's classification based on parallelism in hardware or in software? Explain.
15. Compare the advantages and disadvantages of the two interleaved memory organization.
16. Explain the following terms associated with multiprocessors:
    (a) Loosely coupled multiprocessors
    (b) Tightly coupled multiprocessors
    (c) Crossbar switch
    (d) Time shared common bus
    (e) Multistage interconnection network.
17. What effect does Data Buffering and Busing structure have on the performance of a pipelined computer? Explain with an example.
18. What effect does Pre-fetch and branch handling have on the performance of a pipelined computer? Explain with an example.
19. If the final stage of an NxN Omega Network, with $n=\log_2 N$ stages, is deleted, it destroys its full-access property. Explain the reason.
20. Construct a diagram of 16x16 Omega network using 4x4 switches. Does this network have full-access capability?

APPENDIX A

NUMBER SYSTEMS AND CONVERSION

A. INTRODUCTION

It is simple for humans to understand decimal numbers but computers recognize binary digits only. The fractional numbers represented in the computers have a finite range only, whereas in real life, this range is not finite. Appendix A will discuss about these number systems and their conversions.

A.1 Binary Numbers

Decimal (base 10) numbers have a positional notation. Each digit is multiplied by an appropriate power of 10, depending on the position in the number.

Example A.1:

$853.48_{10} = 8 \times 10^2 + 5 \times 10^1 + 3 \times 10^0 + 4 \times 10^{-1} + 8 \times 10^{-2}$

Similarly, with binary (base 2), each digit is multiplied by the appropriate power of 2.

Example A.2:

$1011.11_2 = 1 \times 2^3 + 0 \times 2^2 + 1 \times 2^1 + 1 \times 2^0 + 1 \times 2^{-1} + 1 \times 2^{-2}$
$= 8 + 0 + 2 + 1 + ½ + ¼ = 11¾ = 11.75_{10}$

It may be noted that binary point separates the positive and negative of 2, just as the decimal point separates the positive and negative powers of 10 for decimal numbers.

A.2 Radix or Base

Any positive integer R (R>1) can be chosen as radix or base. If radix is R, then the digits used are: 0, 1, 2, …, (R-1)

Example A.3:

If R=8, then the digits used are 0, 1, 2, 3, 4, 5, 6, 7.

A.3 Conversion

Any number can be converted from one base to another.

Example A.4:

Conversion from base 8 to base 10.

$147.3_8 = 1 \times 8^2 + 4 \times 8^1 + 7 \times 8^0 + 3 \times 8^{-1}$
$= 64 + 32 + 7 + 3/8$
$= 103.375_{10}$

A.4 For Bases Greater than 10

More than 10 symbols are needed to represent the digits. In this case, letters are used to represent digits greater than 9.

Example A.5:
Base 16 (Hexadecimal):

Digits 0-9, A =10, B=11, C=12, D=13, E=14, F=15

Thus, $A2F_{16} = 10 \times 16^2 + 2 \times 16^1 + 15 \times 16^0$
$= 2560 + 32 + 15$
$= 2607_{10}$

A.5 Conversion of a Decimal Integer to Base R

The base R equivalent of a decimal integer N can be represented as:

$N = a_n R^n + a_{n-1} R^{n-1} + \dots + a_2 R^2 + a_1 R^1 + a_0$

Dividing N by R, the remainder is a_0

$N/R = a_n R^{n-1} + a_{n-1} R^{n-2} + \dots + a_2 R^1 + a_1 = Q_1$, remainder a_0

Divide the quotient Q_1 by R to get quotient Q_2 , remainder a_1
The process is continued until finally a_n is obtained. The remainder obtained at each division step is the desired digit and the least significant digit is obtained.

Example A.6: Convert 53_{10} to binary
$53/2 = 26$ rem $= 1 = a_0$
$26/2 = 13$ rem $= 0 = a_1$

$13/2 = 6$ rem $= 1 = a_2$
$6/2 = 3$ rem $= 0 = a_3$
$3/2 = 1$ rem $= 1 = a_4$
$1/2 = 0$ rem $= 1 = a_5$
$53_{10} = 110101_2$

A.6 Conversion of Fraction

A decimal fraction is converted to binary fraction by successive multiplication with R.

Example A.7:

Convert 0.625_{10} to binary
$F = .625$
$.625 \times 2 = 1.250 \; a_{-1} = 1$
$.250 \times 2 = 0.500 \; a_{-2} = 0$
$.500 \times 2 = 1.000 \; a_{-3} = 1$
$0.625 = 0.101_2$

If the process does not terminate, result is a repeating fraction.

A.7 Fixed Point Numbers

Integers are fixed point numbers which have an implied binary point at the right hand side.

Floating Point Representation

Fractions are represented as floating point numbers. The floating point number has two parts: mantissa and exponent. The mantissa represents the fixed point number. The exponent represents the position of the decimal point.

$N = f \times 10^e$

Here f is the fraction or mantissa, e is the exponent, which may be either positive or negative. The value of exponent represents the actual position of the decimal point.

Example A.8:

Decimal number 2004 may be represented as:

$2004 = 0.2004 \times 10^4$
Fraction = +0.2004
Exponent = +4

Example A.9:

Fraction 2256.117 may be represented as:
2256.117 = 0.2256117 × 10^4
Fraction = +0.2256117
Exponent = +04

Example A.10:

Fraction 0.000001 may be represented as:
0.000001 = 0.1 × 10^{-5}
Fraction = +0.1
Exponent = -5

The range is determined by the number of digits in the exponent and the precision is determined by the digits in the fraction or exponent. As there are more than one ways to represent a number, one form is usually chosen as a standard.

The numbers that have to be represented may be very large, like 6.0247 × 10^{23}, or very small, like 10^{-27}. Therefore, it is needed to have capacity for both very large integers and very small fractions. The decimal point is placed to the right of the first non-zero-digit known as the significant digit. The *scale factor* (10^{23}, 10^{-27} etc.) indicates the position of the decimal point with respect to significant digits. When the decimal point is placed to the right of the first non-zero significant digit, the number is said to be *normalized*.

Example A.11:

Decimal number 204 is normalized, but 0024 is not normalized.

No matter where the decimal point is assumed to be in the mantissa, the number is said to be normalized only if its leftmost digit is non-zero. An un-normalized number can be normalized by shifting its decimal position to the right. Thus, a floating point number is represented by its sign, a string of significant digits called the mantissa, and an exponent to the implied base for the scale factor.

The floating point numbers can be used to represent the real number system of mathematics. The numbers can be represented in a number line, shown in Figure A.1:

Different regions of the real number line are:

1. Negative overflow occurs for negative numbers less than $-(1-2^{-24}) \times 2^{128}$.
2. Negative underflow occurs for numbers greater than -0.5×2^{-127}.
3. Zero.
4. Positive underflow occurs for positive numbers less than 0.5×2^{-127}.

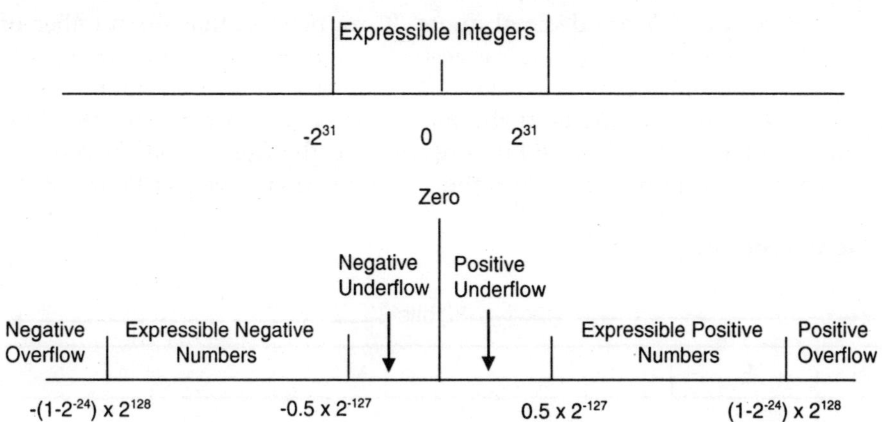

FIGURE A.1 : **Seven Regions of the Real Number Line**

5. Positive overflow occurs for positive numbers greater than $(1\text{-}2^{-24}) \times 2^{128}$.

Overflow occurs when the magnitude of an arithmetic operation is greater than what can be expressed by exponent of 128.

Example A.12:

$2^{100} \times 2^{120} = 2^{220}$. —— Overflow

Similarly underflow occurs when the fractional magnitude is too small to be expressed.

Example A.13:

$2^{-100} \times 2^{-120} = 2^{-220}$. —— Underflow

Underflow is less of a problem than overflow, because in the case of an underflow, the number can be approximated to zero.

A.8 IEEE Standard for Floating Point Numbers

Floating point numbers can be represented in many ways. IEEE has standardized this representation, which is explained in this section.

Floating point numbers in decimal system are represented as:

$\pm X_1 X_2 X_3 X_4 X_5 X_6 X_7 \times 10^{\pm Y1Y2}$

Here X and Y are decimal digits. It can be seen that the number of significant digits are 7 and the range of the exponent is ± 99. The binary range for these numbers is 32 bits, which is a standard computer word length. The 7 decimal digits of the mantissa occupy 24 bits, and the 2-bit mantissa occupies 8 bits. One bit is needed for the sign of the number.

The IEEE standard describes the representation, given in Figure A.2

Single Precision

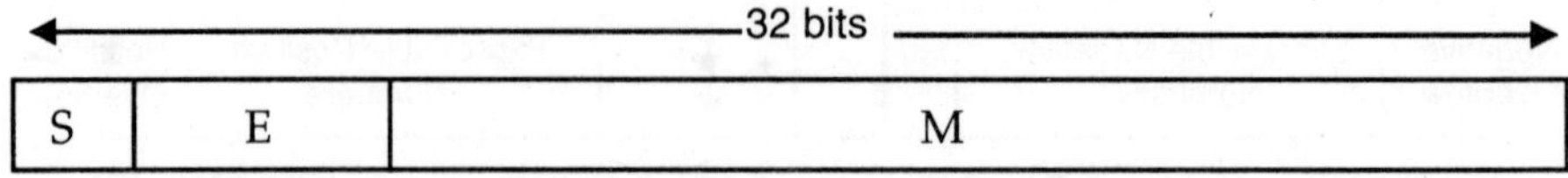

FIGURE A.2 : IEEE Single Precision Floating Point Format

S-Sign of numbers
E-8-bit signed exponent in excess 127 representation
M-23 bit mantissa
Value represented $\pm M \times 2^{E-127}$

Double Precision

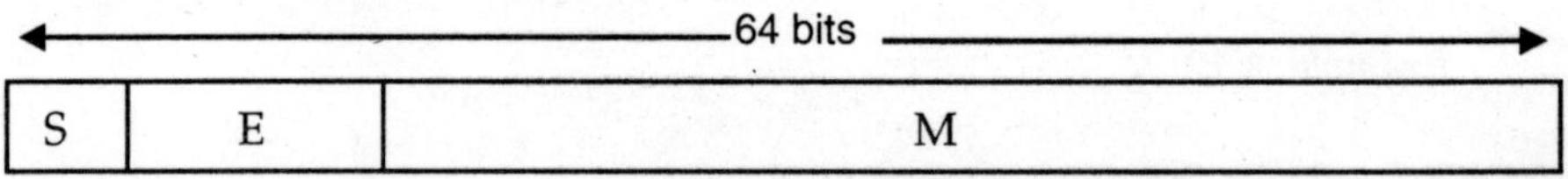

FIGURE A.3 : IEEE Double Precision Floating Point Format

S-Sign of numbers
E-11-bit signed exponent in excess 1023 representation
M-52 bit mantissa
Value represented $\pm M \times 2^{E-1023}$

A fraction with non-zero leftmost digit is called 'normalized' fraction.

Problems

1. Convert octal and then to binary
   (a) 757.25_{10}
   (b) 123.17_{10}
2. Convert octal and then to decimal
   (a) 10111011.1_2
   (b) 1101101.011_2
3. Convert to base 5: 45.75_7

APPENDIX B

CHARACTER CODES

B. INTRODUCTION

Digital computers can understand binary only whereas human beings can understand alphabets and numeric data easily. Character codes are rules to represent alphanumeric characters into binary numbers in the memory. This section will explain the need for character codes and the types of character codes generally used.

B.1 Need for Coding

Alphanumeric data and special characters are the form of data that is to be handled by a computer. An alphanumeric data is a string of symbols where a symbol may be one of the letters A, B, C, …, Z or one of the digits 0, 1, 2, …, 9 or a special character such as +, -, *,/…(), etc. But a computer treats every thing as a number. Even pictures and sounds are also numbers.

For example, consider the word "HERE". Each alphabet has its binary equivalent in a particular binary code, which is listed in Table A.1. Though HERE is just a string of characters for humans, but to a computer, it looks like the strings of ones and zeros as shown in the example below:

TABLE B.1
Binary Code for HERE

Alphabet	*Binary Equivalent*
H	0100 1000
E	0110 0101
R	0111 0010
E	0110 0101

Normally people use base 10 to represent numbers. In a computer, however, all data is represented in base 2 as the electronic switches used in the computer construction have just two possible states. These states are: on and off. On is represented as number 1 and off is represented as number 0 (or *vice versa*). Thus, computer can represent only two numeric values. Hence, programmers realized that they need a standard text code for two numbers. In this standard code, numbers represented the letters of the alphabet, punctuation marks, and other symbols. This standard code system would enable any program to use the same combinations of numbers to represent the same individual piece of data.

B.2 Types of Character Codes

There are various types of codes used by programmers depending on the memory needs and the accuracy of the data to be represented. Some of the representative codes are explained below:

- Binary Coded Decimal
- Extended EBCDIC
- ASCII
- Gray Code

B.2.1 Binary Coded Decimal (BCD) Code

The BCD Code is a weighted code where each digit in the code has a weight. The most commonly used BCD code is the 8-4-2-1 code. In the binary coded decimal (BCD) code, each decimal digit is converted into its binary equivalent rather than converting the entire decimal value into a pure binary form.

The decimal digits are from 0 to 9. Each digit is represented in binary form by using 4 digits. When 4 bits are used, then 16 configurations are possible. But only first 10 of these combinations are used to represent decimal digits. These 10 code words are the valid code words. If any other combination of digits appears in the code, then there is an error in representation. The remaining 6 arrangements (1010, 1011, 1100, 1101, 1110 and 1111) having decimal values from 10 to 15 are not used in BCD coding. That means 1010 does not represent 1010 in BCD. Instead decimal digit 10 is represented in eight digit code, first four digits for '1' and the next four digits for '0'. Thus decimal 10 is not represented as binary (1010), but as the code word (0001 0000) in BCD.

The Table B.2 lists the BCD code and its binary equivalent.

Example B.1:

Convert 4210 into BCD

4210 =0100 0010

whereas in pure binary form

4210=1010102

TABLE B.2
BCD Equivalents of Decimal Digits

Decimal Digits	*BCD Equivalent*
0	0000
1	0001
2	0010
3	0011
4	0100
5	0101
6	0110
7	0111
8	1000
9	1001

Advantages of BCD are that it is a simple code. But the disadvantage is that operations such as addition, subtraction, multiplication and division are difficult to implement.

Instead of using 4 bits with 16 possible characters, computer designers commonly use 6 bits to represent characters in BCD code. In the 6-bit BCD code, the four BCD numeric place positions are retained, but two additional Zone positions are added. With 6 bits, it is possible to represent 64 different characters. Hence coding of decimal digits (10), alphabetic letters (26), and other special characters (28) is possible with this representation.

TABLE B.3
Alphabetic Characters in BCD

Character	*BCD ZONE*	*Code Digit*	*Octal Equivalent*
A	11	0001	61
B	11	0010	62
C	11	0011	63
D	11	0100	64
E	11	0101	65
F	11	0110	66
G	11	0111	67
H	11	1000	70
I	11	1001	71
J	10	0001	41
K	10	0010	42

(Contd.)

L	10	0011	43
M	10	0100	44
N	10	0101	45
O	10	0110	46
P	10	0111	47
Q	10	1000	50
R	10	1001	51
S	01	0010	22
T	01	0011	23
U	01	0100	24
V	01	0101	25
W	01	0110	26
X	01	0111	27
Y	01	1000	30
Z	01	1001	31

TABLE B.4
Numeric Characters in BCD

Character	*BCD Zone*	*Code Digit*	*Octal equivalent*
1	00	0001	01
2	00	0010	02
3	00	0011	03
4	00	0100	04
5	00	0101	05
6	00	0110	06
7	00	0111	07
8	00	1000	10
9	00	1001	11
0	00	1010	12

Example B.2 :

BASE in BCD will be given as defined in the table:

B = 110010
A = 110001
S = 010010
E = 110101

Hence, BASE = 110010 110001 010010 110101

B.2.2 Extended Binary Coded Decimal Interchange Code (EBCDIC)

To overcome the problem of BCD coding, Extended Binary Coded Decimal Interchange Code (EBCDIC) was developed. In this code, the BCD code was extended from 6 bit code to 8 bit code. Thus, it is possible to represent 256 different characters instead of 64.

TABLE B.5
Alphabetic and Numeric Characters in EBCDIC

Character	*EBCDIC Zone*	*Code Digit*	*Hexadecimal Equivalent*
A	1100	0001	C1
B	1100	0010	C2
C	1100	0011	C3
D	1100	0100	C4
E	1100	0101	C5
F	1100	0110	C6
G	1100	0111	C7
H	1100	1000	C8
I	1100	1001	C9
J	1101	0001	D1
K	1101	0010	D2
L	1101	0011	D3
M	1101	0100	D4
N	1101	0101	D5
O	1101	0110	D6
P	1101	0111	D7
Q	1101	1000	D8
R	1101	1001	D9
S	1110	0010	E2
T	1110	0011	E3
U	1110	0100	E4
V	1110	0101	E5
W	1110	0110	E6
X	1110	0111	E7
Y	1110	1000	E8
Z	1110	1001	E9

B.2.3 ASCII

Another computer code that is very widely used is American Standard Code for Information Interchange (ASCII). This code is popular in data communications and its use is restricted to represent data internally in microcomputers.

ASCII-7 and ASCII-8

ASCII-7 is a 7 bit code that allows $128(2^7)$ different characters. The first 3 bits are used as zone bits and the last 4 bits indicate the digit.

Numeric characters in ASCII-7 are listed in Table B.6.

TABLE B.6
Numeric Characters in ASCII-7

Character	*ASCII-7 Zone*	*Code Digit*	*Hexadecimal equivalent*
0	011	0000	30
1	011	0001	31
2	011	0010	32
3	011	0011	33
4	011	0100	34
5	011	0101	35
6	011	0110	36
7	011	0111	37
8	011	1000	38
9	011	1001	39

TABLE B.7
Alphabetic Characters in ASCII-7

Character	*ASCII-7 Zone*	*Code Digit*	*Hexadecimal Equivalent*
A	100	0001	41
B	100	0010	42
C	100	0011	43
D	100	0100	44
E	100	0101	45
F	100	0110	46
G	100	1110	47
H	100	1000	48

(Contd.)

I	100	1001	49
J	100	1010	4A
K	100	1011	4B
L	100	1100	4C
M	100	1101	4D
N	100	1110	4E
O	100	1111	4F
P	101	0000	50
Q	101	0001	51
R	101	0010	52
S	101	0011	53
T	101	0100	54
U	101	0101	55
V	101	0110	56
W	101	0111	57
X	101	1000	58
Y	101	1001	59
Z	101	1010	5A

ASCII-8 is an extended version of ASCII-7. It is an 8-bit code that allows $256(2^8)$ different characters rather than 128. The additional bit is added to the zone bits.

Table B.8 exhibits the representation of numeric characters in ASCII-8 by showing the zone, code digit and the hexadecimal equivalent.

TABLE B.8
Numeric Characters in ASCII-8

Character	*ASCII-8 Zone*	*Code Digit*	*Hexadecimal equivalent*
0	0101	0000	50
1	0101	0001	51
2	0101	0010	52
3	0101	0011	53
4	0101	0100	54
5	0101	0101	55
6	0101	0110	56
7	0101	0111	57
8	0101	1000	58
9	0101	1001	59

Table B.9 shows the representation of alphabetic characters in ASCII-8 by showing the zone, code digit and the hexadecimal equivalent.

TABLE B.9
Alphabetic Characters in ASCII-8

Character	*ASCII-8 Zone*	*Code Digit*	*Hexadecimal Equivalent*
A	1010	0001	A1
B	1010	0010	A2
C	1010	0011	A3
D	1010	0100	A4
E	1010	0101	A5
F	1010	0110	A6
G	1010	1110	A7
H	1010	1000	A8
I	1010	1001	A9
J	1010	1010	AA
K	1010	1011	AB
L	1010	1100	AC
M	1010	1101	AD
N	1010	1110	AE
O	1010	1111	AF
P	1011	0000	B0
Q	1011	0001	B1
R	1011	0010	B2
S	1011	0011	B3
T	1011	0100	B4
U	1011	0101	B5
V	1011	0110	B6
W	1011	0111	B7
X	1011	1000	B8
Y	1011	1001	B9
Z	1011	1010	BA

Example B.3 :

ASCII-8 coding for 'SKY' is as follows:

S=10110011
K=10101011
Y=10111001

B.2.4 GRAY CODE

Many physical systems supply continuous data. But digital systems can process data in discrete form only. The Gray code belongs to such a class of codes called minimum-change codes, in which only one bit in the code group changes when going from one step to the next. The change from any number to the next in the sequence is recognized by a change of only one bit from 0 to 1 or from 1 to 0. The Gray code is an unweighted code, which means that the bit positions in the code groups do not have any specific weight assigned to them. Because of this, the Gray code is not suited for arithmetic operations but finds applications in input/output devices and some types of analog-to-digital converters.

Table B.10 shows the 4-Bit Gray Code and its decimal equivalent.

TABLE B.10
Gray Code with Decimal Equivalent

Binary Code	*Decimal equivalent*	*Gray Code*
0000	0	0000
0001	1	0001
0010	2	0011
0011	3	0010
0100	4	0110
0101	5	0111
0110	6	0101
0111	7	0100
1000	8	1100

The Gray code is often used in the situations where other codes such as binary, might produce erroneous or ambiguous results during transitions in which more than one bit of the code is changing.

Example B.4:

Using binary code and going from 0111 to 1000 requires that all four bits change simultaneously. Depending on the circuit that is generating the bits, there may be significant difference in transition times of the different bits. If the most significant bit changes faster than the rest, following transitions will occur:

0 1 1 1
1 1 1 1
1 0 0 0

The occurrence of 1111 is only momentary but it could possibly produce erroneous operation of the elements that are being controlled by the bits. Obviously, using the gray code would eliminate this problem since only one bit change occurs per transition and no "race" between bits can occur.

APPENDIX C

KARNAUGH MAP

Algebraic equations of digital functions can be simplified by using Boolean algorithms. But as the algebraic equations become complex, other techniques are used to simplify these equations. Karnaugh map is a method used for simplification that is easy and fast. The procedure is explained in this Appendix.

C.1 MINTERM AND MAXTERM

When function is composed of AND gates feeding into OR gates, the expression is composed of minimum cost two-level network. This is identified as sum-of-products (SOP) terms, also known as minterms.

Product-Of-Sums (POS) expression corresponds to a two-level network of OR gates feeding into AND gates. The expression is also known as maxterms.

Therefore, to find minimum expression, the expressions may be in SOP or POS.

Minimum Sum Of Products (SOP) is obtained as follows:

1. Combine terms by using $A\overline{B}+AB = A$. Do this repeatedly.
2. Eliminate redundant terms.

C.2 TWO VARIABLE KARNAUGH MAP (K-MAP)

Just like a truth table, K-Map function specifies value of the function for every combination of variables. A two-variable K-Map is shown in Figure C.1. The possible values of one variable are listed across the rows, and the possible values of the other variables are listed across the columns. For the two variables A and B taken up in the Figure C.1, the possible values 0 and 1 of A are listed on the top, and the possible values 0 and 1 of B are taken on the left side.

The values of A and B in each of the boxes are shown.

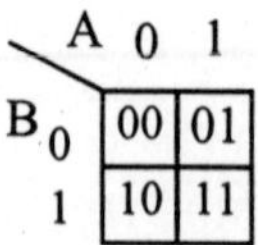

FIGURE C.1: Two Variable K-Map

In the top corner box on the left, A=0 and B=0; this places a value 00 in this box. In the top corner box on the right side, A=1 and B=0; therefore value placed in this box is 01. Similarly, A=0 and B=1 in the left corner in the bottom row, which makes the values listed is 10; in the bottom corner box on the right side, A=1 and B=1, making the value listed as 11.

Example C.1: Minimize $\overline{A}\overline{B}+\overline{A}\,B$

For the expression F = $\overline{A}\overline{B}+\overline{A}$ B, the map is shown in Figure C.2.

1 is placed where $\overline{A}\overline{B}$ is true, which means that in the box of 00. Another 1 is also placed where $\overline{A}$ B is true, that is in the box of 01.

FIGURE C.2: K-Map for F = $\overline{A}\overline{B}+\overline{A}$ B

The adjacent 1's are mapped and the variable that remains constant in the mapping process is the minimized function. As can be seen in the map, only $\overline{A}$ is constant whereas B is varying, being 0 in one box and 1 in the other box.

C.3 THREE VARIABLE KARNAUGH MAP (K-MAP)

Figure C.3 shows a three variable K-Map. Each minterm is located adjacent to 3 terms that it can combine with. Two variables A and B are listed on the top, and third variable C is listed on the left side. All the possible values in the boxes are expressed in binary and decimal notation in various boxes. For example, in the left corner of the top row, A = 0, B = 0 and C = 0, represented as 000, which is decimal 0, representing minterm m0. The rightmost corner in the bottom row has the values A=0, B=1, C=1, represented as 110 or decimal 6, minterm m6.

The brackets indicate in which boxes the variables are true.

If a minterm expansion of a function is given, it can be plotted on the graph by placing 1's in the boxes which correspond to minterms of the function, and placing 0's in the rest of the boxes.

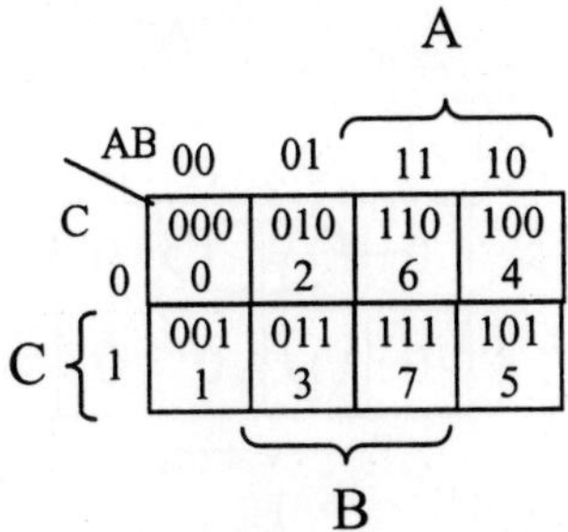

FIGURE C.3: Three Variable K-Map

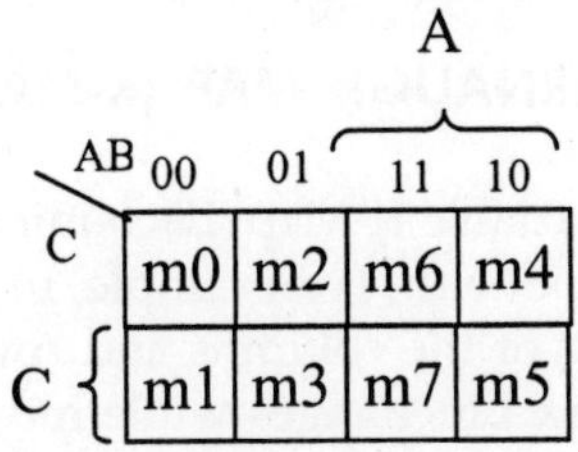

AB \ C	00	01	11	10
C	m0	m2	m6	m4
C	m1	m3	m7	m5

FIGURE C4: Minterms in Three Variable K-Map

Example C.2: Minimize F(a, b, c) = m1 + m3 + m5

From carefully viewing the K-map, the two-1's are placed where m1, m3 and m5 are true; this means the boxes 1, 3, 5. Or in other words, in boxes 001, 011 and 101. The minimized result is obtained for the 1's in the above row where B=1 and C=0. For the two 1's in the column, A = 0 and B=1, which gives the expression as $\overline{A}B$. Thus, the mapped result is $B\overline{C}$. This gives F = $\overline{A}B + B\overline{C}$.

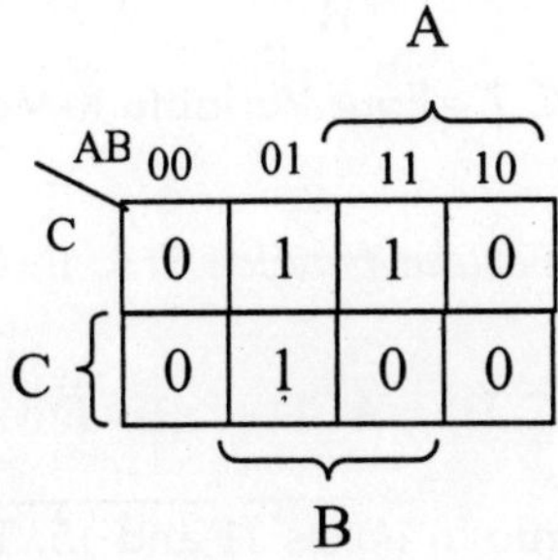

FIGURE C.5 : Plot of F(a, b, c) = m1 + m3 + m5

Mapping is shown in Figure C.6.

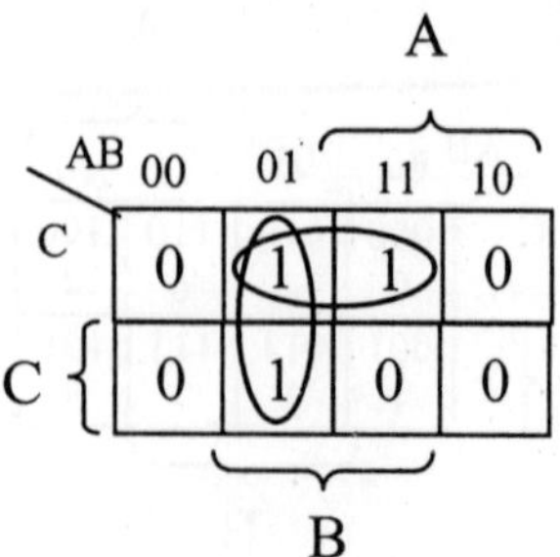

FIGURE C.6 : F(a, b, c) = $\bar{A}B + B\bar{C}$

C.4 FOUR VARIABLE KARNAUGH MAP (K-MAP)

Figure C.7 shows a 4 variable K-Map. Each minterm is located adjacent to 4 terms that it can combine with. For example, m5 can combine with m1, m4, m7 or m13. Numbering of the columns and rows is as depicted in the Figure C.7 such that only one bit changes while moving to adjacent square.

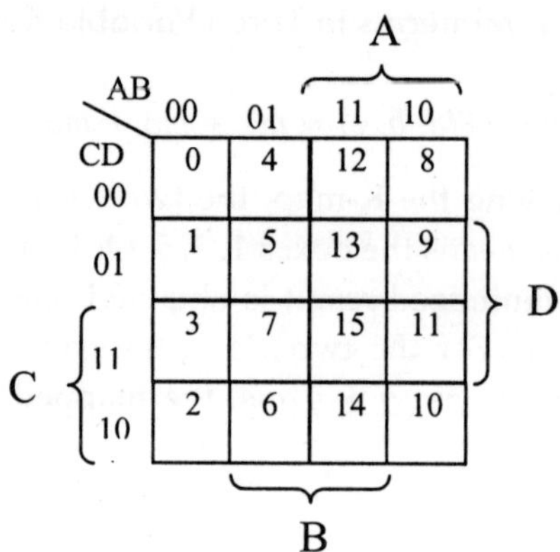

FIGURE C.7 : Four Variable K-Map

Example C.3: Minimize Boolean function F(A, B, C, D) = ACD + $\bar{A}B + \bar{D}$

The plotting of F(A, B, C, D) = ACD + $\bar{A}B + \bar{D}$ is as illustrated in Figure C.8.

The term ACD = 1 is true in boxes 11 and 15. Therefore, a 1 is plotted in these boxes. The term B is true in boxes 4, 5, 7 and 6. So a 1 is plotted in these boxes. $\bar{D}$ is true in boxes 0, 4, 12, 8, 2, 6, 14, 10. The minimized function is F = $\bar{A}B + \bar{D}$ + AC.

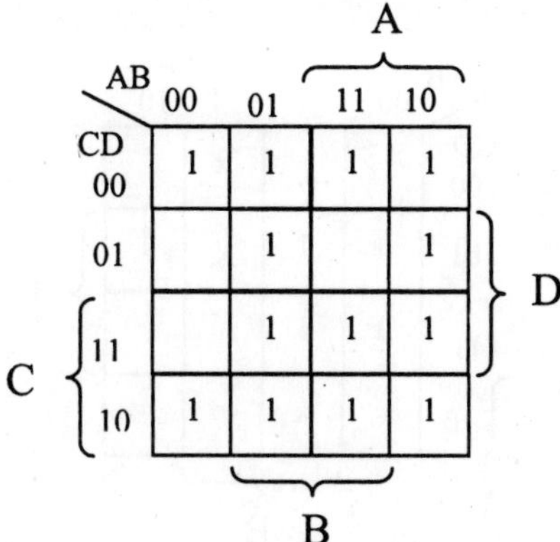

FIGURE C.8 : Four Variable K-Map

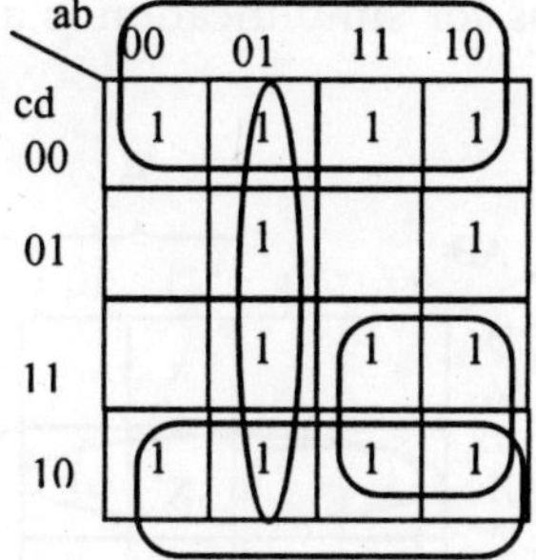

FIGURE C.9 : F $\overline{A}B+\overline{D}+AC$

C.5 DON'T CARE CONDITION

'Don't care' conditions are the conditions where the minterms can take the values of either 0 or 1. While the minterms are indicated as 1, the don't care conditions are indicated as x in the map. When choosing terms to form minimum SOP, all the 1's are covered, but x's are used if they help in simplification of the result.

Example C.4: Minimize $F = \Sigma m(1, 3, 5, 7, 9) + \Sigma d(6, 12, 13)$

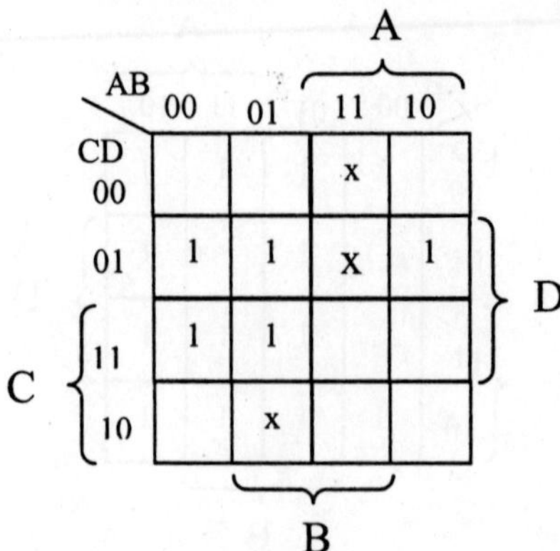

FIGURE C.10 : K-Map for don't care Conditions

Mapping of minterms for simplification is as in Figure C.11.

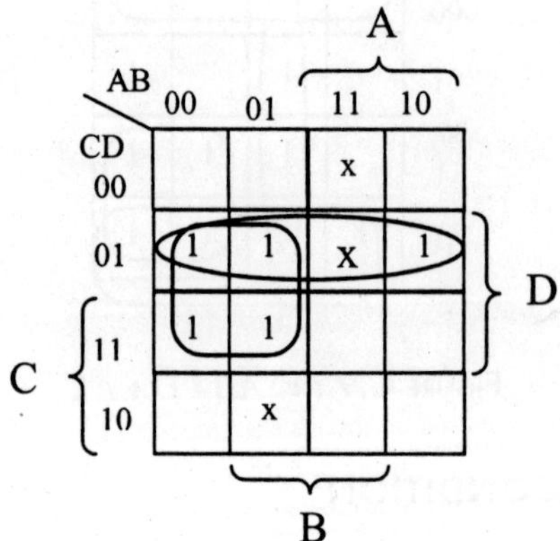

FIGURE C.10 : F = $\bar{A}D + \bar{C}D$

Index